ONE WEEK LOAN

D0995769

Series Standing Order
ISBN 0–333–71691–4 hardcover
ISBN 0–333–69332–9 paperback
(*outside North America only*)

You can receive future titles in this series as they are published by placing a standing order. Please contact your bookseller or, in the case of difficulty, write to us at the addresss below with your name and address, the title of the series and the ISBN quoted above.

Customer Services Department, Macmillan Distribution Ltd
Houndmills, Basingstoke, Hampshire RG21 6XS, England

By the same author

The Catholic Question in English Politics, 1820 to 1830
Politics and the Churches in Great Britain, 1832 to 1868
Politics and the Churches in Great Britain, 1869 to 1921
The Liberal Governments, 1905–15
Disraeli
Churches and Social Issues in Twentieth-Century Britain

The Rise of Democracy in Britain, 1830–1918

Ian Machin

First published in Great Britain 2001 by
MACMILLAN PRESS LTD
Houndmills, Basingstoke, Hampshire RG21 6XS and London
Companies and representatives throughout the world

A catalogue record for this book is available from the British Library.

ISBN 0–333–67227–5 hardcover
ISBN 0–333–67228–3 paperback

 First published in the United States of America 2001 by
ST. MARTIN'S PRESS, LLC,
Scholarly and Reference Division,
175 Fifth Avenue, New York, N. Y. 10010

ISBN 0–312–23544–5

Library of Congress Cataloging-in-Publication Data

Machin, G.I.T.
    The rise of democracy in Britain, 1830–1918 / Ian Machin
        p.   cm. – (British Studies Series)
    Includes bibliographical references (p.) and index.
    ISBN 0–312–23544–5 (cloth)
    1. Great Britain–Politics and government–1837–1901.
    2. Democracy–Great Britain–History–19th century.
    3. Democracy–Great Britain–History–20th century. 4. Great
Britain–Politics and government–1830–1837. 5. Great Britain–
Politics and government–1901–1936. I. Title. II. Series.
DA550 .M28 2000
320.941'09'034–dc21
                                                  00–040448

© Ian Machin 2001

This book is printed on paper suitable for recycling and made from fully managed
and sustained forest resources.

10   9   8   7   6   5   4   3   2   1
10   09 08 07 06 05 04 03 02 01

Copy edited and typeset in *Baskerville* by Password, Norwich, UK.
Printed in China

Contents

Preface

Democracy (rule by the People) is a form of government which has now established itself to a considerable extent in most countries on earth. Yet it was not until a few years ago, in the later twentieth century, that democracy achieved its present degree of triumph.

This has come about after many historical vicissitudes. Even though some degree of democratic ideas and practice was present in Ancient Greece, it declined and vanished for many centuries. Some partial elements of democracy came sputtering into revival, through separate and independent action, in some parts of Europe in mediaeval times. But they were (with exceptions) overlaid by autocratic forms of rule, until the nineteenth century saw a few countries in the world advancing by successive reforms towards what seemed to be permanent forms of democracy. But there were further autocratic or totalitarian challenges and setbacks in the twentieth century, and in many countries a democratic form of rule, which seemed as though it might be achieved quite early in the century, has only been realized in the last decade or so. Democracy, therefore, the political ideal and aim for so many people for so long, could by no means advance continuously to achieve triumph. Rather it appeared sporadically and attained its goals only by protracted, fragmentary, and incomplete means.

In the twentieth century Britain and many other countries have reached a position of fairly full representative democracy, though the questions of how far representativeness is adequate – how far surviving checks on it need to be removed, and how far representation itself can be regarded as democratic – continue to be debated. Countries, such as Britain, which have attained a fairly democratic position have done so by a slow, arduous, and highly disputed process – one which was frequently described as 'democratic' at different stages of attainment, but was far from being so in present-day terms.

Before the later eighteenth century, Britain had contributed a period (the mid-seventeenth century) of democratic aspiration and expression to the fragmented corpus of human democratic evolution. But it was only from the late eighteenth century that Britain – inspired to some degree by the American Revolution, to a greater degree by the French Revolution, and (in the course of time) moved decisively by the social-class changes of the Industrial Revolution – began to evolve continuous democratic aspirations. These led to a long, but by no means inevitable, succession of legal moves towards the large, but still partial, extent of democratic fulfilment which exists today.

Extra-parliamentary publication and combination – including expression of the radical aspirations of religious, commercial, and social reforming groups – provided an important continuous impetus to democratic advance. But unless political revolution was to intervene, which in this country it never did, implementation of democratic claims depended on decisions taken in Parliament. This body, elected in the nineteenth century on a narrow but successively expanded franchise, was motivated mainly by desires for party strengthening and aggrandisement (also, on occasion, but more distantly and less clearly, by the desire to avoid popular revolution) to meet extra-parliamentary demands to the extent that it saw fit. This was always on a limited basis, so important aspects were always left over for democrats or partial-democrats (outside or inside Parliament) to continue demanding.

In 1832 came the first substantial parliamentary enactments which led eventually to a system of democratic representation. After further important enactments following at intervals the measures of 1832, the electoral reform of 1918 largely, though by no means entirely, brought to fruition the system of democracy known in Britain today. This book concentrates on explaining and analysing the reforms which contributed to the advance of democracy, and attempts general surveys of the position of democracy in Britain both before and after the period 1832–1918.

The serious study of the advance of democracy in Britain commenced about the beginning of the twentieth century. But most of the immense flood of publications, and unpublished theses, on this matter or on related subjects has appeared from the 1950s. Two of the earliest works on British democratic developments were by a Russian and an American respectively – Moisei Ostrogorski's useful but opinionated *Democracy and the Organization of Political Parties* (1902), and Charles Seymour's abundantly and fruitfully detailed *Electoral Reform in England and Wales, 1832–85* (1915).

Seymour remains essential reading, but the big impetus to modern study came from two works of the 1950s on nineteenth-century electoral practice, Norman Gash's *Politics in the Age of Peel* (1953), and H. J. Hanham's *Elections and Party Management: Politics in the Time of Disraeli and Gladstone* (1959). W. B. Gwyn's *Democracy and the Cost of Politics in Britain* (1962) was the first book to cover electoral change (concentrating on certain aspects) from 1832 to 1918.

The present book is in the category of attempts at general synthesis, a heavily subscribed genre in itself. It distils some of the matters I have dealt with in a lifetime of university teaching. So it seems desirable to express my thanks here to the students, colleagues, and librarians who have helped me to advance my knowledge and clarify my thoughts on these subjects over a good number of years. I would also like to thank the publishers and Professor Jeremy Black, who obtained for me the invitation to write the book, and Penny Simmons, who did the copy editing.

Ian Machin
Spring 2000

1 Introduction, to 1830

In the history of mankind, democracy has not continuously evolved but has proceeded by fits and starts. It was well known to later ages – not least to those who imbibed a Victorian classical education when this country was beginning to evolve towards democracy – that Athens in the fifth and fourth centuries BC had a fairly democratic, and certainly a directly popular, system of government before succumbing to autocratic rule.[1] All Athenian male citizens over the age of 20 could decide the law on every matter in an assembly which met very frequently. However, since women, slaves and non-natives were excluded from citizenship, this method had marked shortcomings when compared with the nature of democracy in the mid- and later twentieth-century AD.[2]

After the end of Athenian democracy in 323 BC, following Macedonian conquest, forms of government which had democratic elements did not convincingly appear again for 1500 years. They did so in the twelfth and thirteenth centuries, in the contrasting environments of Italian city states and the forest cantons of 'Upper Germany' (soon to become known as Switzerland). Since the preceding Anglo-Saxon *Witanagemot* had, despite the eager assumptions of late eighteenth-century democrats, almost certainly been a consultative council consisting only of the nobles of an absolute monarch, it can hardly be accepted as a serious example of early democracy. Moreover, the sense in which the government of Italian cities in the Middle Ages, and of Swiss cantons before the nineteenth century, can be accepted as democratic is distinctly limited.[3]

There was also no continuity between the flickerings of democracy in these small areas (whether Athens, Pisa or Unterwalden (Switzerland) is in question) and its later development in comparatively large countries such as the USA, France and Britain. One writer has correctly warned us to:

> avoid the unhistorical assumption that any direct line of descent can be traced from the political arrangements of the [Italian]

city-republics to those of modern democratic states ... the city-republics proved to be highly unstable, with the result that their experiments in self-government turned out in almost every case to be sadly short-lived ... Of all the city states ... only Venice survived as a self-governing republic, a status it managed to keep until its collapse in 1797.[4]

In the cases of Athens, the Italian city-states and the Swiss cantons, the signs of democratic government all came in relatively small, compact geographical communities. Any powerful movement to establish democracy in broad nation-states, which were then controlled by the principle of absolute monarchy, had not yet come. When it did appear, it could only be realized by means of a parliamentary representative system, which had not yet (except in rudimentary form) been produced.

The theological and political upheavals of the Reformation did not prevent the extension of absolute monarchy in nation-states. Indeed, in some ways they assisted it. But popular aspirations for more participation in government were encouraged, if only temporarily and unsuccessfully, by some of the effects of the Reformation in the sixteenth and seventeenth centuries. The Levellers, during the English Civil War, produced perhaps the most subversive democratic suggestions yet heard in regard to a nation-state, urging representative popular government based on an ideal of human political equality. In this connection, a recent writer has reviewed 'the great debates at Putney whose resonance is still as striking at the end of the twentieth century as it was in the heady days of 1647'.[5] Oliver Cromwell chaired the meeting of the General Council of the New Model Army at St Mary's church, Putney (near London), in late October and early November 1647. He must have been almost as shocked as King Charles I, upholder of hereditary Divine Right to rule, would have been by the democratic tone of Colonel Thomas Rainsborough:

> For really I thinke that the poorest hee that is in England hath a life to live as the greatest hee, and therefore Truly, Sir, I thinke its cleare, That every Man that is to live under a Government ought first by his owne Consent to putt himself under that Government.[6]

These sentiments were not to be realized as public policy in this country for 300 years. Revived pretensions to absolute monarchy were succeeded, from 1688, by a constitutional monarchy which could, for the most part, only operate through Parliament. Democracy was little advanced by the 1688 Revolution. However extravagant some of the claims made on its hundredth anniversary about the liberty-bestowing benefits of this event, it produced only oligarchical domination of the parliamentary system by the aristocracy and, partially, by the Crown. The House of Lords, filled by unelected peers, most of whom were hereditary, could reject any bill passed by the House of Commons, which itself was filled largely by nominees, and often relations, of the peers. The application by statute of a small landed-property qualification to MPs (except in Scotland) from 1711 emphasized, despite the fact that it was not regularly enforced, the ascendancy of land in the Constitution. The Sovereign could withhold assent from any bill passed by Parliament, though this right fell into disuse in the early eighteenth century and has not been revived to the present day.

Government, therefore, was mainly in the interests of the aristocracy who controlled Parliament. When King George III ascended the throne in 1760, he sought to make use of his constitutional powers in regard to appointments to ministries and the policies which governments might adopt. This was a cause of conflict between the Crown and some of the nobility, and this in turn helped to promote the slowly developing cause of 'parliamentary' (or electoral) reform.

Aristocrats had much influence over the county elections and many of the borough elections. In the case of boroughs with very small electorates, of which there were a great many in the eighteenth century and later, aristocratic control could be practically absolute. Most eighteenth-century elections were uncontested, and this helped greatly to maintain the unbroken influence of the patron. The largest amount of control was obtained from the right to nominate the members for a constituency. Influence which did not include the right of nomination was not so tight, but could still be powerful and extensive. Some constituencies, especially small-borough seats, were regarded as family appendages. Some peers were extensive borough-owners, the number of seats virtually owned by them amounting, in one or two cases, to ten or eleven. The right to be returned, or to nominate the member, could be sold for money until this practice was forbidden by Curwen's Act of 1809.

Electoral contests were comparatively few in the eighteenth century, but when a contest arose it was often intensely fought. Control of the electorate was exercised by various means, with the aim of vindicating the 'interest' of the Crown or an aristocratic patron and securing the return of the desired candidate. These means included the compulsory open voting (which might be followed by publication of the giving of votes in a poll book), so that it could be dangerous to vote against the wishes of a patron. They also included the illegal, but widespread, bribery of electors through money or food and drink – forbidden by the 'Treating Act' of 1696 and other measures. It has been noted that:

> To evade the bribery laws, less direct methods were frequently used. The friends and relations of voters, and often … the voters themselves, were sometimes employed in large numbers during a campaign ostensibly as messengers, chair-men, flagbearers, watchers, or something of the sort but in reality only to influence votes. Until the law hindered the practice, it was easy under the guise of paying electors' travelling expenses to give them bribes.[7]

The power of electoral influence might also be demonstrated by the eviction of tenant farmers who voted against the interest of their landlord. The exercise of these methods was by no means uniform, and depended very much on individual decision. But collectively it indicated that voting was often performed to satisfy the patron rather than the opinions of the elector.

Huge amounts could be spent by patrons and candidates by means which, though traditional and deeply rooted, were illegal and corrupt. Perhaps the best-known case of massive electoral expenditure was the Yorkshire contest of 1807, when William Wilberforce and Viscount Milton, the two successful candidates, spent £3 million and £11 million respectively (in today's monetary values), and Henry Lascelles (who lost) spent £11 million.[8]

The total electorate was small, well under half a million; but (especially in England) it varied very greatly in size between constituencies. Tiny English boroughs with only a handful of voters returned two MPs, the same number as the large popular constituencies of Westminster and Preston which, in the early nineteenth century, had at least 10 000 voters each – a figure which was about three times as large as the entire electorate in Scotland. Some areas, particularly in the south of England, were plentifully supplied with 'rotten' boroughs (very small places, some practically vanished, which had decayed and had only minuscule electorates) and 'pocket' boroughs (constituencies 'in the pocket' of a patron). Cornwall was clearly the chief of these areas: its abundance of small boroughs meant that it returned 44 MPs to Scotland's 45, though it had only about a sixth of Scotland's population in 1801. By contrast, some large and growing towns returned no MPs separate from the surrounding county. The creation of separate MPs for such towns, in association with a demand for elective town councils, was increasingly pressed by the 1820s. The pronounced economic and social changes of the time had a fundamental influence on encouraging the demand for electoral reform, both nationally and locally.[9]

There was a good deal of popular, communal participation in elections, including that of interested people who did not have the vote. Elections sometimes had an air of festivity and jollification, but this could not disguise the hard self-interest which lay at the root of them. If an elector displeased his patron by the way he gave his vote, he could incur economic ruin; but if he satisfied his patron, he could receive further material rewards. It clearly paid to be deferential; and this applied to candidates supported by a patron as well as the electors who formed his 'interest'. A successful candidate who did not satisfy his patron by his subsequent actions in the House of Commons might forfeit the patronage, and consequently his seat.[10]

The system bore no resemblance to any attempt to represent numbers. It was claimed instead that it represented major sectional interests in the country, and indeed to some extent the overseas empire. But although there was legal, financial, mercantile, and even some manufacturing, representation in the Commons, it could not be seriously pretended that any interest was fully and properly represented apart from the landed class. The hereditary landed interest in Parliament had also the almost exclusive advantage (apart from the same right possessed by Anglican bishops) of being able to reject in the Lords any bill passed in the Commons. Nor could it be seriously argued, at a time when so many small and unthriving boroughs still had their own representation apart from that of the surrounding county, that growing towns should not have their own MPs merely because they had a part in returning those of the county.

The origins of criticism of this oligarchical governmental system, and of desires to reform it, lay in the earlier eighteenth century, when the 'Commonwealth Whig' tradition was still decidedly alive, and helped to carry political questioning into the more contentious era of the later decades of the century.[11] In the 1760s and later, the revived political activity of the Crown caused resentment and adverse reactions. These helped to promote reforming ideas and proposals, and to give rise, from the 1770s, to a halting but fairly continuous movement demanding more democracy in the political system.[12] In the case of Scotland especially, calls for political change included the desire for elective local councils as well as a reformed Parliament.

The anti-Crown and anti-ministerial activities of John Wilkes in the 1760s aroused a popular stir, but did not seriously attempt to establish effective and lasting popular organization. Determined popular organization did not occur until the 1790s (and then it did not last). In the meantime, external influences were important in encouraging the development of radicalism at home. The cry of the American colonists for 'no taxation without representation', and a statement in the Declaration of Independence in 1776 that governments should derive their powers from the consent of the governed, aroused echoes among those in Britain who wanted an expanded representative system.[13] Radical reformers in this country therefore supported the cause of American independence against the Crown and the government. After radical fervour had faded for some years after the early 1780s, it was revived, first by centennial commemorations of the 1688 Revolution and then, from 1789, by the influence of the Revolution in France.

Aristocrats were the main political beneficiaries of the existing system, but they were not exclusively concerned with trying to maintain it. Some of them, influenced perhaps by Rousseau and other thinkers of the Enlightenment, reacted against the more obvious interests of their class by trying to subvert or at least to reform the system. This became a noticeable trend in British politics for over a century, and included such figures as Wilkes, Sir Francis Burdett, Jeremy Bentham, Henry Hunt, Fergus O'Connor, Ernest Jones, Sir William Harcourt and Bertrand Russell. Major John Cartwright and the Revd Christopher Wyvill were two of the earliest members of the landed-gentry class to play a large part in the gradual launching of the Parliamentary Reform movement. This name is usually given to the general aim of extending and purifying parliamentary representation, which lasted well beyond 1918 and still – in regard to the question of the constitutional powers and composition of the House of Lords – remains in existence today. Cartwright, who was of a Northamptonshire landowning family, was a clear forerunner of the Chartist movement of the mid-nineteenth century. His seminal reforming pamphlet of 1776, *Take Your Choice*, included four of the Six Points of the People's Charter of 1836 (manhood suffrage, annual Parliaments, equal electoral districts and the secret ballot). The second edition in 1777 added the two other points which appeared in 1836 – abolition of the property qualification for MPs (standing at £600 a year for a county MP and £300 a year for a borough MP), and State payment of MPs.[14]

The fact that the same aims as Cartwright's were revived 60 years later (after other revivals in the meantime) indicates the lack of success for democracy in this long period. Cartwright supported Christopher Wyvill and the County Association movement of 1779–85, which aimed to increase county representation at the expense of borough representation (much of which was under government control). In 1780 Cartwright also founded the reforming Society for Constitutional Information, which declined after a few years, but revived by the end of the 1780s and formed a link with the popular radical agitation of the 1790s. In that turbulent decade Cartwright, unlike Wyvill, gave his support to the radical democratic societies.

But it was reformers of a lower social status, skilled worker or lower middle class – the staymaker Thomas Paine and the shoemaker Thomas Hardy – who were more characteristic of the democratic agitation of the 1790s than the landowners. They were the heralds of another, working-class trend in democratic leadership over the following century, comprising such as Place, Cobbett, Carlile, Hetherington, Lovett, Harney and Howell. In the ideological battle between the conservative Edmund Burke and the radical Tom Paine which followed the French Revolution, Paine's *Rights of Man* condemned hereditary monarchical and aristocratic government and advocated manhood suffrage. The book, based on the idea that mankind had natural rights which included that of deciding on their own government, provided a bible for democrats for many years, until by the 1820s 'natural rights' tended to be superseded by more utilitarian arguments for a wide popular franchise. Officially banned from 1792, *Rights of Man* was freely published again from the 1820s. As well as the repression of subversive radical publications, the popular democratic societies of 1791–3 were destroyed by government decrees and legislation and by legal verdicts.

Official reaction against radical democratic claims was supported by growing patriotic feeling and by anti-radical societies and publications during the war with revolutionary France which broke out in 1793. With the support of this popular loyalist wave, the government tightened its grip during the mid- and later 1790s. Government strength in parliament also grew, against an increasingly weak opposition. After long negotiations between William Pitt (the premier) and the more moderate leaders of the Whig Opposition, several Whigs accepted posts in Pitt's ministry in 1794, and over half the Whigs in the House of Commons gave the government their support. After this, Charles James Fox, Charles Grey and the other Whigs who continued in opposition, had no hope of carrying reform against ministerial policy, and the government encouraged scarcely any important reforms until the 1820s. The Whigs found it impossible to achieve any success with electoral reform motions in the 1790s, and after a forlorn effort in 1797 (when a motion by Grey was heavily defeated) there was no further motion in the Commons to reform the franchise until 1810. Comparatively little argument for franchise extension based on the continuing industrial urban growth, was heard before the 1820s.[15]

Gradually, the issue of Parliamentary Reform revived in the first decade of the nineteenth century. In 1809 J. C. Curwen's bill to abolish the sale of seats was successful, but Thomas Brand's motion for enfranchisement and redistribution was defeated in 1810 by 234 votes to 115.[16] In 1811 the veteran Cartwright and other leading radicals founded 'The Union for Parliamentary Reform according to the Constitution'. This was renamed the Hampden Club in 1812 and formed numerous branches, providing a powerful stimulus to renewed radical popular organization over the next eight years.[17] Their successors in 1818–9 were known as Political Union societies. The beginning of a cheap edition of Cobbett's *Political Register* in 1816 also helped to spread Reform ideas among the poorer classes.

But, as in the 1790s, there came government reaction in the form of fresh repressive legislation. The popular agitation generally faded after the 'Peterloo' massacre of 1819 and the subsequent Six Acts. These measures, mostly lasting only for three years, covered familiar ground by restricting meetings and publications (a stamp duty being placed on all cheap political pamphlets, similar to that on newspapers).[18] There was renewed defeat on six occasions for Parliamentary Reform motions in the Commons (and no successes) from 1817 to 1826. Apart from the disfranchisement of a few small-borough seats in 1821 and 1828, on the grounds of excessive corruption, Parliamentary Reform had no success (except for a partial one over Catholic emancipation in 1829) until Grey's bill was carried in 1832.

What was particularly notable in the 1820s, compared with the popular upheavals of 1815–20 and 1830–2, was that while meetings in favour of Parliamentary Reform or local council reform often occurred, there was an absence of popular organization. This was perhaps explained by the effects of the Six Acts or the fear that the government would adopt further repressive legislation, and also perhaps by improved economic circumstances. Certainly the mass agitation in Ireland, fomented from 1823 by Daniel O'Connell on behalf of Catholic emancipation, found no echo in Britain on behalf of Parliamentary Reform until 1829–30. This was in spite of the fact that the radical (and anti-radical) press was continuing to grow substantially.[19]

Social change resulting from industrialization had added greatly to the actual or potential pressure for Parliamentary Reform. But, on account of the effectiveness of government policy, organizations working for this cause had come and gone. When Cartwright died in 1824, aged 84, his lifetime's agitation seemed to have turned full circle without result. There was a general absence of petitions to Parliament for electoral reform from the beginning of 1824 to the end of 1829.[20] The Whig efforts within Parliament did not have the backing of powerful popular organization without. Repeated heavy defeats for these efforts in the Commons were counter-balanced only by a gradual swing of individual Whig opinion towards Reform.[21] A mild motion by Lord John Russell in 1822, proposing to remove one of the two seats from the 50 smallest boroughs and transfer them to counties and large towns, was defeated by the smallest margin for a Parliamentary Reform motion since 1785; but the margin, at 269 votes against to 164 in favour, was still large. In any case, the promise in this result was not followed up. In 1827 Russell referred somewhat despairingly in the Commons to 'a great lukewarmness on the subject throughout the country'.[22] In two years, however, the position was changing once again, to indicate more of a confluence between potential Whig effort in Parliament and revived radical agitation and organization in the country.

The swing of circumstances to produce more favourable prospects for Parliamentary Reform in the late 1820s owed more to party political developments and to changes in government policy than to the revival of radical agitation. There was not very pronounced agitation until a bill had been put before Parliament in 1831. But the agricultural 'Swing Riots' of 1829–30 in southern counties of England were linked with popular franchise demands. So, more obviously, was the London Radical Reform Association, founded in July 1829 in emulation of O'Connell's Catholic Association in Ireland, whose goal of emancipation had just been reached through the passing of the Tory Government's measure. The financial reforms advocated by Thomas Attwood's Birmingham Political Union for the Protection of Human Rights (which was formed in December 1829 and held its first meeting in the following month) were firmly connected to calls for expansion of the representative system.[23] A more radical Metropolitan Political Union was formed in London in March 1830, and a great many other reforming societies were founded. The reviving clamour for Reform was led, among others, by Daniel O'Connell in both Ireland and Britain.[24]

The general election of July and August 1830 reflected the reforming revival, providing several radical interventions and exciting contests, and unexpected defeats for Tories (though also some for Whigs). After the election the Tories still had a majority, though a much reduced one. Wellington's ministry became increasingly beleaguered by conflicting Tory groups and by the more and more confident Whigs. But the Duke remained stoutly opposed to any general scheme of Parliamentary Reform, against which he delivered a resounding declaration in the Commons on 2 November 1830, saying that 'the legislature and the system of representation possessed the entire confidence of the country'.[25] On 15 November his government was defeated by 233 to 204 over a relatively minor question concerning Civil List expenditure, and he resigned the next day, hence being able to escape the direct defeat over Parliamentary Reform which he might otherwise have incurred. A Whig ministry, led by Grey and containing a number of secessionist Tories from both 'liberal' and 'ultra' wings of their former party, came into office on 17 November, and the question of electoral reform was taken up by the new government.

Only the coming to power of a Whig ministry initiated a change of policy on Parliamentary Reform. Together with the winning of a decisive majority by the Whigs in the election of 1831, the support of much popular agitation in the country, and the exertion of determined pressure on the House of Lords, this led to the passage of the first major Reform Act in 1832.

The Whigs acted from a mixture of dedication and expediency, a combination of commitment to the principle of Parliamentary Reform and desire to keep government office, now that they had finally got it, out of the hands of the Tories. They did not act out of fear of popular revolution, as this was not threatened at the time (though it might have been if a Reform Bill had not been passed in 1832). Given the combination of conservatism, reforming inclinations and regard for party expediency and property which characterized the average moderate Whig, the nature of the Whigs' Reform Act is not difficult to explain. Aristocratic dominance was to be preserved, and democracy kept at bay, by maintaining a much larger element of small-borough and county representation than was justified on grounds of population. But small-borough representation was nevertheless to be considerably diminished. This was because it gave much less support to the Whigs than it did to the Tories, and because much more large-town representation was desirable since, despite encouraging radicalism, it would probably benefit Whigs more than Tories. Qualified town-dwellers would not be prevented from voting in the neighbouring county, as the counties were more Tory than Whig, and Whig elements should be encouraged to influence them.

It is through such considerations, in regard not only to the 1832 Act but also to subsequent Parliamentary Reform legislation, that the formidable obstacles as well as the substantial encouragements to attaining democracy in Britain can be seen. A traditional aristocratic regime had to be persuaded, on grounds of idealism or expediency, to dilute itself. In view of the strength of tradition, and the absence of the threat of revolution, Britain was likely to struggle only slowly into democracy and not to attain it swiftly and decisively. But the Whig Act of 1832 did, without intending to, give the country a substantial start in a democratic direction. Most of the Whig ministers probably intended that the Act (or rather Acts) would be final, and that their odd combination of tradition and innovation would rule the country as far as they could see. But the social changes which contributed influentially to the 1832 Acts continued to gather pace after the latter had been enacted; and this, together with the encouragement given to future radical campaigning by the 1832 measures, made it not unlikely that there would be further Parliamentary Reform.

Notes

1. E. F. Biagini, 'Liberalism and direct democracy: John Stuart Mill and the model of ancient Athens', in E. F. Biagini (ed.), *Citizenship and Community: Liberals, Radicals and Collective Identities in the British Isles, 1865–1931* (Cambridge, 1996), pp. 22–7, 36–7.

2. M. I. Finley, *Democracy Ancient and Modern* (London, 1973), pp. 15, 18–20; S. Hornblower, 'Creation and development of democratic institutions in Ancient Greece', in J. Dunn (ed.), *Democracy: The Unfinished Journey, 508 BC to AD 1993* (Oxford, 1992), pp. 12–29; J. Thorley, *Athenian Democracy* (London, 1996), pp. 4, 31, 77–8, 81–2.

3. For the transformation of Swiss constitutional arrangements in a democratic direction from the 1830s, see A. V. Dicey, *Introduction to the Study of the Law of the Constitution* (9th edn, London, 1945; first published 1885), pp. 604–19; and J. Bryce, *Modern Democracies* (2 vols, London, 1921), I, 415–53. For government in Italian city-states, see Q. Skinner, 'The Italian City-Republics', in J. Dunn, op. cit., pp. 57–60. For Swiss mediaeval and early modern political developments, see E. Bonjour, H. S. Offler and G. R. Potter, *A Short History of Switzerland* (Oxford, 1952), pp. 102–5 and ff. See also R. W. Davis (ed.), *The Origins of Modern Freedom in the West* (Stanford, 1995), pp. 2–5, 28–9, 59–60, 101–8, 133–4. On the fragmentary appearances of democracy in history, cf. J. W. De Gruchy, *Christianity and Democracy* (Cambridge, 1995), pp. 15–19, 35.

4. Q. Skinner in J. Dunn, op. cit., pp. 58–9.

5. Frances Henderson, 'Putney Debates', *Oxford: The Journal of the Oxford Society*, XLIX (Nov. 1997), 60.

6. Quoted ibid., p. 59.

7. W. B. Gwyn, *Democracy and the Cost of Politics in Britain* (London, 1962), pp. 64–5.

8. E. A. Smith, 'The Yorkshire elections of 1806 and 1807: a study in electoral management', *Northern History*, II (1967), 86. Cf. P. Burroughs, 'The Northumberland elections of 1826', *Parliamentary History*, X (1991), 86–

97; D. Williams, 'The Pembrokeshire elections of 1831', *Welsh History Review*, I (1960–3), 37–64; R. D. Rees, 'Election ideals current in South Wales, 1790–1832', ibid., II (1964–5), 233–50; D. Wager, 'Welsh politics and parliamentary reform, 1780–1832', ibid., VII (1974–5), 127–49.

9. A careful and extensive account of the exercise of nomination and influence and their limits before 1832, challenging some exaggerated assumptions, is given by F. O'Gorman, *Voters, Patrons and Parties: The Unreformed Electoral System in Hanoverian England, 1734–1832* (Oxford, 1989). Cf. J. V. Beckett, *The Aristocracy in England, 1660–1914* (Oxford, 1988), pp. 418–48. The Scottish unreformed system is well depicted, on a similarly challenging basis, by R. M. Sunter, *Patronage and Politics in Scotland, 1707–1832* (Edinburgh, 1986). For the activities of non-electors, see J. Vincent, *The Formation of the Liberal Party, 1857–68* (London, 1966), pp. 100–4, and J. Foster, *Class Struggle and the Industrial Revolution* (London, 1974) pp. 52–6.

10. A. S. Turberville, *The House of Lords in the Age of Reform, 1784–1837*, ed. R. J. White (London, 1958), pp. 247–8.

11. H. Dickinson, *The Politics of the People in Eighteenth-Century Britain* (Basingstoke, 1994), pp. 190–220.

12. K. Robbins, *Great Britain: Identities, Institutions and the Idea of Britishness* (London, 1998), p. 148.

13. K. Perry, *British Politics and the American Revolution* (Basingstoke, 1990), pp. 121, 123; D. Hay and N. Rogers, *Eighteenth-Century English Society* (Oxford, 1997), pp. 177–8.

14. Naomi C. Miller, 'John Cartwright and radical parliamentary reform, 1808–19', *English Historical Review*, LXXXIII (1968), 707. For the reform movements, cf. D. G. Wright, *Democracy and Reform, 1815–85* (London, 1970), pp. 3–31.

15. R. Quinault, 'The Industrial Revolution and parliamentary reform', in P. K. O'Brien and R. Quinault (eds), *The Industrial Revolution and British Society* (Cambridge, 1993), pp. 192–5.

16. Naomi Miller, op. cit., 714–15; J. Cannon, *Parliamentary Reform, 1640–1832* (Cambridge, 1973), p. 148. For the nature and elements of Conservative reaction in this period, see B. Coleman, *Conservatism and the Conservative Party in Nineteenth-Century Britain* (London, 1988), pp. 17–54.

17. See Miller, 716–24; J. Cannon, op. cit., pp. 167–72.

18. A. Prentice, *Historical Sketches and Personal Recollections of Manchester: The Progress of Public Opinion, 1792–1832* (3rd edn, London, 1970; first published 1851), pp. 177–8.

19. D. Eastwood, *Government and Community in the English Provinces, 1780–1870* (Basingstoke, 1997), pp. 74–5; P. Jupp, *British Politics on the Eve of Reform: The Duke of Wellington's Administration, 1828–30* (Basingstoke, 1998), pp. 347–57.

20. M. Brock, *The Great Reform Act* (London, 1973), p. 15.

21. Cannon, pp. 183–5.

22. Ibid., p. 187; J. Prest, *Lord John Russell* (London, 1972), pp. 29–31; M. Bentley, *Politics without Democracy, 1815–1914: Perception and Preoccupation*

in British Government (London, 1984), p. 55.

23. M. Brock, op. cit., pp. 86–105; E. J. Evans, *Britain before the Reform Act: Politics and Society, 1815–32* (London, 1989), pp. 68–75; P. Jupp, op. cit., pp. 417–28; C. Flick, *The Birmingham Political Union and the Movements for Reform in Britain, 1830–9* (Hamden, Conn., 1978), pp. 17–18.

24. Cannon, pp. 194–5; Brock, pp. 58–9, 124–9; F. O'Gorman, *The Long Eighteenth Century: British Political and Social History, 1688–1832* (London, 1997), p. 363.

25. Quoted Cannon, p. 201. Cf. M. Bentley, op. cit., pp. 74–5. See also D. Southgate, *The Passing of the Whigs, 1832–86* (London, 1962), pp. 13–17.

2 Moves for a More Democratic System, 1830–48

The Great Reform Act

The first Parliamentary Reform Bill and its passage remain one of the most intriguing features in British history. The episode revealed a clear contrast between the relentlessly reassuring, moderate tone of Lord Grey and the provisions of his bill, which were apparently enough to throw half the members of the House of Commons into near-apoplexy when they first heard them. Those whose seats it was proposed to abolish would, of course, have been particularly upset. Strong Tory resistance in Parliament was a continuous feature of the episode, though it conceded the fight in the end. Popular vociferousness outside Parliament was no less in evidence, sometimes against the moderation of the bill but more often showing sympathy with the government against its opponents. The popular upsurge followed rather than preceded the parliamentary introduction of the bill, and was particularly evident at times when parliamentary opposition was effective and it seemed that the Whig enterprise might collapse, and Reform receive banishment to an indefinite future. At these times the popular agitation was of obvious value to the government and played an important part in helping to keep their scheme alive and forcing the bill through.

So intense and dramatic did the struggle become that it might well be imagined that a larger reform was at stake than a measure which, according to one view of the subject, was largely, and deliberately, intent on reinforcing the existing political system of deference towards the aristocracy. It is not easy to see why, if this was the main intention, there was a Reform Bill at all, especially one which carried out very substantial changes in the franchise and the distribution of seats. The Reform Bill intended to modify and indeed to weaken deference, as will be seen. But at the same time, it was moderate and restricted enough to cause a large movement to take shape and to campaign for much more democratic reform a few years later. It was not only the alarming changes proposed by the bill itself, but the prospects of wider reform along the same lines, that caused such contention in 1831 and 1832. Conservatives feared these prospects, radicals looked forward to them with eager anticipation, and this largely explains the bitter conflict which arose.

The intentions, vicissitudes and eventual success of the Reform scheme have been well and thoroughly charted.[1] Soon after Grey's Government was formed, a committee of four ministers was appointed to draft proposals for parliamentary reform, and commenced its meetings on 11 December 1830. The chairman of the committee was Grey's son-in-law, Lord Durham, who was much more radical than most Whigs and had, in 1821, introduced a bill for equal electoral districts, a ratepayer franchise, and triennial Parliaments. On the basis of cautious statements already made by Grey, it seemed that proposals such as Durham's in 1821 would be too radical for the new government's bill. But a secret ballot in parliamentary elections – strongly advocated in the committee by Durham, but opposed by Lord John Russell – was included in the committee's proposals to the Cabinet. Durham did not succeed, however, in getting triennial Parliaments adopted by the committee, which would only accept quinquennial. Quite sweeping changes in the franchise and the distribution of seats were also included.[2] Three draft bills (for England and Wales, Scotland, and Ireland respectively) were forwarded to Grey by the committee on 14 January 1831.

When the Cabinet met on 24 January, it struck out the secret ballot and quinquennial Parliaments. Although these had appeared so early in proposals for parliamentary reform drawn up by government direction, the ballot was not enacted until 1872 and quinquennial Parliaments not until 1911. The ballot, however, had only been adopted by the committee after a proposed £10 household qualification in boroughs had been doubled to £20, and after eliminating the ballot, the Cabinet adopted the original £10 proposal in mid-February.[3]

On 1 March Russell announced the government scheme in the House of Commons, and the first scenes of opposition and support in the Lower House took place. Under the plan there would be a large transfer of seats from small boroughs to counties and large towns, and a uniform £10 male household franchise in the boroughs. Leave was obtained to introduce a bill, and the second reading was carried by only one vote on 23 March. Not long afterwards, on 18 April, an amendment in committee, proposing that the representation of England and Wales should not be reduced, was carried against ministers by eight votes. In effect the bill was lost. King William IV, who had been reluctant to consider granting a dissolution, which would lead to a general election, now agreed to do so. The ensuing contest produced a big reduction in Tory strength in the Commons and a large government majority of about 130.[4] But extreme radical opinion outside Parliament, wanting manhood suffrage and the ballot and therefore rejecting the bill, was shown in a new National Union of the Working Classes, formed by William Lovett (later one of the authors of the People's Charter) and Henry Hetherington, editor of the *Poor Man's Guardian*.[5]

Armed with their enlarged parliamentary support, ministers introduced a second Reform Bill. The second reading was carried by 367 votes to 231 on 6 July. At the committee stage, however, the famous (or notorious) ultra-Tory amendment known as the Chandos clause was inserted by a majority of 84. This enfranchised £50 'tenants at will' in the county constituencies (tenants only at the will of the landlord, without guaranteed occupancy for any period, whose holdings had an annual value of £50 or above). These £50 tenants-at-will were quite common, and the clause was an obvious boost to the political influence of landowners. The government was against the clause. But the implications of the clause were ambivalent, and some radicals (including Henry Hunt and Joseph Hume) voted for it because at least it enfranchised more people and they thought it might compel acceptance of the ballot in a short time.[6]

On 22 September the third reading was carried by 111 votes and the bill was brought up to the House of Lords, which had a substantial Tory majority. Here on 8 October it was thrown out on second reading by 41 votes. The bishops, 21 of whom had voted against the second reading and only two for it, were stigmatized as having seemingly played a crucial role in the rejection, and were very unpopular with angry crowds.

The new parliamentary setback produced the first of two periods of widespread and intense popular demonstration during the

Reform crisis. The radical Political Unions became more militant and a new National Political Union, organized by the veteran Francis Place, held its first meeting on 31 October. The windows of Tory peers (including those of Wellington) were broken; the castle of the Duke of Newcastle at Nottingham was burned; and the gaol at Derby was destroyed before troops quelled the rioting. At Bristol a mob ran riot for three days, breaking into and destroying several buildings including the bishop's palace. It was suggested that an armed National Guard should be formed to protect property. A radical answer to this was that a Popular Guard should be formed to support Reform.[7]

The government hoped that some concession to the Tories would reduce opposition, especially in the Lords. The extent of the proposed disfranchisement of seats was therefore somewhat reduced in the next bill. But Grey insisted that there must be disfranchisement of decayed ('rotten') boroughs, more represent-ation for large towns, and a £10 borough household franchise. Russell announced the third Reform Bill, slightly different from its predecessor, on 12 December in the Commons. The second reading passed by 324 to 162 on 18 December, and the third by 355 to 239 on 22 March 1832. The Lords had then to be faced again. The delicate matter of creating enough Whig peers, if necessary, to surmount the opposition in that House, had come under serious discussion.[8] Grey decided not to ask for new peers before the Lords had voted on the second reading. But he warned the King, who disliked the bill, that a creation of 50 or 60 might be necessary. On 15 January 1832 the King wrote to Grey, in reply to a cabinet Minute, agreeing to create peers if this course of action seemed unavoidable in order to pass the bill.[9]

The extensive Lords' debate on the second reading of the third bill spread over several days, from 9 to 14 April. To the gratification of ministers in their impasse, a group of 'waverers', prepared to consider conceding support to the bill, had appeared among Tory peers. Grey attempted to win over peers with moderate words about the bill. But his son-in-law Durham did the opposite, threatening their Lordships with revolution unless they yielded: 'are you prepared to live in solitude in the midst of multitudes – your mansions fortified with cannon ... and protected by troops of faithful, perhaps, but, if the hour of danger come, useless retainers?'[10] Thus 'Radical Jack' tried to shock the predominant

Tory side of the Upper Chamber into a calculated submission in order to avoid a deluge. Thanks to the transfer of 16 Tory votes, coming from waverers, to support of the bill, and the absence of 15 other Tories, the second reading squeezed through the peers by nine votes (184 to 175) on 14 April.

But the saga of the bill produced yet more twists and turns. There was much Tory criticism and attempted amendment of the bill in committee. On 7 May an amendment to postpone consideration of the disfranchisement clauses was carried by a majority of 35 (151 to 116). Ministers thought this setback so serious that Grey gave in his resignation. The King accepted it, but the ministers did not relinquish their seals of office and so they technically kept their places during the brief period of fruitless search for successors.

The question now was, would government revert to the Tories, and would this happen with or without a Tory scheme of Reform? The King urged that any new government must adopt a substantial plan of Reform for the sake of restoring tranquillity. The leading Tories appeared uncertain and fractious, surprised at having practically dislodged the Whig Government and far from ready to form another in its place. Sir Robert Peel and the Earl of Harrowby (a waverer) both refused to try and form a ministry. Wellington was ready to make the attempt, but his record as an opponent of Reform hitherto would render his leadership of a Reform ministry somewhat absurd. Tremendous furore had broken out in the country, representing the second wave of mass agitation during the Reform crisis. A great many popular meetings were held, mainly concerned with resisting the Tories. Arming himself with the slogan 'to stop the Duke, go for gold', Francis Place urged a run on the banks to withdraw deposits and deprive a new government of funds, though his initiative came too late to have much effect. Although there were divisions among them, 'the people' did appear on the whole to want both 'the bill' and the Whigs.[11]

The upshot was that no Tory attempt was made to form a ministry, and the King had to continue putting up with the Whigs. He assured Grey on 18 May that, if the bill still met obstruction in the Lords, he would create enough peers who supported it to see it through the Upper House. So the Whigs, instead of leaving their offices, had their places and plans confirmed. Most Tory peers who were still against the bill stayed away from the remaining debates. Only 22 were sufficiently 'die-hard' to vote against the third reading of the bill for England and Wales (106 peers voted for) on 4 June. The Royal Assent to this bill was given three days later. The Scottish bill received the Royal Assent on 17 July, and the Irish bill on 7 August.

The amount of effort and outcry that had gone into the passage of the bill, making it seem a joint concern from both inside and outside the walls of Parliament, seemed to exceed the fairly modest proportions of the measure. However, the weight of the measure lay not only in its details but also in its general nature. It was the first widespread reconstruction of parliamentary representation for several centuries. If it had not been enacted, democracy would not have evolved in Britain in the way it did. It was also significant that the representative House – however unrepresentative it appeared to democrats – had persuaded the hereditary Upper House and the hereditary monarch to yield. The latter had accommodated the government by promising to create peers in order to get the bill through. The Lords mostly resisted the bill until this threat was clearly before them, when they yielded to the measure of a party which was in a minority in their House. Their eventual concession did not of course signify any permanent acquiescence in democratic tendencies. Similar constitutional disputes could arise in which the Lords might take a more determined line.

The Reform Acts of 1832 set a precedent, even if they were not meant to; and their function as a precedent must have seemed likely to many even in 1832. Although some of the Whigs stressed the finality of their measure, the continuing economic and social change of the mid-nineteenth century, and the further calls for political reform to which it could hardly fail to give rise, must have made them doubt the reliability of their own words. It has been said: 'Precisely what the argument [of finality] meant varied with the pressures of debate. Sometimes the Whigs talked as if they were concerned with the distant future, but at other times finality seemed to refer to the foreseeable future, perhaps a period of twenty years or so.'[12] It did, in fact, take the Whigs precisely 20 years from 1832 to introduce their next Reform Bills for Britain, and 18 years for Ireland.

Moreover, the actual terms of the 1832 Acts, though not revolutionary, were far from lacking in significance. They were of both an enfranchising and a disfranchising kind. Enfranchisement lay, first, in the adoption of a uniform £10 male household

qualification in the boroughs; former electors who
under this franchise kept their votes for life, and
freemen, could transfer their votes to heirs. The incre
was particularly large in Scotland, and particularly sm
In Scotland the increase was not surprising, as there l   ...ily
some 4500 voters; under the Scottish Reform Act this number rose
to 64 500 (and reached 84 000 by 1839).[13] Enfranchisement also
lay, secondly, in the creation of new categories of tenant elector in
the counties, which were added (in the case of England and Wales)
to the traditional 40-shilling freehold franchise. The total electorate
in the United Kingdom grew by less than half, to about 800 000.
There was further enfranchisement through the creation of new
seats – five in Ireland; eight in Scotland; and 130 in England and
Wales (65 in counties, and 65 in boroughs). Disfranchisement was
effected by the large-scale removal of seats from small boroughs to
counties and large towns, the same number of seats as previously
being in the new House of Commons.

The vote still rested firmly on property and privilege. Because of
the rising value of real property the electorate as a whole increased
in future years. But in some constituencies, rising values did not
compensate for the death rate among 'ancient right' voters, and
the electorate declined in these places for the next few decades.
New electors as well as old electors might feel compelled to follow
a patron's wishes, rather than their own, in giving their votes; and
the few democratic purists of that time would have found nothing
to satisfy them in the 1832 Acts. There was no manhood suffrage,
proportional representation, creation of equal electoral districts,
secret ballot, ban on the publication of poll-books, provision against
bribery, or reduction in the election expenditure required of
candidates. There was no abolition of the property qualification
for MPs, payment of MPs, restriction of the Lords' veto on bills
passed in the representative Chamber, or abolition of the official
veto of the monarch over bills. In the 1832 Acts it was pronounced
for the first time in statutory form that women could not vote, thus
formalizing an existing exclusion. There were also elaborate and
expensive requirements to register the names of electors, which
stimulated party rivalry to register voters, but obstructed rather
than encouraged the practice of voting.[14]

Popular agitation had been important in keeping the reform-
pot boiling during the crisis, but it had assisted the achievement of

the Whig scheme rather than enlarging it. As has been recently stated afresh:

> The Government would have been both surprised and alarmed if it had been portrayed as inaugurating a 'British tradition' by introducing the first in a series of changes in the franchise which would lead, within a hundred years, to every adult man and woman in Britain possessing the 'right to vote'. The claim by the Tory opposition that the Reform Bill was indeed but the first step down a democratic slippery slope was strongly rejected by the Government.[15]

It is true that much in the electoral system remained the same after the Acts. Traditional aristocratic influence, and the deference with which it was accepted, continued to be a marked feature, especially because many small boroughs survived and continued to return MPs.[16] But the maintenance of deference was not pursued in the Acts with the single-minded zeal and mathematical exactitude which have tended to be assumed in a famous, but highly controversial, account.[17] If the retention of 'deference communities' had been so important to the Whigs, they would not have risked bringing in a Reform Bill at all, unless it had proposed a Reform in reverse, which would abolish the 'open boroughs' where there was little deference to aristocracy and give their seats to new proprietorial and nomination boroughs. The Whigs did intend to retain much aristocratic deference, as is shown by their maintenance of many small boroughs and their substantial increase of county constituencies. But they also challenged and weakened traditional deference by doubling the number of large-borough seats, which bore out their party hopes by usually returning Liberals (though often of a problematic radical hue), and by permitting the continued increase of urban-dwelling voters in county constituencies. The large increase in urban seats was the most progressive aspect of the Reform, the one which was most encouraging to radicals in trying to build on the 1832 measure in order to achieve further electoral change. The large towns proved to be the most reliable source of Liberal returns for several decades. In the general elections between 1832 and 1867, Conservatives never reached 30 per cent of the number of MPs returned for large towns.[18] All in all, the 1832 Reform Acts produced notable changes in the representative system, though it was many years before the social composition of the House of Commons became markedly different through the effects of gradually moving away from traditional landed predominance. The limited and undemocratic though the measure was, it has been rightly said that 'the 1832 Act, not the subsequent Reform Acts of 1867, 1884 and 1918, was the decisive move' towards democracy in Britain.[19]

The Reform of 1832 was both a measure of principle and a measure of party interest. It was far more of a compromise between different political forces and interests than an attempt to meet ideals. Radical accusations of 'betrayal' made against the Whigs were beside the point: no promises had been made to introduce a wide popular suffrage, and in any case the Whigs' reform was wider than had been generally expected. Radicals expressed their disappointment with the measure, but they were glad to see it enacted. It provided for them a useful and encouraging basis on which to campaign for greater democracy.

The Ballot, Registration, and Elective Municipal Councils

After the Homeric struggle over the Reform Bills, the Whigs won a huge overall majority of about 300 seats in a general election in December 1832. At that point it seemed that the franchise they had created might well keep them in office for a very lengthy period. But, ironically, they soon encountered problems which made them weaker than would have appeared at all likely at the end of 1832. A dispute in 1834 over appropriation of surplus revenues of the Church of Ireland for secular purposes caused Lord Stanley, Sir James Graham, the Duke of Richmond, and a sizeable number of others to secede from government ranks and drift slowly over to the Tories. In the election of January 1835 the Whigs were reduced to an overall majority of 108, hardly more than a third of the figure of two years before. The election of 1837 saw their majority slump further to 40. They carried several important reforms in the first half of the 1830s. In the second half of the decade they remained concerned with reform measures, trying (and usually succeeding, sometimes after a long struggle) to pass reforms for Ireland, for the Church of England, and, to a degree, for Protestant Dissenters. As the Liberals' (a name applied increasingly to the Whig Party from about 1835) majority sank, the aristocratic leaders of the party would at least have drawn relief from the reduction of seats held by radicals and by Irish repealers (the former officially within, the latter allied to, their own party). In regard to the very difficult matter of preserving party unity, this decline of awkward factions was some compensation for a strong Conservative revival from the mid-1830s.[20]

In this situation of decline for the Liberals, government initiatives for further Parliamentary Reform were only likely to occur if there was strong radical demand inside and outside Parliament. Inside Parliament there was a diminishing radical voice. Outside Parliament reforming organization was shown for a few years after 1832, mainly in the form of Dissenters' committees working for civil equality, Short Time committees seeking a ten-hour working day in factories, and trade union combination on a national scale which collapsed in 1834. After this, radical association languished somewhat for two or three years. It by no means died out, however, and became stronger from 1836.[21]

The existence of reforming associations showed that various groups wanted to achieve greater democracy in parliamentary representation in order to assist the realization of their own causes.[22] Protestant Dissenters were sometimes feared as a vanguard of democracy. A book entitled *Dissent and Democracy*, published in 1864, said that some Dissenters wanted a more democratic system because this would hasten the separation of Church and State. What would happen after this separation had been achieved? 'I believe that the downfall of the aristocracy and monarchy will follow close upon the downfall of the Established Church ... we will suppose that the dust of the Established Church is given to the four winds of heaven ... about AD 2000. Well, soon after that event, I doubt not, an agitation would be commenced against the aristocracy and monarchy.'[23] In time, however, the advance of democracy showed the relative political weakness of the aim of Church disestablishment in England and (to a lesser extent) Scotland. Pressure groups might hope that extension of the franchise would enhance their aims, but the reverse could also happen. Expansion of voting to a wider social field than that which provided many supporters for a particular reform could 'swamp' that reform and frustrate hopes that it could be realized.

The weakening of radicalism in Parliament was paralleled by

repeated defeats for attempts to carry the secret ballot between 1833 and 1839. Demand for the ballot was a staple feature in radical schemes to reform the parliamentary system. Secret voting was seen, from the reforming point of view, not as undermining British pluck and bravery, but as an essential means of counteracting influence and coercion, and of producing more democratically credible elections in which voting would more closely represent the opinions of the electors. An influential article advocating the ballot by James Mill, a leading Utilitarian, in the *Westminster Review* of July 1830, won the thorough approval of Francis Place. In October of that year William Cobbett also argued in his *Political Register* for introduction of the ballot.[24] It was disappointing to radicals that, though recommended by the cabinet committee which prepared draft Reform bills, the ballot was turned down by the Cabinet in January 1831. It took 41 years and some 20 parliamentary attempts before the ballot was gained, but despite this long struggle it was the first major radical point to be enacted in the evolution of British democracy.

During the rest of the 1830s the introduction of the ballot was debated on several occasions in the Commons. It was consistently opposed by Tories and by many Whigs, and this combination ensured that the question was always defeated. Peel, significantly, said in April 1833 that he opposed the ballot 'because it would make that House more democratic than it was already, and he thought it was democratic enough':

> He would confidently assert, that if the influence of property in elections were destroyed, the security of all property and the sta-bility of all Government would be destroyed with it. It was surely absurd to say, that a man with ten thousand pounds a year should not have more influence over the Legislature of the country, than a man of [*sic*] ten pounds a year. Yet each was only entitled to a single vote. How could this injustice, this glaring inequality, be practically redressed excepting by the exercise of influence? How could the Government end but in a democracy, if the influence were merely accorded to numbers?[25]

Among the leading Whigs who opposed the ballot was Lord John Russell. His opposition probably helped to inspire his 'finality' speech of 20 November 1837, when he declared that the settlement of 1832 should not be disturbed in any important way:

> I cannot conceal the disadvantages and the injuries to which the
> Reform Act is subject. I admit that at the late elections [1837]
> corruption and intimidation prevailed to a very lamentable ex-
> tent ... I admit that with respect to the registration of voters in
> particular, great amendments may be made. But these are ques-
> tions which are totally different from those now brought forward,
> such as the question of the ballot, the extension of suffrage, and
> triennial parliaments, which are, taken together, nothing else but
> a repeal of the Reform Act, and placing the representation on a
> different footing. Am I prepared to do this? I say certainly not.[26]

Perhaps Russell would not have been so ready to express 'finality'
if the radicals had not sunk to a much weaker position in the
Commons than in the earlier 1830s, and if the Tories (now
becoming known as Conservatives) had not been so clearly gaining
in strength.[27] Melbourne, the premier, held the opinion – though
he soon relaxed it, as will be seen – that 'the Ballot was only put
forward in the first instance and that all the other points, extension
of the suffrage, [and] reformation of the House of Lords, would
be pressed necessarily in the same manner'.[28] Opponents of the
ballot believed that a vote should continue to be given openly as a
matter of public trust, and open voting was seen as a means of
enabling non-electors to feel that they had a part in deciding how
an elector used his vote. Certainly, there was indifference, and even
hostility, to the ballot among workers as long as they did not have
the vote; in these circumstances, introduction of the ballot could
be seen as taking political participation further away from them.[29]

Appropriately for a country in which classical example was often
cited in support of contemporary democratic aims, George Grote,
a historian of Ancient Greece and a radical MP for the City of
London, championed the ballot in the 1830s as a feature of
Athenian democracy which Britain should emulate. He tried six
times in the Commons to have the ballot adopted. In 1833 his
motion was lost by 211 votes to 106; in 1835 by 310 to 146; in 1836
by 139 to 88; and in 1837 by 267 to 155. The division of 1837 was
thus hardly more favourable to the ballot than that of 1833. But
towards the end of 1837 and in 1838, there was, coinciding
appropriately with the beginnings of the Chartist movement, a

notable growth of public interest in the ballot question. In February 1838 Grote moved again for the ballot, but he got no further, meeting another defeat by 317 votes to 200. From these figures, however, it seems that, in spite of the lack of progress made, the ballot was the one radical electoral demand which had won over a sizeable number of moderates.[30]

Allegedly because of this, but also with an eye to reversing its weakening position *vis-à-vis* the Conservative revival, Melbourne's Cabinet made the ballot an open question in 1839 among government ministers. As in the case of Catholic emancipation previously, they could vote and speak in accordance with their own convictions. Despite this encouragement, parliamentary interest in the ballot fell away in that year, perhaps because of its inclusion in the ultra-radical Charter, and Grote met another defeat (by 333 to 216) on 18 June 1839.[31] Strange to say, this was the end of the great days of the ballot as a parliamentary issue. There was a further effort in June 1842, when the radical H. G. Ward (a member for Sheffield) lost a ballot motion by 290 to 157, soon after a second Chartist petition including the ballot had been rejected. Apart from these instances, and the inclusion of the issue once again in a monster Chartist petition in 1848, the question in the Commons awaited a series of attempts by another radical, Francis Henry Berkeley, who represented Bristol. Berkeley's ballot motions stretched over 20 years, from 1848 until he died in 1868. But despite his attempts to win over the House with humorous electoral anecdotes, he was no nearer obtaining the ballot in 1868 than he had been in 1848. During this period, the question did not arouse as much interest as it had done in the wake of the Reform Act or when it was brandished before the people by the Chartists. Although victory for the ballot came at last in 1872, the issue was then attracting less attention than it had done in the 1830s.

Not only the ballot failed in the 1830s. So did attempts to reform the House of Lords. Daniel O'Connell – chiefly known in the 1830s for his leadership of the Irish Party which aimed to repeal the Union, but also for other radical efforts – was then to the fore in campaigning to remove hereditary peers from the Upper House. No doubt this was partly because of the Lords' frustration of government reforms for Ireland, some of which took several years to get through and succeeded at last only in a form substantially altered by the peers. In a speaking tour of Scotland and the north of England in 1837, O'Connell advocated that the existing membership of the Second Chamber be replaced by 150 elected peers. John Arthur Roebuck and Francis Place also urged Lords' reform, the former proposing to deprive the peers of all power to reject bills passed by the Commons.[32] But, although some publications appeared on the subject, there seemed to be little popular support for such a campaign. The Chartists did not appear to be strongly tempted to include Lords' reform in their programme.

Another reforming effort that failed at this time was an attempt to remove the landed-property qualification for MPs (£600 a year for a county member, £300 for a borough member) which operated under English law but not Scottish, and was not, in fact, regularly applied in England and Wales. A Parliamentary Committee on Electoral Expenses in 1834, which made large but fruitless proposals to reduce election expenses by legal provision, recommended that the qualification law be reconsidered. But abolition did not come until 1858, when the question beat the ballot as the first of the Six Points of the People's Charter to be carried. In 1838 the qualification was actually extended to include personal as well as real property, though perhaps this was at least a recognition that the supreme political power of land had begun to diminish.

Finally, there was disappointment for Joseph Hume's attempt in March 1839 to carry male household suffrage in the Commons. This did not go far enough to meet the manhood suffrage demand of the Chartists, who in July that year suffered the first massive rejection of a petition that the Commons should consider their programme. Grote and O'Connell spoke in support of Hume, but Russell said that the introduction of household suffrage would only encourage the more extensive Chartist demand for manhood suffrage. A thin House indicated general lack of interest in Hume's motion, which failed by 85 votes to 50.[33]

Failure to achieve these changes emphasized the abundant resemblances between the unreformed (pre-1832) parliamentary system and the new semi-reformed one.[34] So too did the failure to impose effective restrictions on bribery and corruption. These abuses probably increased after 1832 because there was an increase in contested elections and in activity by party agents. Between the first and second Reform Acts, 130 petitions were presented to the Commons, claiming that an election should be declared void on account of corruption, and two-thirds were successful. Russell failed in 1832 to carry a small measure extending the scope of petitioning and complaint against bribery. Bills with similar aims failed to pass in 1835, 1836, and 1837. However, Russell carried a small measure to restrict bribery in 1841. Another Act in 1843 strengthened the powers of parliamentary election committees against corruption. Following this, Parliament, as well as continuing to pass minor reforms, reverted to its pre-Reform method of disfranchising constituencies found guilty of particularly gross and extensive illegal practice. Twelve boroughs were disfranchised from 1844 to 1884. In 1854 came the Bribery Act, the first comprehensive measure against electoral corruption, but its intentions proved all too easy to evade.[35] Until the much more effective Corrupt and Illegal Practices Act of 1883, widespread bribery continued to frustrate the attainment of a more democratic system.

Similarly, democratic aspirations were also frustrated by one of the provisions of 1832 – that there should be (for the first time) a system for the registration of all who were to be allowed to give their vote. This showed that it was not simply failure to correct the old, but the adoption of some new aspects, which kept the reformed system very clearly undemocratic. It was not so much the intention of the registration provision, as the uses and abuses to which it was widely subjected, which amounted to a significant frustration of democracy. The monetary charges to become registered could be a deterrent to receiving the right to vote, despite the fact that one was otherwise qualified. Full means were provided for making objections to names on the register, and for having them decided by revising lawyers in election courts. Consequently, party agents and committees became busy in trying to remove voters from the register who were known to be inclined to the other party, and to get supporters of their own party registered. It has been said that the registration system, at least in its earlier stages, 'restricted the operation of the franchise' and:

> offered a means to the election agents and the party associations for the making and unmaking of qualifications. By the organized system of objections on the one hand and the manufacture of faggot [i.e. specially created] votes on the other, the party com-mittee either destroyed or controlled a large proportion of the suffrages supposedly conferred in 1832.[36]

Apathy or objection towards voting under the new system led to several small bills being introduced in the mid-1830s to try and make the procedure more attractive. But none of these was successful. Similar bills of 1839, 1840, and 1841 also failed. Finally, in 1843 one was passed, on a non-party basis, easing and improving the system in various ways. But it left grounds for complaint, and public apathy and party exploitation of the system were still present. Peel said in 1837 that 'the battle of the Constitution will be fought in the registration court', and this was indeed the ground level of party warfare. Different organizations with political interests (the Anti-Corn Law League being an outstanding example) concerned themselves with the niceties of registration and their possibilities for gaining advantage, and sometimes with purchasing and allocating property to create votes.[37]

Apart from the Reform Acts of 1832, the most important changes in political participation in the years 1830–48 were the Acts establishing elective municipal corporations. These were passed soon after the first Reform Acts, and (in England and Wales) were intended to establish political power in urban local government on a wider basis than the male £10 household franchise in parliamentary government. They were also intended to remove power from the existing unelected, mostly Tory, local councils and transfer it to elected bodies which, the government hoped, would be mostly Liberal.[38]

The municipal reform Acts, in 1833 and 1835, appeared (perhaps especially in historical retrospect) to be under the shadow of the 1832 measures, but they were by no means passed simply as an adjunct to them. Since the 1780s, demand for elective municipal councils had paralleled and reinforced the demand for Parliamentary Reform. But support and organization for municipal reform ('burgh reform' in Scotland) had a good deal of weight in its own right, and its contribution was becoming very marked in the 1820s.[39] Two Scottish Burgh Reform Acts, applying to burghs of different origin, were passed in 1833, following a special Act which in 1831 had granted an elective council to Dundee, after a strong local campaign.[40] The government gave prior attention to Scotland in this matter because the case for reform was traditionally stronger there, and opposition seemed likely to be weaker than in the case of England. The Scottish measures of 1833 repeated the recent Reform Act in establishing a male £10 household qualification, in this case for the municipal vote. The first municipal elections to replace the old self-electing Scottish councils were in December 1833.[41]

The Municipal Corporations Bill of 1835 for England and Wales, following the report of a commission appointed in 1833, was a more novel venture and it aroused more opposition. It was proposed that there should be a ratepaying franchise conditional on three years' continuous residence in the borough, and (in another significant move) it included single women who paid their own rates. Receiving a fairly easy passage in the Commons, the bill had a much more difficult time in the Lords. In fact the measure provided one of the instances in the 1830s when the Conservative majority in the Upper House was distinctly awkward over a Liberal measure. The Lords initially proposed that, to accompany the elected councillors, an unelected category of aldermen should be appointed for life to the new councils. The Commons rejected this, but compromised by accepting that a third of the councillors should be selected (by the council) as aldermen and serve for six years, and that councillors would have to meet a property qualification. The Act, under which the first elections took place in December 1835, applied to the existing corporate boroughs, and new incorporated boroughs were added later. For many decades the councils were dominated by the middle class, for whom they provided a much more attainable outlet than Parliament for the realization of political ambition, and in some councils Nonconformity was in the ascendant.[42]

The municipal reforms thus reflected some of the broad social developments of nineteenth-century Britain. By the 1833 and 1835 Acts, municipal government was largely turned over (at least for the next few years) to the Liberal Party, and the reforms have been described as 'a much greater blow to Toryism than the Reform bill itself'.[43] They were certainly a major blow to the old deferential urban politics, and an important stage in the development of democracy in the towns.

The People's Charter

By the later 1830s demands for radical reform were again strengthening, and were shown in pressure-groups outside

Parliament far more than in the weakening radicalism inside. The extent of middle-class and working-class co-operation in the Reform struggle of 1830–2 has probably been exaggerated. There was certainly more class conflict than class co-operation in the radical movements from 1832 to 1848. A national Anti-Corn Law League emerged out of scattered local associations in 1838, and seemed menacing to aristocratic interests on quite a wide front. By then, demands were being made more openly for disestablishment of the Church, and a strong movement was taking shape in support of the Six Points of the People's Charter, which were published and circulated in 1838. Support for both the mainly middle-class Anti-Corn Law League and the mainly working-class Chartist movement – organizations which developed a bitter rivalry – swelled on account of serious economic depression commencing in 1837 and lasting for about five years, causing business failures, unemployment, and short-time working.

It is probably true to say that radicals of both the middle and the working class were not disappointed with the Reform Acts of 1832, as these had brought greater change than had seemed likely previously and contained wider provisions than, at some points in the Reform crisis, the Whigs had seemed likely to get through. Radicals were, however, frustrated after the Acts because, following the encouragement of 1832, they wanted much more electoral reform, but neither political party was yet interested in supporting this aim.

On account of long-term radical hopes, directed towards achieving a large amount of democracy in the Constitution, it was clear that the Reform Acts would be widely regarded as anything but final, and rather would be seen as opportunities to work for further electoral reform. It could also be fairly clearly discerned that, since there was in the provisions of the Reform Acts a strong element of trying to serve Whig interests and to undermine Tory ones, party interest would bulk large in any further extension of the franchise or the redistribution of seats. Even a substantial Conservative Reform Bill might be introduced in an effort to preserve or revive party strength in an age which often appeared to be dominated by Liberalism. It was very unlikely that there could be finality over electoral reform in a country which was committed to a representative system of government, where social change was proceeding apace and continuing to fuel the desire for political change, and in which politics was dominated by party rivalry.

The continuance or revival of radical groups aiming at further electoral reform in the six years or so after 1832 demonstrated the gap between the provisions of the Reform Acts and aspirations to establish a more democratic system. Thomas Attwood's Birming-ham Political Union, which had played an originating role in the recent radical upheavals, continued until 1834. It was then suspended, but was revived in 1837 with a programme of manhood suffrage, secret ballot, and frequently-elected Parliaments. However, it broke up through internal disagreements in 1839.[44] North of the border a Scottish Radical Association was formed in December 1836, having as president Dr John Taylor (soon to become a close ally of Fergus O'Connor), developing several branches, and aiming at manhood suffrage, the ballot, annually elected Parliaments, and an end to Established Churches.[45] Defence of the unstamped (or 'pauper') press and campaigns for the repeal of taxes on newspapers combined the efforts of middle- and working-class radicals. An alliance between them was seen in the Society for Promoting a Cheap and Honest Press, which was founded in April 1836 and shortly became the London Working Men's Association (LWMA).[46]

The LWMA aimed at wide electoral reform and in May 1838 published the 'People's Charter', which had been prepared by a joint committee consisting of radical MPs and some of its own members.[47] This provided the unifying basis of the Chartist movement, which lasted officially for 20 years (and unofficially into the indefinite future). From 1838, Chartism was, until at least ten years later, the main extra-parliamentary organization working for Reform in a period when there was little pressure for electoral change within Parliament itself.[48]

The fact that Chartism led the demand for Parliamentary Reform in these years represented a notable change from 1830–2, when the government had taken the lead and much of the extra-parliamentary effort had acted in a supporting capacity. In the later 1830s and the 1840s, there was no government initiative for major Parliamentary Reform and there was very little support in Parliament for the Chartist initiative. Government and Parliament were to revive as leading motivating centres of electoral change, but not until the extra-parliamentary force of Chartism had failed in its last major plea for parliamentary consideration of its programme in 1848.

The wide separation between Parliament and the Chartists is probably to be explained by the extremism of the Chartist movement. This was shown not only in some of the Six Points of its political demands, but in some of its activities, which were easily condemned as subversive and resulted in imprisonment or transportation for some of its leaders; also in its representation of growing working-class industrial solidarity in a period (culminating in 1842) of depression, strikes, and bitter opposition to the New Poor Law and its workhouse system.[49] Chartism not only had its own cause, the Six Points of the Charter, but drew practically every other radical cause within its ambit, resulting in a protean diversity which brought both strength and weakness to the movement. It has recently been said that, by the summer of 1838:

> a lively and assertive movement had been born, providing a common banner under which a variety of existing causes, grievances and organizations could be marshalled, and fusing together potentially contradictory elements (embracing, for example, the full spectrum of views on political economy and of religious attachment, and bringing representatives of employers and workpeople into uneasy alliance) in pursuit of a common political goal. How it was to be achieved, and what was to be done with it if success were attained, remained highly problematic and divisive issues.[50]

But although it had connections with social (and to a lesser extent religious) reform, Chartism was primarily working for a large advance towards democratic government through the adoption by Parliament of the Six Points of the People's Charter.[51] The six claims were manhood suffrage, secret ballot, equal electoral districts, payment of MPs, abolition of the property qualification for MPs, and annually elected Parliaments. These were not baldly stated in this way, however, but were accompanied by brief explanatory glosses which emphasized the democratic nature of the aims. The object of a secret ballot was 'to protect the elector in the exercise of his vote'. Abolition of the property qualification was to enable constituencies 'to return the man of their choice, be he rich or poor'. Equal electoral districts would 'secure the same amount of representation for the same number of electors, instead of allowing small constituencies to swamp the votes of large ones'. Annual Parliaments were linked to the need to stop bribery and intimidation. This reform was seen as a check on both bribery and the actions of MPs:

> since though a constituency might be bought once in seven years (even with the ballot), no purse could buy a constituency (under a system of universal suffrage) in each ensuing twelve-month; and since members, when elected for a year only, would not be able to defy and betray their constituents as now.[52]

The Six Points were a restatement of aims which, at one time or another, had appeared as the staple of radical democratic demand since Cartwright's *Take your Choice* in 1776. Thus the Points were not original or innovative. Though very radical in nature, they were of a conventional and familiar radicalism, and did not venture into the outrageous by asking for votes for women, abolition of the House of Lords, or institution of a republic. The demand for annual Parliaments was dropped as a reforming claim after the Chartist era, perhaps partly because bribery was eventually quashed, and perhaps partly because the claim did not accord with the desire of parties to hold power for substantial periods. All the other Points were gained by 1918 (manhood suffrage being the last), and this indicates that they were indispensable to the democratic demand as a whole. After 1848 it was not until the militant campaigning for the women's vote in the early twentieth century that a democratic upsurge occurred that was similar to Chartism in sustained and diverse activity. When limited women's suffrage was gained in 1918, at the same time as full manhood suffrage, it appeared like the appropriate winning of a Seventh Point, additional to the Charter.

The changing fortunes of Chartism were influenced by the state of the economy and its effect on employment, also by the reactions of the House of Commons. Chartist efforts displayed examples of direct physical action. The more physical side of the movement was rarely encouraged by the leaders, but was seen in the Newport Rising in South Wales in 1839 and, to a lesser extent, in disturbances in other industrial areas in that year and soon afterwards; also in riots in 1848, and in examples at different times of meetings of other groups being broken up by Chartists. Generally, the law and government informers triumphed in these encounters, and the power of civil authority was never challenged by a concerted attempt at revolution under Chartist auspices. Also defeated were the more mainstream, constitutional efforts of Chartists to have their national petitions for the Six Points considered by the Commons. Three major efforts were made – two of them in the most hopeful period for Chartism, a time of pronounced economic depression (1839–42), and the third in 1848, a briefer time of economic recession which coincided with the inspiration of the continental 'Year of Revolutions'. These petitioning attempts were promoted by the Chartist annual Conventions which were held every year from 1839 to 1858. The three pleas to consider the Charter achieved only low levels of support in the Commons. In July 1839 the petition was rejected by 235 votes to 46, and in May 1842 by 287 to 59. The petition was presented again, in very discouraging circumstances, on 10 April 1848, but was withdrawn without a vote. Later, smaller efforts were also unsuccessful.

Chartism never recovered from its parliamentary fate in April 1848 and from repressive action by the authorities throughout the country during the next few months. Chartism lasted as an organized body for ten more years; and after this, its aims (still mostly unrealized by that time) continued to be at the centre of radical democratic demand. But after its effort in 1848, it lost its position as the leading democratic force in the country. It declined into being one of several not very effective bodies working for political reform in the less promising economic and social conditions of the 1850s, when at times it seemed that only support for the causes of foreign refugees was keeping British radicalism consistently alive. The Chartist leadership disintegrated and dispersed for various reasons in the 1850s – the tendency of some prominent Chartists to leave Britain being some indication of the changed political circumstances, even if these individuals continued their radical activities (as did George Julian Harney) in their new habitats.[53] The year 1858, in which Chartism terminated as a movement, was the same year in which Parliament first conceded, in effect, a Chartist Point – the abolition of the property qualification for MPs – and not long before the slow beginnings of revived interest in radical reform. It was not until 1865, however, that there emerged, in the Reform League, a popular body which bore marked resemblances to Chartism.

The Six Points may have received a bad setback in 1848, but most of them were alive at the end of the 1840s and in the early 1850s. Ironically, they now seemed to gain more attention inside

Parliament than outside, as though Parliament had been awaiting the decisive weakening of Chartism before considering some of its demands. Radical MPs, especially Joseph Hume, moved for the adoption of selected points from the Charter, though they failed to win them.

From the time of the Chartist failure of 1848, indeed, electoral reform moved back more positively into Parliament and party politics. From 1848, both Lord John Russell and Benjamin Disraeli, the Liberal and Protectionist leaders in the House of Commons, contemplated initiating a further reform of parliamentary representation, though of a mild kind compared with the contemporary back-bench radical motions. The new party efforts at Parliamentary Reform probably owed very little to fears of revolution after the example of 1848.[54] They were not sufficiently swift, determined, or extensive to support the view that they were attempts to introduce hedges against revolution. It is more likely that they were seen as methods of benefiting one or other of the parties in their search for more electoral support amidst the unrewarding doldrums of mid-century politics. This was probably an important reason behind Russell's abortive Parliamentary Reform Bills of 1852, 1854, 1860, and 1866, Disraeli's of 1859, and finally Disraeli's successful one of 1867. The social changes which had encouraged Parliamentary Reform in 1832 were continuing, and party interest supplied a reason for appealing to the people who were experiencing these changes. Party interest in Reform in the 1850s was also doubtless stimulated by the changed conditions of party politics after the disruption and fall of Peel's Conservative Government in 1846.

The political crisis of that year was caused by a Conservative split which had the effect of keeping that party out of majority government for many years. A Liberal Government succeeded to office, led by Lord John Russell, and managed to retain it for six years. But in seeking to strengthen itself in a general election in 1847, it obtained the slimmest of overall majorities, and largely depended for its continued power on the division between the two Conservative groups, Protectionists and Peelites. The Liberals were stronger than they had been when they lost office to Peel after a defeat by a majority of 78 in the election of 1841. But they were divided and unstable, and it was not surprising that Russell turned by 1849 to the planning of franchise extension as a means of obtaining more party strength (or, in the case of Ireland, as one of the means of restoring a country which had been pulverized by famine).[55] Among some Conservatives, the division of 1846 and consequent party weakness also suggested the adoption of franchise extension. From 1848, Disraeli was weighing the possibilities of introducing a Conservative Reform Bill, and by the early 1850s he was openly advocating this line of policy, to the alarm of more cautious colleagues.[56]

So it was that, by the 1850s, the centre of gravity in electoral reform swung away from Chartist extra-parliamentary demands and back to parliamentary political efforts, in which back-bench radicals proposed some of the Chartist Points and rival party leaders took up more limited objectives. However, apart from the Irish Franchise Act of 1850 and the abolition of the property qualification for MPs in 1858, these efforts bore the common characteristic of failure, and it was not until 1867 that this situation markedly changed.

Notes

1. The fullest modern treatment, which will be difficult to supersede, is by M. Brock, *The Great Reform Act* (London, 1973). Important recent examinations on a smaller scale are by J. W. Derry, *Charles, Earl Grey, Aristocratic Reformer* (Oxford, 1992), pp. 184–210; and W. D. Rubinstein, *Britain's Century: A Social and Political History, 1815–1905* (London, 1998), pp. 37–46. Reference should also be made to the contrasting interpretations of J. Cannon, *Parliamentary Reform, 1640–1832* (Cambridge, 1973), pp. 204–63; and D. C. Moore, *The Politics of Deference: A Study of the Mid-Nineteenth Century English Political System* (Hassocks, 1976).
2. For the committee's proceedings, see M. Brock, op. cit., pp. 136–41; and J. Cannon, op. cit., pp. 205–10.
3. Brock, pp. 141–2.
4. Ibid., p. 196.
5. D. Fraser, 'The agitation for Parliamentary Reform', in J. T. Ward (ed.), *Popular Movements, c.1830–50* (London, 1970), p. 42.
6. See Brock, pp. 228–9; C. Seymour, *Electoral Reform in England and Wales: The Development and Operation of the Parliamentary Franchise, 1832–85* (Newton Abbot, 1970; 1st edn 1915), pp. 18–20.
7. Cannon, p. 227; Brock, pp. 247–57. On earlier popular rioting in the Reform crisis, see D. J. V. Jones, 'The Merthyr riots of 1831', *Welsh History Review*, III (1966–7), 173–205; idem, 'The Carmarthen riots of 1831', ibid., IV (1968–9), 129–42.
8. Brock, pp. 268–70 and ff.; J. W. Derry, op. cit., p. 201.
9. Cannon, pp. 231–2; Brock, p. 269; Derry, p. 204.

10. Quoted Cannon, p. 232.

11. Brock, pp. 294–9.

12. Derry, p. 191. Cf. I. Newbould, *Whiggery and Reform, 1830–41* (London, 1990), p. 79.

13. J. I. Brash (ed.), *Papers on Scottish Electoral Politics, 1832–54* (Edinburgh, 1974), pp. xi–xii. Cf. I. G. C. Hutchison, *A Political History of Scotland, 1832–1924* (Edinburgh, 1986), p. 1; M. Dyer, *Men of Property and Intelligence: The Scottish Electoral System Prior to 1884* (Aberdeen, 1996), pp. 23–47; J. Parry, *The Rise and Fall of Liberal Government in Victorian Britain* (London, 1993), p. 154.

14. J. M. Bourne, *Patronage and Society in Nineteenth-Century England* (London, 1986), p. 141; C. Seymour, *Electoral Reform in England and Wales, 1832–85* (Newton Abbot, 1970), p. 5.

15. K. Robbins, *Great Britain: Identities, Institutions, and the Idea of Britishness* (London, 1998), p. 154. Cf. F. O'Gorman, *The Long Eighteenth Century: British Political and Social History, 1688–1832* (London, 1997), pp. 369–71.

16. J. Parry, op. cit., p. 83. Cf. M. Bentley, *Politics without Democracy, 1815–1914* (London, 1984), pp. 86–8; K. T. Hoppen, 'Roads to democracy: electioneering and corruption in nineteenth-century England and Ireland', *History*, LXXXI (1996), 555–8.

17. This argument is encapsulated in D. C. Moore's celebrated article, 'The other face of reform', *Victorian Studies*, V (1961–2), 7–34, and elaborated in his book, *The Politics of Deference: A Study of the Mid-Nineteenth Century English Political System* (Hassocks, 1976). Among the numerous criticisms of Moore's thesis are Cannon, pp. 246–53; R. W. Davis, *Political Change and Continuity, 1760–1885: A Buckinghamshire Study* (Newton Abbot, 1972), pp. 9–10; idem, 'The Whigs and the idea of electoral deference: some further thoughts on the Great Reform Act', *Durham University Journal*, LXVII (1974), 79–91; and, more recently, D. Eastwood, 'Contesting the politics of deference: the rural electorate, 1820–60', in J. Lawrence and M. Taylor (eds), *Party, State and Society: Electoral Behaviour in Britain since 1820* (Aldershot, 1997), pp. 27–49.

18. Parry, p. 83. Cf. A. Howe, *The Cotton Masters, 1830–60* (Oxford, 1984), pp. 93–5.

19. E. J. Evans, *The Forging of the Modern State: Early Industrial Britain, 1783–1870* (London, 1996), p. 229.

20. Cf. I. Newbould, op. cit., pp. 228–44.

21. J. K. Walton, *Chartism* (London, 1999), p. 8.

22. For detailed illustrations of the numerous pressure groups and their aspirations for democratic advance, see Patricia Hollis (ed.), *Pressure from Without in Early Victorian England* (London, 1974); D. A. Hamer, *The Politics of Electoral Pressure: A Study in the History of Victorian Reform Agitations* (Hassocks, 1977); B. Harrison, *Drink and the Victorians: The Temperance Question in England, 1815–72* (London, 1971); P. J. Waller, *Democracy and Sectarianism: A Political and Social History of Liverpool, 1868–1939* (Liverpool, 1981); K. Young and Patricia L. Garside, *Metropolitan London: Politics and Urban Change, 1837–1981* (London, 1982).

23. Quoted I. Machin, 'Disestablishment and democracy, c.1840–1930', in E. F. Biagini (ed.), *Citizenship and Community: Liberals, Radicals, and Collective Identities in the British Isles, 1865–1931* (Cambridge, 1996), p. 120. See R. Masheder, *Dissent and Democracy: Their Mutual Relations and Common Objects* (London, 1864), pp. 4–6, 312 ff.

24. Bruce L. Kinzer, *The Ballot Question in Nineteenth-Century English Politics* (New York, 1982), pp. 11–13. For a detailed examination of the ballot question, see also C. Seymour, op. cit., pp. 205–15. See also W. Thomas, *The Philosophic Radicals* (Oxford, 1979), pp. 406–38 (ch. on 'George Grote and the Ballot').

25. Quoted in B. L. Kinzer, op. cit., p. 20.

26. Quoted ibid., p. 23.

27. Cf. J. Prest, *Lord John Russell* (London, 1972), p. 122.

28. Kinzer, p. 26.

29. Ibid., pp. 29, 50; J. Prest, op. cit., p. 122. Cf. B. Harrison, *The Transformation of British Politics, 1860–1995* (Oxford, 1996), p. 38.

30. Kinzer, pp. 34–41.

31. Ibid., pp. 42–5; Prest, *Russell*, p. 147; Newbould, pp. 244–6.

32. E. A. Smith, *The House of Lords in British Politics and Society, 1815–1911* (London, 1992), pp. 136–8, 142.

33. Ronald K. Huch and Paul A. Ziegler, *Joseph Hume, the People's MP* (Philadelphia, 1985), pp. 114–15.

34. These resemblances are emphasized in a large amount of published work, for example N. Gash, *Politics in the Age of Peel: A Study in the Technique of Parliamentary Representation, 1830–50* (London, 1953), p. 66 ff.; M. Brock, *The Great Reform Act*, pp. 329–30; K. T. Hoppen, 'Roads to democracy: electioneering and corruption in nineteenth-century England and Ireland', *History*, LXXXI (1996), 552–71.

35. W. B. Gwyn, *Democracy and the Cost of Politics in Britain* (London, 1962), pp. 79–83; Seymour, pp. 171–204, 215–27.

36. Seymour, p. 163. For detailed examinations of the operation of the registration system and attempts to reform it, see ibid., pp. 104–64; and J. Prest, *Politics in the Age of Cobden* (London, 1977), pp. 11–76.

37. Seymour, pp. 116–35.

38. D. Fraser (ed.), *Municipal Reform and the Industrial City* (Leicester, 1982), p. 11.

39. D. Eastwood, *Government and Community in the English Provinces, 1700–1870* (Basingstoke, 1997), p. 75. See also A. Prentice, *Historical Sketches and Personal Recollections of Manchester: The Progress of Public Opinion, 1792–1832* (2nd edn, London, 1851).

40. J. Cannon, *Parliamentary Reform, 1640–1832*, p. 112; D. Southgate, 'Politics and representation in Dundee, 1832–1963', in J. M. Jackson (ed.), *The City of Dundee (Third Statistical Account of Scotland*, vol. 25, Arbroath 1979), pp. 287–8; W. Ferguson, *Scotland, 1689 to the Present* (Edinburgh, 1968), pp. 282–3, 303.

41. N. Gash, *Aristocracy and People: Britain, 1815–65* (London, 1979), pp. 166–7.

42. J. Prest, *Russell*, pp. 95–7; D. Fraser, op. cit., pp. 4–5; N. Gash, *Aristocracy*

and People, pp. 167–8; Alice Russell, *Political Stability in later Victorian England: A Sociological Analysis and Interpretation* (Lewes, 1992), pp. 253–7; G. I. T. Machin, *Politics and the Churches in Great Britain, 1832 to 1868* (Oxford, 1977), pp. 54–6. See also G. B. A. M. Finlayson, 'The politics of municipal reform, 1835', *English Historical Review*, LXXXI (1966), 673–92.

43. Quoted M. Brock, *The Great Reform Act*, p. 317.
44. C. Flick, op. cit., pp. 109, 131, 172.
45. A. Wilson, *The Chartist Movement in Scotland* (Manchester, 1970), p. 35.
46. Patricia Hollis, *The Pauper Press: A Study in Working-Class Radicalism of the 1830s* (Oxford, 1970), pp. 304–5.
47. E. Royle, *Chartism* (3rd edn, London, 1996), p. 18.
48. J. K. Walton, *Chartism* (London, 1999) is a useful recent guide to the subject.
49. E. Royle, op. cit., pp. 16, 90–1; Shona Paul, 'Dundee radical politics, 1834–50' (M. Phil. thesis, University of Dundee, 1999), pp. 98–167; J. Charlton, *The Chartists: The First National Workers' Movement* (London, 1997).
50. J. K. Walton, op. cit., p. 10.
51. Royle, p. 91; G. Stedman Jones, *Languages of Class: Studies in English Working-Class History, 1832–1982* (Cambridge, 1983), pp. 96, 100.
52. F. C. Mather (ed.), *Chartism and Society: An Anthology of Documents* (London, 1980), p. 47.
53. G. I. T. Machin, 'George Julian Harney in Jersey, 1855–63: a Chartist "abroad"', *Annual Bulletin of the Société Jersiaise*, 23:4 (1984), 478–95.
54. Cf. R. Quinault, '1848 and Parliamentary Reform', *Historical Journal*, XXXI (1988), 835, 837, 848.
55. See Prest, *Russell*, pp. 305–11.
56. R. Stewart, *The Foundation of the Conservative Party, 1830–67* (London, 1978), p. 353; I. Machin, *Disraeli* (London, 1995), pp. 81–2.

3 Further Moves to Advance Democracy, 1848–68

Introduction

The year 1848 formed a break in the history of democratic pressure in Britain, and of government reactions to it. But it was not a break which pointed decisively in any direction. A phase of powerful and ambitious extra-parliamentary campaigning had ended, but in Parliament a new, though narrower, phase of radical motions and moderate government bills commenced. The negative aspect of this turning point was the recession, for some 16 years, of wide and popular political campaigning. The positive aspect was a stream of parliamentary motions and bills, many more than in the 1840s, coming from both radical and moderate reformers, usually from Liberals, but in 1859 from a Conservative Government. The radical motions seemed like attenuated Chartism; indeed, they proposed the adoption of some of the Six Points, and they commenced in the Commons only five weeks after the Chartist *débacle* on 10 April 1848.

For 12 years or so from 1848, radicalism in the country declined but did not die out. There was a fair amount of extra-parliamentary radical activity during this time, shown by the existence of radical societies urging various causes and by the continuance of a flourishing radical press. The National Freehold Land Society, formed in 1849, emulated the defunct (because successful in its aim) Anti-Corn Law League by buying land in order to create votes, and had 85 000 members by 1852.[1] But the radicalism of these years was notably uneven in character, and small-scale compared with that of most of the 1840s. On occasion, British radicalism seemed almost to be relying on the presence, from time to time, of Continental exiles to keep it going – such as Kossuth, Mazzini, Marx and Louis Blanc, who variously advocated nationalism, individualism, and socialism.[2] Failure clearly marked some of the radical organizations of these years, such as the National Parliamentary and Financial Reform Association (1849–54), which advocated Free Trade, a more open foreign policy, and a watered-down version of the Six Points.[3] As the 1850s advanced, electoral reform seemed less and less likely in spite of all the activity in Parliament. There was not enough demonstrated radical force outside Parliament to support the efforts inside. Radical prospects sometimes looked bleak indeed. 'As for Parliamentary Reform', wrote Cobden in September 1856, 'I hold that we might as well call out for the millennium.'[4]

In considering possible reasons for the recession of radicalism, it is difficult to deny the dominating presence of simple apathy, arising from the gradually growing prosperity and the low unemployment of the time, in contrast to the depression of 1837–42 which had stimulated radicalism. A marked interest by British radicals in overseas political questions could not compensate for the lack of popular support for the advance of democracy at home.

Radicalism and Electoral Reform, 1848–51

The radical parliamentary motions for democratic reform in the late 1840s and the 1850s did not influence specific government intentions, but they helped to keep the cause alive at a time when interest was flagging in the country.[5] Only one motion to enact the secret ballot – Henry George Ward's unsuccessful attempt in 1842 – had been brought before the Commons between 1840 and 1848. In the latter year Francis Henry Berkeley's series of motions for the ballot began, and lasted until 1867.

On 8 August 1848 Berkeley brought in his first ballot motion. The result was striking, being the first majority for the secret ballot in the Commons. But it was gained by a very narrow margin in a very small House (86 votes to 81), and there was no opportunity to present a bill based on the motion before the end of the session.[6] Berkeley was defeated in 1849 and 1850. In 1851, however, he succeeded again (by 87 votes to 50) in an even smaller House than in 1848. Again he could not introduce a bill because of the late stage which had been reached in the session. Another defeat followed in 1852. But in 1853 the formation of the Society for Promoting the Adoption of the Vote by Ballot – with Berkeley as president and supported strongly by Cobden, Bright, and other leading radicals – seemed to put more stiffening into this demand. This came after the National Parliamentary and Financial Reform Association (NPFRA), which included the ballot among its aims, had failed to achieve any obvious success. But the Ballot Society, hampered by lack of adequate finance, was no more successful than the NPFRA, though it managed to last until the late 1860s.

Moreover, although Berkeley's motions had a good deal of support in the reforming press, dislike of secret voting remained strong even among some radicals. John Stuart Mill, formerly an advocate of the ballot, began to turn against it about 1853 and denounced it in his *Thoughts on Parliamentary Reform*, published in 1859. Berkeley's motions had no success in the years 1852–8, but in 1859 he obtained a third victory, by 102 votes to 99. Although they sometimes squeezed through in thin Houses, the ballot motions could make little headway against the usual majority opposition, which included many Liberal MPs as well as almost all Conservative ones. Russell, who wanted some franchise extension, opposed the ballot together with Palmerston, who was against franchise extension. But Russell's opposition to Berkeley was weakening by the late 1850s, just as Mill's was strengthening.[7]

The attempt to gain the ballot was paralleled by other radical efforts at electoral reform in the late 1840s and the 1850s. Although these were despised by Fergus O'Connor and the hard-line Chartists, they were a clear, if weakened, extension of the attempts to gain the Six Points. Though the last major Chartist effort failed in 1848, support was growing in Parliament at this time for a less ambitious radical programme of electoral change.[8] A meeting of radical politicians was held on 11 April 1848, one day after the ill-fated Chartist assembly on Kennington Common. The meeting appointed a committee which had Joseph Hume as chairman and Richard Cobden as deputy chairman. Hopes that this initiative would produce a strong reforming movement were eventually disappointed, and disagreements continued among leading radicals. But Hume was active in urging radical reforms in the Commons. As these were decidedly less than the Charter as a whole, it was hoped that they would attract more support in Parliament and have more success in uniting middle-class and working-class radicals. Payment of MPs was not supported by many parliamentary radicals because it was suspected that it would lead to the increase of government patronage, and it was not included in Hume's proposals.[9] Abolition of the property qualification for MPs was also absent. The ballot was included; but there were only watered-down versions of some of the other Chartist Points – male household suffrage instead of manhood suffrage, triennial Parliaments instead of annual Parliaments, and a more equitable distribution of seats instead of equal electoral districts.

When Hume moved, on 20 June 1848, for leave to bring in a Reform Bill, his scheme had become known as the 'Little Charter'. It was too little for O'Connor, but too large for both Government and Opposition. Consequently, it was opposed in the Commons debate by Russell, the Liberal premier, and Disraeli, the chief spokesman of the Protectionists (the larger of the two post-1846 Conservative groups). Both of these were soon to take up much milder versions of Parliamentary Reform; Russell, indeed, said in his opposing speech that the time for some reform of the electoral system was near.[10] Thus the first notable crack in Whig intransigence had been made in a parliamentary declaration; it was the first glimmering of a new governmental approach to the franchise question.

After a postponement of the debate, Hume's motion was decisively defeated on 6 July by 351 votes to 84. On introducing a similar motion on 5 June 1849, he lost again, by 268 to 82. Russell had again discouraged the scheme, and Hume and O'Connor joined in condemning the ineffectuality of the government on the electoral question. A month later, on 3 July, Hume was one of only 13 MPs who voted to consider the People's Charter when O'Connor introduced this *en bloc* once again. A third effort by Hume to bring in the Little Charter was defeated by 242 to 96 in February 1850. The margin of opposition remained very decisive.

Hume did not try to introduce the Little Charter in 1851. But in February that year Peter Locke King, radical MP for East Surrey, carried the second of five motions he introduced in the 1850s (1850–2, 1857–8) to extend the county franchise. He unexpectedly defeated the government, by 100 votes to 52, in obtaining leave to introduce a bill enfranchising £10 occupiers in towns within county constituencies; though the consequent bill was lost on the second reading.[11] Also in February 1851, Hume asked Russell whether he intended to introduce a Reform Bill that year, and Russell said he would consider doing so at 'a fit time'.[12] He did, in fact, commence preparation of a Reform Bill in the following autumn, for introduction in 1852.

Already, however, Russell's ministry had carried a Reform Bill for Ireland in 1850. This was naturally encouraging at the time for reformers in Britain as well as Ireland.[13] The Great Famine and the scarcity of leases for tenants had caused a rapid reduction in the number of Irish electors. After the Famine, it has been said, 'voters simply melted away':

> Tipperary's effective electorate slumped from 2,369 in 1832 to about 200 in 1849. Armagh was down from 3,342 to 700, Tyrone from 1,151 to 800, Mayo from 1,350 to 250. Even the total 'nominal' county electorate had fallen from 60,597 to 27,180, though the latter figure was still grossly inflated and a reasonable estimate of *effective* county voters in 1849–50 would probably lie in the region of 15,000 to 18,000. In the boroughs, where leasing was less important and the population dropped less rapidly, numbers held steady at about the 29,471 of 1832. Overall, however, the electorate had fallen from 121,194 to around 45,000.[14]

In post-1832 Britain, some borough electorates dropped for a while, because of the deaths of 'ancient right' voters, until the rise in occupation values restored them and raised them further, but decimation of this special Irish magnitude was never experienced. The government could hardly ignore the situation, or (in the circumstances) meet it simply by reducing the number of Irish seats in proportion to the fall in electors and keep the same franchise qualifications. Russell's Irish Franchise Bill was passed fairly rapidly, though there were differences over it between the Commons and the Lords. The Act provided a £12 household franchise in the counties and an £8 one in the boroughs. The total electorate shot up from about 45 000 to 163 546 (135 245 in the counties and 28 301 in the boroughs).[15] The new total was not spectacularly higher than the pre-Famine one, but in post-Famine conditions it represented a very large proportional enfranchisement.

Questions of Bribery and Proportional Representation in the 1850s

Apart from the Irish Franchise Act and the passage, after efforts from 1854, of a bill of Peter Locke King to abolish the property qualification for MPs in June 1858, a third electoral reform measure was passed between 1848 and 1867. This was the Corrupt Practices (or 'Bribery') Act of 1854. The bill was introduced by Russell during the Aberdeen Coalition of Peelites and Liberals, after a vast amount of bribery was discovered to have taken place in the 1852 election and after a previous bill, introduced by Spencer Walpole, had been dropped.[16] But the 1854 Act's power to eliminate political corruption – an insidious and massive obstacle to free democratic expression – was not very great.

Attempts to reduce bribery had been no stranger to Parliament since the Reform Act. An Act of 1843, to strengthen the investigative powers of parliamentary election committees into charges of corruption, had had little effect.[17] Parliament disfranchised Sudbury for gross electoral corruption in 1844, after two previous efforts had been foiled by the Lords. St Albans was disfranchised for similar reasons in 1852. Four more boroughs lost their representation on account of corruption in 1867, and a further four between then and 1884.[18]

Russell's bill of 1854 was the first anti-bribery measure which set out to be a comprehensive reform. It clearly defined bribery, treating, and undue influence (which was stated to include abduction of voters during an election). It laid down a more realistic penalty of £50, in place of the previous one of £500, for anyone found guilty of administering or receiving treating. Its most important provision was that an election auditor should be appointed in every constituency by the returning officer every year. The auditor was to be informed of all money spent by candidates and for what purposes. However, a vast and fatal flaw in the measure was that the auditor was given no power to investigate expenditure, and had to take a candidate's returns on trust. Some reduction in direct bribery probably occurred as a result of the Act. But soon after the bill had passed it was widely believed that candidates and their agents who were intent on influencing voters by corrupt means could easily escape the eye of the election auditor. This could be done by informing him only about the legal portions of their expenditure, and concealing the rest. It has been concluded that 'the effect of the statute upon bribery and treating was very slight', and that, as before, 'the electors could see little reason to fear prosecution for accepting bribes'.[19] Moreover, it has been pointed out, the Act 'made no attempt to prevent bribery by rendering it useless, nor did it impose any real check upon undue influence'.[20]

Attempts to suppress bribery awaited another enactment in 1868, but this also proved unsuccessful. It would naturally be difficult to eliminate bribery when so many of the sitting MPs and peers were involved in it as a matter of accepted habit. But from the timid, tentative, and slipshod nature of anti-bribery Acts before the strong measure of 1883, it could have been alleged that the reformers were trying to bring about change through collusion with corruption rather than cleaning out the Augean stables for good and all.

In the 1850s there were not only motions and bills for Parliamentary Reform, based on ideas conceived previously. There was also, outside Parliament, the revived advocacy of proportional representation, as well as discussion of other electoral changes in a variety of publications. Proposals made previously for the fairer representation of minorities had included proportional represent-ation, the 'limited vote', and the 'cumulative vote'. The limited vote would have provided that electors in the seven three-member English counties (and the four-member City of London constituency) established in 1832 could vote for no more than two candidates.[21] The limited vote was established in these and in five large urban constituencies (Birmingham, Glasgow, Leeds, Liverpool, and Manchester) in the Reform Acts of 1867–8, and it was abolished when a system of mainly single-member consti-tuencies was adopted in 1885. The cumulative vote, which allowed electors to accumulate an allocation of votes on one candidate if they wished, was adopted only in elections for some local government bodies, including Poor Law Guardians and School Boards. Proportional representation was adopted in the United Kingdom for the first time for Northern Ireland elections held from 1920 to 1929. It did not appear again until a new Northern Ireland Assembly was established in 1973, and it figured to a sizeable extent in the electoral system for a Scottish Parliament and a Welsh Assembly, first used in 1999. But proportional representation for British parliamentary elections has been continuously advocated from the 1850s, battling to no avail against the argument of stable and lasting government which has coincided with the interests of large parties in obtaining big majorities.

The issue of proportional representation really began to be put on the map in this country in 1857, when Thomas Hare, a friend of John Stuart Mill (who supported his aims), published a long pamphlet on *The Machinery of Representation*, which he followed in 1859 with a lengthy and widely read *Treatise on the Election of Representatives, Parliamentary and Municipal*. Hare's intriguing scheme involved drawing up a list of all the candidates in a general election (probably over a thousand), and a register of all the electors (about a million at that time), and allowing any elector to state his preferred candidates in order and to vote for them. Candidates would qualify for entry to the House of Commons in order of votes obtained, provided they had reached the required 'quota' of votes, which was calculated by dividing the total number of registered electors by the number of seats in the Commons. Thus far the scheme was not unduly complex, but it was accused of becoming so when further aspects of it were considered, such as the recommended three polling days and the details of allocating surplus votes among candidates after the one given first preference. But Hare simplified some of his suggestions in a second edition of his 1857 pamphlet; now, for example, recommending only one polling day.

Hare was certain that his plan would aid democracy, by circumventing patronage, liberating MPs from the straitjacket of representing a small constituency, and giving the elector much more responsibility and choice. The purity of voting and the quality of representation would greatly improve.[22] The expectation of universal benefit from the scheme was typical of the age which produced the far-reaching, optimistic ideals of the Utilitarians, the Free Traders, and Karl Marx. Mill thoroughly supported Hare's publications. When Hare's *Treatise* appeared in January 1859, Mill 'read it at once, and by 7 February was recommending Edwin Chadwick to read it without delay'. In March he told Hare that he seemed to have 'exactly, and for the first time, solved the difficulty of popular representation'. In 1867 Mill argued unsuccessfully for the inclusion not only of women's suffrage, but also of Hare's scheme in the Reform Bill of that year.[23] Largely through Mill's urging of Hare's plan, proportional representation became an important part of the ideas of some radicals for the advance of democracy.

Government Efforts at Franchise Reform in the 1850s

As well as a series of unsuccessful radical motions representing attempts to enact parts of the People's Charter, the period 1848–60 saw a parallel series of government efforts to carry fairly modest extensions of the franchise and redistributions of seats. This revival of party political interest in Parliamentary Reform – which widened into direct party rivalry when the Conservatives entered the lists with their own Reform Bill in 1859 – replaced, for the time being, the lead which had been taken in the question by extra-parliamentary agitation.

In the case of neither party were the Reform Bills of the 1850s and of 1860 introduced with unanimous agreement. The bills revealed divisions among both Liberals and Conservatives over the desirability of franchise extension and the redistribution of constituencies. Both parties continued to be dominated by the aristocracy, and the leaders of neither party wanted an extension and a redistribution so great that they would bring about a marked reduction in landed influence. This meant that none of the parallel radical efforts at electoral reform was then likely to be adopted as a government-sponsored issue. On the other hand, both parties were rather weak in the Commons – the Conservatives in seats, the Liberals in cohesion[24] – and both wanted to increase their electoral support. A fairly modest extension of the franchise and redistribution of seats by a Liberal ministry, and another by a Conservative ministry, could be expected to give each party an electoral boost without overturning the remaining substantial influence of the aristocracy.

The Conservatives were, more clearly than the Liberals, in the position of wanting to reform the representative system in such a way that it might win them more seats. They might then hope to regain the Commons majority which they had lost on account of their split over Corn Law repeal in 1846. The Liberals won a majority in every general election from 1847 to 1868. But their majority depended on two precarious successive factors – the division between Conservative groups from 1846, which did not last in a substantial way beyond 1857, and the Liberal dominance of Palmerston for most of the decade from 1855 to 1865, attracting a certain amount of Conservative support on account of his home and overseas policies. Without these factors, the Liberals would be all the more grateful for the increased electoral support they might gain through franchise extension and redistribution of seats.

Lord John Russell, Prime Minister from 1846 to 1852, was the most enthusiastic advocate of Parliamentary Reform among the leaders of the Liberal Party, and his rival Palmerston was no advocate at all of such a policy. Russell's plans for Reform, indeed, encountered marked indifference, and sometimes opposition, among his cabinet colleagues. After beginning to consider adopting Parliamentary Reform once more, immediately after the Chartists' last great effort in 1848, Russell first thought of reforming the House of Lords, especially through the creation of life peers. But he gained little support for this idea in 1849 and turned instead to franchise extension.[25]

In October 1849 Russell told his Cabinet that he hoped to introduce a bill for this in the parliamentary session of 1850, and suggested a reduction of the borough qualification to £5 and a county household qualification of £20. The Cabinet were taken by surprise by the announcement. When they next met in mid-November, they decided against having a Reform Bill.[26] In the session of 1850 the only Parliamentary Reform measure was the Irish Franchise Bill, which was amended by the House of Lords to the annoyance of the government. In August 1850, just after the end of the session, Russell told his Cabinet that a bill for life peers should be introduced in 1851. But this proposal met with strong disapproval from his colleagues, as did his suggestion that a Reform Bill for a £6 borough household franchise and a £20 county household franchise should be introduced in the 1851 session.[27] There was no Reform Bill in 1851, but on 24 February that year Locke King's motion to extend the county franchise was carried against the government. Russell resigned, but the failure to form another ministry soon caused his government to resume office.

Russell persisted in his reforming intentions despite the opposition in Cabinet, which came chiefly from the Marquess of Lansdowne and Lord Palmerston but also from others. In October 1851, harking back to the great Whig Reform days of 20 years before, he appointed a committee of four, including himself, to draft a Reform Bill. This immediately set to work and agreed on extended borough and county franchises, but did not propose a redistribution of seats. In Cabinet on 6 December it was decided not to propose a secret ballot. But more exciting events supervened in the form of Palmerston's disgrace for having signified, as Foreign Secretary but without consulting the Cabinet or the Queen, his approval of Louis Napoleon's *coup d'état* which gave him supreme power in France. Russell dismissed Palmerston on 27 December on account of this action. The ministry was disintegrating. Russell had the satisfaction of introducing a Reform Bill in the Commons at last (his first since 1831) in February 1852, proposing a household franchise of £5 in boroughs and £20 in counties. The bill got no further, however, because Palmerston, seeking his revenge on Russell, carried an amendment to a Militia Bill against the government. The Russell ministry resigned for the second time on 21 February, and Russell withdrew his Reform Bill on 12 March.

Russell's next opportunity to introduce a Reform Bill came two years later, when he was a member of the Earl of Aberdeen's Coalition ministry of Peelites and Liberals, formed after the defeat of a Conservative minority government in December 1852. The Coalition found no time for a Reform Bill in 1853, but in February 1854 Russell introduced one in the Commons which was more extensive than its predecessor of 1852. The terms were likely to alarm any markedly conservative person, whether he sat on the Opposition or the government benches. There would be a £10 household qualification in counties; and a £6 one in boroughs, dependent on residence in the same borough for at least the past two-and-a-half years. There would be disfranchisement of all boroughs with fewer than 300 voters, and removal of one member from two-member boroughs which had between 300 and 500 voters. The released seats would be redistributed, 46 going to counties and 17 to boroughs, two to the Inns of Court and one to London University. There would be a limited vote in the largest constituencies. As in 1852, males who paid at least £2 a year in direct tax would get the vote, and there would be more of these provisions (later called 'fancy franchises') in order to emphasize the importance of probity, respectability, and independence in the electorate. Eligibility to vote would go to men who earned at least £100 a year, paid quarterly or at longer intervals; men who obtained at least £10 a year in income from gilt-edged securities; those who were graduates of any university in the United Kingdom; and those who had £50 deposited for three consecutive years in a savings bank (in the borough in which they resided).[28]

The bill thus contained many provisions, but this only multiplied the reasons to attack it, and opposition came abundantly from Conservatives, Whigs, and radicals, the two latter groups being, of course, in Russell's own party. The bill had only a short life in Parliament. Russell postponed it in March and withdrew it in April. This was officially because Britain became involved in the Crimean War, but Russell might well have been glad of this fortuitous reason in order to escape the embarrassing dissension which had broken out in his party.[29] Palmerston's adverse reaction to the bill had been profound. As happened 12 years later in the case of another Liberal, Robert Lowe, he saw a moderate measure as encouraging a dangerous slide into a democratic abyss. He wrote to Russell asking him whether he really supposed that 'men who murder their children to get £9 to be spent in drink, will not sell their vote for whatever they can get for it?'[30] Because of the bill's fate he did not need to worry about his vision materializing immediately. Palmerston was dead before Lowe's anti-democratic campaign of 1866. But in the meantime, he had probably adopted the view that a reform more modest than that proposed in 1854 might be supported. For in the autumn of 1857, when Prime Minister, he established a committee of Cabinet to consider another Reform measure.[31] At the same time, Disraeli was continuing, without avail for the moment, to try and persuade his party leader Lord Derby that the Conservatives should press for Reform as a means of revival: 'Our party is now a corpse, but ... in the present perplexed state of affairs, a Conservative public pledged to Parliamentary Reform ... might ... put us on our legs.'[32]

In 1858–9, during the second Derby Government, this Conservative approach was first attempted through the introduction of a Reform Bill. On the basis of opinions obtained from Conservatives by party agents, a bill was drafted in meetings of a cabinet committee in November 1858. Apart from the small boroughs where landed patronage of either party was still dominant, Conservatives looked to county seats as their main strength, just as Liberals looked to the large towns as theirs. The Reform Bill of 1859 emerged from the Cabinet discussions with its original proposals much altered. As well as extending the £10 household franchise in boroughs to the counties, preventing 40s. freeholders living in boroughs from voting in the counties, and establishing a franchise for lodgers, the measure initially proposed to disfranchise 70 small boroughs and transfer the bulk of their seats (52) to counties and only 18 to large towns. While the franchise proposals were retained in the bill, the redistribution aims had been strongly contested in Cabinet by Spencer Walpole and J. W. Henley. They preferred to continue defending Conservative interests through the hallowed safety of small-borough seats rather than entrust this object to the greater hazards of more county representation. In order to try and keep Walpole and Henley from resigning, the number of small-borough seats to be transferred was reduced drastically to only 15, and some 'fancy franchises' were added, resembling those in Russell's bills. All university graduates, members of certain professions, government pensioners receiving at least £20 a year, and holders of at least £60 in a savings bank would be enfranchised.

But when Disraeli introduced the bill in the Commons on 28 February 1859, Walpole and Henley had not been reconciled to the measure. Both spoke against it and resigned. Disraeli, moreover, was disappointed in his hope of obtaining support from many in the Liberal majority in the House. Rather there was considerable (though by no means complete) Liberal unity against a bill which seemed to be shaped primarily for the purpose of obtaining a Conservative majority. Radicals, in particular, objected to the narrowness of both the franchise and the redistribution proposals, finding very little in either which would give more votes to the industrial working class. Even Palmerston and Russell began to get over their differences in opposition to the bill. It was Russell, appropriately, who finished off the bill by carrying a resolution against it, by 330 votes to 291, on 31 March.[33]

The last Reform Bill in the period up to and including 1860 was another moderate measure, introduced in March that year by Palmerston's second ministry, which had been formed after Conservative defeat in the previous June. Russell had accepted office as Foreign Secretary in this government, on the understanding that there would be a ministerial Reform Bill. In November 1859 Palmerston duly appointed a cabinet committee to draft a Reform scheme. A bill was produced and accepted by the Cabinet, to be introduced in the 1860 session. The franchise proposals were similar to those of 1854, reducing the borough household franchise from £10 to £6, and establishing a £10 household franchise in the counties. Some small boroughs would be disfranchised and their seats redistributed, but fewer than in the 1854 bill. Russell insisted on introducing the bill in the Commons on 1 March, the anniversary of his epoch-making speech of 1831, although this necessitated changes in the parliamentary timetable.

But a Russellite triumph, similar to the eventual results of the previous Reform initiative on a 1 March, was not to follow. The conditions both inside and outside Parliament on the two widely separated occasions could hardly have been more different. In 1831 not only had marked extra-parliamentary agitation commenced, but most of the Whigs in Parliament had been enthusiastic for Reform. In May 1860, on the other hand, the chief Liberal whip, Henry Brand, reported growing opposition in the party to any franchise extension at all. Outside Parliament there was perhaps more obvious support for Reform, but only from limited groups, especially political Nonconformists and trade union leaders. In June a motion was carried in the Commons in favour of postponing the question until the results of the next decennial census in 1861 were known and digested. Inadequately supported, the bill died of inanition, and Russell dropped it. He was left complaining to Palmerston – not the most sympathetic of hearers on this subject – that 'the apathy of the country was undeniable'.[34] This was similar to Cobden's view after the failure of a Reform campaign in northern England in 1859: 'What is wanting is some multitudinous demonstrations by the unenfranchised in favour of Parliamentary Reform.'[35]

Russell announced early in the 1861 session that he must give up the question, at least for the time being. He said that Reform was impossible 'without "a great tide of public opinion" to carry it through Parliament'.[36] The years 1861–3 were probably the lowest point for Parliamentary Reform in the period since 1848. It has been said that 'even Locke King, Berkeley and [Edward] Baines grew tired, for during 1862 and 1863 there were no franchise or ballot motions'.[37] There was, in fact, a ballot motion in 1863, when the indefatigable Berkeley obtained the support of only 102 MPs, a drop of 63 since his last effort in 1861. When he moved again on the subject in 1865, he experienced a further drop to only 74.[38] Other radical issues had drifted into a similarly unhopeful state, for example the campaign to abolish compulsory payment of church rates.[39] Palmerston would certainly have been gratified by the almost unbroken stagnation in domestic reform. His basic anti-democratic feelings were displayed again in a letter to Russell in

October 1862: 'Power in the Hands of the Masses throws the Scum of the Community to the surface, and ... Truth and Justice are soon banished from the Land.'[40] With such views being maintained by the apparently indestructible old premier, who did not even mention Reform in his 1865 election address, it was no wonder if radicals looked to his death as a chink of light for their causes in a general atmosphere of gloom.

There was little revival of the wider national demand for electoral reform until 1864. Some previous stirrings of renewed interest, shown in organized form, had come to little. Some new Reform societies had been founded in 1857–8, including the Political Reform League, led by Joseph Sturge, and the Northern Reform Union at Newcastle, led by Joseph Cowen, both of which argued for enacting some of the main Points of the Charter. But by the end of 1858 the Political Reform League was defunct.[41] There was also the beginning, and the subsequent development on a continuous basis, of a more obvious political reforming role by the trade unions. This was seen after the formation of a committee or 'junta' of trade union leaders in 1859 and the London Trades Council in 1860, and in the beginning of the Trade Unionists' Manhood Suffrage and Vote by Ballot Association in 1862 (revived in 1864) and the commencement of the *Bee-Hive* newspaper in 1861.[42] Among the *Bee-Hive*'s stated aims were 'to claim for the working classes a complete Reform of Parliament', and to obtain 'the natural and God-given rights of every man to equal political rights'.[43] Stimulus to a reviving radicalism also came from support for overseas causes – that of Garibaldi in Italy, of the Northern States in the American Civil War, and of the Polish rebels against Russia.[44]

Parliamentary Reform Crisis, 1864–8

In April 1864 the foundation of the Reform Union – a mainly middle-class body led by John Bright and campaigning for household suffrage, the ballot, and triennial Parliaments – contributed to the slowly swelling stream of radical revival. In the same year, Garibaldi visited London. A London Working Men's Garibaldi Association was formed in his honour, and this provided the nucleus of the mainly working-class Reform League, founded in 1865 and calling for manhood suffrage.[45] From September 1866 it had the alliance of a newly formed Scottish National Reform League. The Marquess Townshend in 1863 had founded a Universal League for the Material Elevation of the Industrious Classes, whose offices later also housed the famous International Working Men's Association (the 'first International'), formed in September 1864.[46] Edward Baines, a radical MP, in 1864 introduced the second of his trio of bills (of 1861, 1864, and 1865) to lower the borough household qualification to £6; but the second reading was lost by 272 to 56, Robert Lowe and 24 other Liberals voting against. In the debate, however, there was a notable declaration on 11 May 1864 by the Chancellor of the Exchequer, W. E. Gladstone, in which he seemed to commit himself to manhood suffrage (though he later indicated that this exceeded his intention): 'every man who is not presumably incapacitated by some consideration of personal unfitness or of moral danger, is morally entitled to come within the pale of the Constitution.'[47] Intellectual ruminations and deliberations on the benefits of movement towards democracy were fed by new publications on the subject in these years, particularly a succession of books and pamphlets by John Stuart Mill, including *Thoughts on Parliamentary Reform* (1859), *Considerations on Representative Government* (1861), and *The Subjection of Women* (1869). Altogether, Russell might not yet have been seeing the 'great tide of public opinion' which he believed the Reform cause needed, but he was seeing varied tendencies towards producing such a tide.[48] The cause was being lifted out of the doldrums.

A London meeting on 23 February 1865 at St Martin's Hall inaugurated the Reform League, which aimed to obtain manhood suffrage (with residential qualifications) and the ballot. The League soon became a powerful organization, extending to over 400 branches and 60 000 members. Mainly working class in membership and including the trade union leaders, it had also some middle-class support. The League was usually in financial difficulties, though its annual income rose to £3000 in 1867, mainly through middle-class donations. Some members of the League were also members of the Reform Union. Among these was Samuel Morley, a very rich hosiery manufacturer, who was the League's chief benefactor despite giving twice as much money to the Union. The League did not grow close to merging with the Union, but it did sometimes share platforms with it.[49] Relations were a great deal better between these two bodies than they had been between the Chartists and the Anti-Corn Law League.

Palmerston died in October 1865, and the introduction of a Reform Bill by the new premier, Earl (the former Lord John) Russell, with the support of Gladstone as Leader of the Commons, seemed very likely. Nevertheless, Russell had contemplated postponing the Reform question, perhaps for as long as two years, by appointing a commission of enquiry into the electoral system. It was perhaps radical pressure from W. E. Forster, and others, that caused another moderate government bill to be introduced as the most important item in the session of 1866.[50] Despite the current agitation for Reform, which had been almost entirely absent in 1860, the bill decided on in Cabinet (after much dispute) in February 1866 was more modest than its predecessor of six years before. As yet, there was clearly no breakthrough from the restricted nature of the 1850s government proposals to a higher level of enfranchisement.

Gladstone introduced the bill in the Commons on 12 May. There would be a reduction of the borough household qualification from £10 to £7, a £14 rental qualification in the counties, and admittance to the franchise of lodgers occupying premises worth £10 a year and of holders of at least £50 in a savings bank.[51] There were moves to allow additional residents in boroughs to vote in the counties, in order to encourage more Liberal voting in county constituencies. Altogether, about 400 000 new electors would be created, and in the towns most of these would be working class. There would also be a modest redistribution of about 50 seats in a separate bill, the new seats being split almost equally between counties and boroughs, with one going to London University. Radicals disagreed about whether the bill should be supported. The Reform League endorsed it after internal disputes. The Chartist Ernest Jones resigned from the League rather than sanction 'a measure which is a deliberate insult to the working class', but he resumed membership when the bill had been defeated.[52] The League's Secretary, George Howell, could just about accept the measure, and wrote: 'The Bill is small enough ... and if it be tampered with in Committee it will become a contemptible farce, unworthy of the Liberal Party, an insult to the people.'[53]

The bill was soon destroyed by a combination of Conservatives and dissident Liberals. The latter formed, in John Bright's Old

Testament language, the 'Cave of Adullam', a gathering of malcontents consisting mainly of Whig aristocrats, together with a few middle-class MPs. The group was led by Robert Lowe, a middle-class Liberal intellectual who genuinely feared that even such a moderate measure as the bill in question could form a slippery slope to ultimate democratic chaos, to government by the drunken, the illiterate, and the ignorant – the 'impulsive, unreflecting, and violent people' at the bottom of society.[54]

The bill was virtually defeated on 18 June, on an amendment in committee by the Adullamite Lord Dunkellin to raise the proposed borough qualification by substituting rateable for rental value. This would have reduced the enfranchisement in the boroughs by over a third.[55] The vote in favour of the amendment and against the government was 315 to 304. After a week of flurried and fruitless activity, the ministry resigned and was replaced by another minority Conservative administration.

The Liberal measure had clearly failed to impress the more pronounced radicals. But when the bill was lost, the radicals showed their determination not to lose the current chance of Reform. They redoubled their agitation, and kept it at a high pitch, until a bill finally passed in 1867. As in 1832, the decisions on the bill were made in Parliament (as, of course, they had to be unless the Constitution were overturned), and much of the drama over the measure occurred again within the parliamentary walls at Westminster. But, as before, a great deal of the pressure came from outside. The passage of bills in both 1832 and 1867 should be seen as the fruits of partnership between parliamentary and extra-parliamentary activity.

To the radicals, having no reform at all was worse than the enactment of the Liberal Government's unsatisfactory bill. It was therefore not surprising that, having seen a Reform Bill defeated, radicals should campaign strongly to try and ensure that another Reform measure would soon be introduced and passed. The Conservatives who now came into office had played a large part in defeating the Liberal bill. But this was no bar to the presentation of a Conservative Reform Bill, particularly when one had been introduced by the previous Conservative ministry.

The Reform League and John Bright were well to the fore in the extra-parliamentary agitation over the next year, Bright allying with the League without accepting its main objective of manhood suffrage. The public pressure for Reform did not attain the dramatic heights of 1831–2. But it played an important role in helping to keep the question afloat, and in pushing a Conservative ministry towards adopting a Reform Bill – which it might otherwise have been reluctant to do on account of the renewed threat of division in the party it was likely to bring.

After Russell's defeat and resignation, a demonstration was held in London at the end of June. This adopted resolutions stating that Russell should have dissolved Parliament and – ironically, in view of the passage of a much wider Reform Bill by the Conservatives in the following year – deploring 'the advent of the Tories to power as being destructive to freedom at home and favourable to despotism abroad'. A much larger gathering, organized by the Reform League, was held in Trafalgar Square a few days later, and voted to hold a national demonstration in Hyde Park on 23 July in protest against the frustration of Reform.[56] An official ban on this meeting by the Commissioner of Police, acting on instructions from the Home Secretary (Spencer Walpole), was ignored after Bright had condemned it as a denial of popular liberty by the ruling class and the Reform League's executive committee had voted to proceed with its plans. On 23 July a large crowd pressed against the police guarding Hyde Park gates, broke down the railings and surged into the park. On the following two days, crowds invaded the park again. Spencer Walpole reached an understanding with the League that it would keep order amongst the crowd in return for withdrawal of the police.[57] The League naturally gained much confidence from this episode and expanded its activities: the Secretary, George Howell, was able to list 427 branches by March 1867.[58]

But the Hyde Park riots did not spur the new government to introduce a Reform Bill, even one as modest as the recent Liberal measure. The government's intentions on the subject at this stage were tentative and leisurely. Resolutions would be moved in the Commons, then (assuming they were adopted) there would be a Royal Commission to enquire into the electoral system and propose changes; perhaps after this there would be a cautious government bill in 1868.[59] It was only at the end of 1866 that this programme received a notable injection of speed and purpose, from the government leaders (Derby and Disraeli) themselves. In the preceding five months, popular clamour had not continued at the level of the Hyde Park riots. But Bright had conducted a sustained autumn campaign of mass meetings in major towns in Scotland and in the north and midlands of England.[60] Some of these had huge attendances, and further large meetings were held in London. Not since the first Chartist decade had there been such vast overt interest in Reform. The Reform League's campaign was revived in May 1867 with a further large meeting in Hyde Park, which took place despite another official ban.[61]

The autumn campaign probably had some effect in quickening government action. On 16 September 1866, a fortnight after Bright's speaking tour began, Derby told Disraeli that he was 'coming reluctantly to the conclusion that we shall have to deal with the question of Reform'. He was referring to the planning of the government programme in the next parliamentary session, and he thought that the moving of resolutions should come first, providing the basis of a bill.[62]

This more purposeful turn towards Reform reflected both the continued pressure from extra-parliamentary activity and the persistent minority position of the Conservatives since 1846. In later 1866, the Conservatives were in office only because of manifest divisions in the Liberal majority in the Commons, and they faced the prospect of being turned out as soon as the Liberals reunited on a particular issue. They needed to try and enhance their strength, from the *éclat* of carrying a Reform Bill and from the prospect of maintaining (over such a bill) the divisions amongst Liberals. The position was well noted by F. B. Smith:

> The primary impulse to plan for some gesture towards Reform in the next session undoubtedly arose from the growing impressiveness of the mass meetings, but the necessity to take up the question also stemmed from the Government's minority position in the House.[63]

Resolutions were prepared by Derby and accepted by the Cabinet on 8 November 1866. They stated that the electorate should be widened in accordance with a male occupation franchise requiring payment of rates, and that there should be a Royal Commission to enquire into the boundaries of borough constituencies. The government appeared to be turning to the view that a larger bill than the Liberals' measure would be desirable. Not least, this might have been because, by going below the Liberals' 'respectable' £6 limit in the boroughs, they could tap a layer of popular Tory support.[64] In a crucial letter to Disraeli of 22 December, Derby proposed household suffrage in the boroughs: 'Of all possible hares to start I do not know a better than the extension of household suffrage, coupled with plurality of voting.'[65] After the leading ministers had individually accepted that male household suffrage should be proposed in the government's resolutions, it was decided, on Disraeli's suggestion, that Reform should be specifically mentioned in the Queen's Speech at the opening of the parliamentary session.

There was now considerable Conservative enthusiasm for a Reform Bill. The idea that a minority government might help its prospects by carrying a major measure over the heads of its squabbling opponents was a very tempting one. There was already an air of adventure and daring about the scheme, well suited to Disraeli's political gifts, when the Reform intentions announced in the Queen's Speech were approved at the opening of the session on 5 February 1867. However, some Conservative alarms were already taking hold, and it began to appear that household suffrage would not be adopted without causing a degree of secession.

Government resolutions on Reform were introduced in the Commons by Disraeli on 11 February, but ministerial opposition to household suffrage was shown by Viscount Cranborne (the later Marquess of Salisbury), the Earl of Carnarvon, and General Jonathan Peel.[66] Moreover, it was pointed out to ministers that from calculations which had been made, household suffrage in the boroughs would provide a large working-class majority in the electorate as a whole. Despite this prospect, which on the face of it would not have seemed promising to Conservatives, Derby and Disraeli decided to retain borough household suffrage as the basis of Reform, though the need to counteract it by means of other provisions must also have seemed important to them. On 23 February the Cabinet accepted borough household suffrage (conditional on rates being paid in person, not compounded by means of payment through a landlord), together with some 'fancy franchises' and a plural voting plan based on property levels. But these important counteractions to household suffrage were not enough to remove the prospect of resignation by Cranborne, Carnarvon, and Peel.

The threat of losing these ministers caused the Cabinet reluctantly to abandon household suffrage and to adopt a more restricted and conventional bill, proposing a £6 household qualification in the boroughs and £20 in the counties. But the appetites of many Conservative MPs had been whetted by the prospect of 'dishing the Whigs' by a wider measure, and the new proposal was so unpopular that it was given up in turn and qualified household suffrage was re-adopted. At a meeting of Conservative MPs at the Carlton Club on 28 February, a return to a household suffrage measure (restricted by plural voting, a formidable residence requirement of three years in the same constituency, and personal payment of rates) was preferred, by a majority of 150, to the more limited plan.

On 2 March the Cabinet re-adopted the wider scheme, with a two-year rather than a three-year residence requirement. Cranborne, Carnarvon, and Peel resigned on the grounds that the plan would, on the whole, undermine Conservative prospects and aid the Liberals.[67] Cranborne, an accomplished writer in journalistic vein, denounced Derby and Disraeli in the *Quarterly Review* (with an Old Testament allusion), for the 'treachery' to Conservative principles in the new reforming intentions, which had apparently transformed the party's attitude:

> It was certainly a startling change, and one that naturally per-
> plexed those who had adopted their opinions after calm consid-
> eration, and did not see what had happened to refute them. Sud-
> denly the whole of the forces of resistance that had rallied so
> numerously, and fought with so much resolution last year [1866],
> disappeared like Rabshakeh's army, in a single night.[68]

A bill embodying the re-adopted scheme was presented to the Commons on 18 March. Gladstone strongly challenged the bill. But while the vexed Adullamites mostly returned grumblingly to support him against their Conservative allies of the previous year, the radicals in his ranks supported the Conservative measure as a reasonably wide enfranchisement. In this situation, Gladstone found himself able to make no headway as his rival Disraeli triumphed. Gladstone's amendments to the bill were defeated, while broader amendments from the radicals were accepted by Disraeli and carried. The divisions in Liberal ranks seemed as wide as ever; the Conservatives, after losing the three dissidents, were comparatively united. The amendments adopted included one by A. S. Ayrton, MP for Tower Hamlets, to reduce the two years' residential qualification to one year; one by W. T. M. Torrens, MP for Finsbury, to enfranchise lodgers occupying premises of £12 annual value; and the notable and controversial one of Grosvenor Hodgkinson, member for Newark, abolishing compounding for rates in order to establish personal payment only and hence drawing an extra half-million people in England and Wales (compounding did not apply in Scotland) into the franchise. Later, however, on account of widespread protests about the end of the financial benefits of compounding, the latter practice was continued, and the Poor Rate Assessment Act of 1869 allowed ratepayers both to compound and to register as electors.[69] The new half-million intended electors were often unable to register for the 1868 election.

The fancy franchises in the bill were dropped – and, as it turned out, such things had gone forever from Reform schemes. The qualification for the vote in counties was lowered from £15 to £12 in England and Wales (it was fixed at £14 in Scotland), after Locke King had moved for a £10 qualification. The county requirement for the vote thus remained much higher than the borough qualification.

The first women's enfranchisement motion ever introduced in Parliament came in these debates from John Stuart Mill, then in a three-year period as radical MP for Westminster. He moved an amendment to give the vote to women in the bill on the same basis as men – though this would not actually have enfranchised many women, as married females did not qualify as householders. His amendment was lost by 196 votes to 73 – an encouragingly large minority for the female suffrage cause on its first parliamentary airing. The arguments on the issue, both favourable and unfavourable, had now been launched in Parliament, and were given at least 30 opportunities to be heard there again before legislative success came at the end of a long saga in 1918.[70] It took longer to enact women's suffrage than the secret ballot. Outside Parliament, Mill's motion helped to encourage the formation of local societies, which joined in a federal organization, the National Society for Women's Suffrage, in November 1867.[71] Thus, the year 1867 saw not only the first parliamentary motion, but also the first national organization for female suffrage.

The third reading of the bill for England and Wales passed in the Commons without a division on 15 July; in the debate, Disraeli countered fierce attacks from Cranborne and Lowe by pointing out that he had favoured extending the franchise for nearly 20 years. Most of the amendments to the bill by the House of Lords were rejected by the Lower House, but one establishing the 'limited vote' (providing that electors in the three-member constituencies could vote for no more than two candidates) was accepted by the Commons, and this form of electoral procedure lasted until 1885.[72] The bill became law on 15 August 1867. The corresponding bills for Scotland and Ireland, discussion of which had been postponed, passed in the 1868 session. The reformed Scottish system was on a basis similar to that for England and Wales. But the reformed Irish system remained distinct (the proportion of enfranchised adult males being only about half that in the rest of the United Kingdom) until the three systems were amalgamated on a new basis in 1884–5.

The hope of advancing Conservative Party interests through the electoral changes of 1867–8 is seen especially in the narrowness of the redistribution of seats and the extensiveness of constituency boundary changes.[73] The Redistribution Act in 1867 followed the traditional interests of Conservatism by transferring only a relatively small number of seats (52, little more than a third of the total transferred in 1832) from small boroughs to large ones or to counties or new university seats. The electorate in the United Kingdom doubled, to nearly two and a half millions, but most of the new householder voters were in large urban constituencies which were given only a few additional seats. To have created a lot more urban seats would have made the redistribution much more favourable to the Liberals. The survival of large numbers of boroughs with small and easily influenced electorates had prevented the 1832 Reform from being anything like satisfactory on democratic grounds, and the same criticism could be levelled with only slightly diminished force at the Reform of 1867–8. The enfranchisement in 1867–8 was the largest in the nineteenth century in Great Britain, but the redistribution was the smallest. The small-borough electorates, mostly in England, continued to swamp the representative system, and after 1868 Scotland lagged behind England by at least 20 seats in terms of population. In 1881, 72 boroughs with a population of under 10 000 each still returned MPs.[74]

The proposals of a Boundary Commission, consisting mostly of Conservative landowners, to change numerous constituency boundaries were modified by a parliamentary Select Committee, whose recommendations were unsuccessfully opposed by Disraeli. But even after the revision, 700 000 suburb-dwellers were transferred from county constituencies to borough constituencies – thereby, it was hoped, making the counties purer for Conservatism.[75]

Finally, in this bulging package of electoral changes, there were passed in 1868 a Registration of Voters Act and a Corrupt Practices at Elections Act. The latter provided that petitions against the results of elections would be considered not, as hitherto, by the House of Commons (which might contain too many interested parties), but by the High Court of Justice which would institute a special election court in each case. This measure also stiffened the penalties for bribery. Any candidate found guilty of administering bribes was barred from being an MP or from any national or local public office for the next seven years. But nothing was done to reduce the very high cost of election petitions, and they were rarely pressed in consequence.[76] As usual, the effort against electoral corruption was inadequate, and corruption remained a widespread pursuit until really effective steps were taken against it by the Corrupt and Illegal Practices Act of 1883 and the Redistribution Act of 1885.

While it is highly doubtful whether such important Reform Bills as those of 1832 and 1867 could have been carried without considerable public pressure behind them, it is also doubtful whether they would have proposed the changes they did if these had not been in keeping with the party interests of the governments which introduced them. Both measures moved only slightly towards democracy. The main benefit which both of them brought to democracy was to whet the appetites of reformers for further change. Much wider demands for democracy than were represented by the Reform Bills of 1832 and 1867 were seen in the years between them, in the form of attempts to enact the People's Charter or parts of it, and in the emergence of demands for proportional representation and women's suffrage and of moves to reform the House of Lords. These wider demands remained to be fought for in the years from 1868.

Notes

1. R. Wallace, *Organise! Organise! Organise!: A Study of Reform Agitations in Wales, 1840–86* (Cardiff, 1991), p. 98.
2. Margot Finn, *After Chartism: Class and Nation in English Radical Politics, 1848–74* (Cambridge, 1993), pp. 9–10, 108, 116–22; E. D. Steele, *Palmerston and Liberalism, 1855–65* (Cambridge, 1991), pp. 245–316.
3. N. C. Edsall, 'A failed national movement: the Parliamentary and Financial Reform Association, 1848–54', *Bulletin of the Institute of Historical Research*, XLIX (1976), 108–31; M. Finn, op. cit., 96.
4. Cobden to George Wilson, 23 Sept. 1856; quoted R. Robson (ed.), *Ideas and Institutions of Victorian Britain* (London, 1967), p. 114.
5. Cf. M. Taylor, *The Decline of British Radicalism, 1847–60* (Oxford, 1995), pp. 163–70.
6. Bruce L. Kinzer, *The Ballot Question in Nineteenth Century English Politics* (New York, 1982), pp. 50–4.
7. Ibid., pp. 55–79.
8. R. Quinault, '1848 and Parliamentary Reform', *Historical Journal*, XXXI (1988), 836–9.
9. M. Taylor, op. cit., p. 31.
10. C. Seymour, *Electoral Reform in England and Wales: The Development and Operation of the Parliamentary Franchise, 1832–85* (Newton Abbot, 1970), pp. 240–1; R. Quinault, op. cit., 840–6; J. Prest, *Lord John Russell* (London, 1972), pp. 303–6; R. K. Huch and P. R. Ziegler, *Joseph Hume, the People's MP* (Philadelphia, 1985), pp. 139–44.
11. C. Seymour, op. cit., p. 241; F. B. Smith, *The Making of the Second Reform Bill* (Cambridge, 1966), pp. 30–1.
12. Huch and Ziegler, op. cit., pp. 148–50; N. C. Edsall, *Richard Cobden, Independent Radical* (London, 1986), pp. 192–215.
13. J. Prest, *Politics in the Age of Cobden* (London, 1977), pp. 104–6; K. T. Hoppen, *Elections, Politics and Society in Ireland, 1832–85* (Oxford, 1984), pp. 16–20.
14. K. T. Hoppen, op. cit., pp. 16–17.
15. Ibid., pp. 17–19.
16. J. B. Conacher, *The Aberdeen Coalition, 1852–5* (Cambridge, 1968), pp. 344–6. For abolition of the property qualification, see Helen E. Witmer, *The Property Qualifications of Members of Parliament* (New York, 1943), pp. 192–215 (also see pp. 39–191 on the previous operation of the qualification).
17. W. B. Gwyn, *Democracy and the Cost of Politics in Britain* (London, 1962), pp. 80–2.
18. Ibid., pp. 82–3.
19. Ibid., pp. 84, 91.
20. Seymour, p. 232 (and see pp. 226–33, 385–416 for further details of the Act and the extent of bribery after it).
21. Jenifer Hart, *Proportional Representation: Critics of the British Electoral System, 1820–1945* (Oxford, 1992), pp. 6–23.

22. Ibid., pp. 24–9.
23. Ibid., pp. 37–52.
24. R. Blake, *Disraeli* (London, 1966), pp. 270–80.
25. Prest, *Russell*, pp. 304–5.
26. Ibid., pp. 305–6.
27. Ibid., pp. 319, 324; Huch and Ziegler, op. cit., pp. 152–3; F. B. Smith, op. cit., pp. 32–3.
28. F. B. Smith, op. cit., pp. 34–7.
29. Ibid., pp. 37–8; J. B. Conacher, op. cit., pp. 215–32, 291–311; Muriel Chamberlain, *Lord Aberdeen* (London, 1983), pp. 465–8; Huch and Ziegler, pp. 158–9.
30. Prest, *Russell*, p. 363.
31. Ibid., p. 380.
32. Quoted F. B. Smith, p. 38. Cf. R. Blake, op. cit., p. 396; I. Machin, *Disraeli* (London, 1995), pp. 81–2.
33. A. Hawkins, *Parliament, Party and the Art of Politics in Britain, 1855–9* (London, 1987), pp. 177–225; F. B. Smith, pp. 39–44; M. Taylor, pp. 318–22; I. Machin, op. cit., pp. 91–2; R. Stewart, *The Foundation of the Conservative Party, 1830–67* (London, 1978), pp. 353–4.
34. Quoted Prest, *Russell*, p. 392.
35. F. B. Smith, p. 40.
36. Ibid., p. 47.
37. Ibid.
38. Bruce L. Kinzer, pp. 82–4.
39. G. I. T. Machin, *Politics and the Churches in Great Britain, 1832 to 1868* (Oxford, 1977), pp. 305–10; J. P. Ellens, *Religious Routes to Gladstonian Liberalism: The Church Rate Conflict in England and Wales, 1832–68* (Pennsylvania, 1994), pp. 167–222.
40. Quoted Prest, *Russell*, p. 393; F. B. Smith, pp. 46–7; M. Taylor, p. 171.
41. R. Wallace, op. cit., pp. 94–5.
42. Margot Finn, op. cit., pp. 192–4; F. M. Leventhal, *Respectable Radical: George Howell and Victorian Working Class Politics* (London, 1971), p. 46.
43. Finn, p. 194; F. M. Leventhal, op. cit., pp. 20–42, 46.
44. Finn, pp. 206–24; E. F. Biagini, *Liberty, Retrenchment and Reform: Popular Liberalism in the Age of Gladstone, 1860–80* (Cambridge, 1992), pp. 257–8.
45. T. A. Jenkins, *The Liberal Ascendancy, 1830–86* (Basingstoke, 1994), p. 101.
46. Leventhal, pp. 50–2.
47. Quoted E. J. Feuchtwanger, *Democracy and Empire: Britain, 1865–1914* (London, 1985), p. 29.
48. M. St John, *The Demands of the People: Dundee Radicalism, 1850–70* (Dundee, 1997), pp. 13–25.
49. Leventhal, pp. 55–6, 63–5.
50. D. G. Wright, *Democracy and Reform, 1815–85* (London, 1970), pp. 67–8.
51. F. B. Smith, pp. 61–8; E. J. Feuchtwanger, op cit., pp. 29–34.
52. Quoted Leventhal, p. 72.
53. Quoted ibid., Cf. Seymour, pp. 247–56; R. Harrison, *Before the Socialists: Studies in Labour and Politics, 1861–81* (London, 1965), p. 82.
54. F. B. Smith, pp. 75–89. For anti-democratic opinions at this time, see W.

Bagehot, *The English Constitution* (London, 1993; 1st edn 1867), pp. 25, 163, 271–3, 282.
55. F. B. Smith, pp. 97–111.
56. Leventhal, p. 74.
57. Ibid., p. 75; F. B. Smith, pp. 127–31.
58. Leventhal, p. 83.
59. Ibid., p. 88; F. B. Smith, pp. 131–4.
60. E. F. Biagini, op. cit., pp. 257–75; F. B. Smith, pp. 139–43; M. Cowling, *1867: Disraeli, Gladstone and Revolution* (Cambridge, 1967), pp. 12, 161; I. G. C. Hutchison, *A Political History of Scotland, 1832–1924* (Edinburgh, 1986), p. 132.
61. R. Harrison, op. cit., pp. 91–5.
62. F. B. Smith, p. 134.
63. Ibid. Cf. Harrison, pp. 132, 134; M. Cowling, op. cit., p. 122.
64. Feuchtwanger, *Democracy and Empire*, p. 38.
65. F. B. Smith, p. 139.
66. Ibid., pp. 148–51. For the 1867 bill, see also D. G. Wright, op. cit., pp. 72–85; and M. Bentley, *Politics without Democracy, 1815–1914* (London, 1984), pp. 189–94.
67. Blake, *Disraeli*, pp. 456–63; F. B. Smith, pp. 156–64; Cowling, pp. 12–13, 137–66.
68. P. Smith (ed.), *Lord Salisbury on Politics: A Selection from his Articles in the Quarterly Review, 1860–83* (Cambridge, 1972), p. 280 (see also editor's comments, pp. 104–9, 256–7).
69. F. B. Smith, pp. 184–203; Cowling, pp. 166–216; Seymour, pp. 264–72.
70. For the arguments employed for and against women's suffrage, see the extracts and commentary in Jane Lewis (ed.), *Before the Vote was Won: Arguments For and Against Women's Suffrage* (London, 1987).
71. A. Rosen, *Rise Up, Women!: The Militant Campaign of the Women's Social and Political Union, 1903–14* (London, 1974), p. 7.
72. F. B. Smith, pp. 212–14. See Jenifer Hart, op. cit., pp. 119–21 for effects of the limited vote.
73. See Seymour, pp. 300–10, for an examination of party benefit from the new franchise system, and pp. 329–38 for the redistribution of seats.
74. J. Parry, *The Rise and Fall of Liberal Government in Victorian Britain* (London, 1993), p. 217; M. Dyer, *Men of Property and Intelligence: The Scottish Electoral System Prior to 1884* (Aberdeen, 1996), pp. 100–20.
75. Blake, p. 473; F. B. Smith, p. 219–27.
76. Gwyn, p. 85.

4 Crucial Years in the Advance of Democracy, 1868–85

Introduction

The various electoral reform measures of 1867–8 continued a trend of making some advances towards democracy but frustrating others. Included in the latter were the defeat of female suffrage and the passage of another inadequate bribery bill. As before, however, the encouragement given by the electoral changes of 1867–8 to hopes of further democratic progress was probably more important than the scope of the changes themselves. The grant of household franchise in the boroughs led to demands for household suffrage in the counties. The introduction of a motion for women's suffrage in the Reform debates stimulated a long series of similar parliamentary efforts, supported by extra-parliamentary associations. The continuance of obvious electoral influence, especially in the numerous small boroughs which still returned members, motivated the persistence of attempts to obtain the secret ballot, to end electoral bribery and intimidation, and to transfer seats from small boroughs to counties and large towns. The continuance of great numerical discrepancies in the numbers of voters in different constituencies maintained efforts to obtain more equal electoral districts. By 1885 it could be said that all of these objectives, except votes for women, had been largely attained.

The recent concentration of popular organization and agitation for Reform was not maintained at the same pitch after 1867. But organization by no means died away completely. The Reform Union lasted for many years. It declined in the early 1870s, but revived after the Liberal defeat in 1874. It produced a new constitution in 1875 which called for a number of radical reforms, including household suffrage in counties and more equal constituencies. The number of branches grew from 173 in 1875 to 423 in 1891.[1] The Reform League, on the other hand, was dissolved in March 1869.

This followed bitter internal conflict over George Howell's and Randall Cremer's agreement to accept Liberal funding in order to give important support to that party in the 1868 election; this was seen by some members of the League as abandoning its working-class identity and independence.[2] As an offshoot of the Reform League, the Labour Representation League was formed in 1869, and aimed to return working-men to Parliament. This was in order to demonstrate 'the strength of the operative classes as an electoral power, so that when necessary it may be brought to bear with effect on any important political, social, or industrial question'.[3] The new body did not intend to become an independent Labour Party, however, but to function as a 'Lib-Lab' pressure group. It could not afford to give much financial assistance to candidates in the 1874 election.[4] But it lasted precariously, and in a state of growing weakness, until 1879, when it was replaced by the National Liberal League. This was another working-class organization which continued the 'Lib-Lab' connection of 1868, and it was not greatly concerned with returning working-class MPs.[5] Another offshoot of the Reform League was the Representative Reform Association, founded in 1868 with George Howell as secretary. This helped to sustain the cause of proportional representation, but lasted for only six years.[6] The absence of a powerful popular movement demanding electoral reform, from 1867 until the suffragette campaign began in 1903, may have helped to account for the meagre electoral changes in Gladstone's first ministry and the almost complete lack of them in Disraeli's Government of 1874–80.

Growth of Party Organization

After the 1867–8 Acts, fierce party battles continued over getting supporters on to the register and excluding opponents from it. This, together with the greatly increased number of voters, led to the institution of more extensive, efficient, and centralized party organizations, replacing the rather sketchy and rudimentary ones commenced in the 1830s: 'As the size of the electorate expanded so party bureaucracy grew.'[7] In this development Conservatives led the way, not altogether surprisingly in view of their seizing of the Reform initiative in 1867. The National Union of Conservative and

Constitutional Associations (NUCCA) was founded in that year. It was not immediately very influential. But in the early 1870s the number of its constituency branches, including Conservative Working Men's Associations (replacing the Conservative Operative Associations), rapidly grew under the enthusiastic leadership of John Gorst. By 1877 there were 791 affiliated associations. The NUCCA worked closely with the new Conservative Central Office (established in 1870), where Gorst transacted his business, and the two bodies practically merged as one.[8]

The new Conservative national organization was founded well in advance of its eventual Liberal parallel. This was probably because the Conservative Party, despite showing divisions over Reform in 1867, was more homogeneous than its rival. On the Liberal side, the Birmingham Liberal Association, which commenced in 1865 under Joseph Chamberlain's leadership (and was soon saddled with the detrimental American designation of 'caucus'), was only one of a series of urban Liberal societies which had been established since the 1830s.[9] But its strength and activity was shown in its strategic deployment of Liberal voting so as to surmount the restrictions of the 'limited' vote and win all three Birmingham seats in the elections of 1868, 1874, and 1880. This feat was not repeated (in the case of all three elections) in any other three-member constituency. The Liberal parallel to the NUCCA, the National Liberal Federation (NLF), was inaugurated at Birmingham in 1877, although as this proved to be a radical organization, it had the effect of intensifying the differences between Whigs and radicals in the party which became more marked in the next decade.

Whether the new party organizations and their attached social clubs clearly assisted the spread of democracy has been a matter of debate. Moisei Ostrogorski, a Russian observer of British political practices in the last third of the nineteenth century, saw the 'caucus' as an undesirable new oligarchy, composed of a rising business and professional *élite*, which was gradually replacing (in a political sense) the declining aristocracy. In his view the party organization was narrow and ingrown, claiming to speak for the many but, in fact, representing only a select few, especially those who held official positions in the organization. These few activists, he held, were not necessarily estimable persons: in the case of some at least, they aspired merely to spend a day or two each year gaining reflected social glory by hobnobbing with the national bigwigs of their party.[10]

The 'select few', however, were really quite numerous, and were becoming increasingly so as political associations spread and multiplied. They reached a new peak after the very popular Primrose League was founded in 1883 and, as it spread, was a striking example of growing Conservative influence in the late nineteenth century. The Birmingham Liberal Association contained representatives who were nearly 600 strong – ranging pyramidically from ward committees at the base, through executive and general committees in the middle stages, to a managing subcommittee at the top. Ostrogorski was no doubt correct in pointing out the poor attendance at some committee meetings; the fact that some committee members were co-opted rather than elected; and the frequent control of business by small groups.[11] But he neglected to note the genuine advance of democracy which was represented by these new political organizations. They were all trying, to some degree, to channel public desires into party policy and government legislation – and to some extent they succeeded, though exactly how far was a matter of contention. 'Our constitution', wrote Francis Schnadhorst about the new NLF (of which he was Secretary) in 1878, 'represents an honest attempt to put the management of the party ... where we think it should rest – in the hands of the people themselves.'[12]

The spread of these organizations greatly increased political participation, and they ran parallel to the growing national and local press in disseminating political information and interest. After the stamp duties on newspapers were removed in 1855, newsprint extended to larger sections of the population, boosted by the removal of most of the remaining illiteracy after the passage of the 1870 and 1872 Education Bills and the coming of compulsory school attendance.[13] 'We must educate our masters', said a disappointed Robert Lowe after the events of 1867, though the electoral restrictions of the new Reform meant that the workers were still very far from being political masters. The number of newspapers published in the United Kingdom grew from 795 in 1856 to 2093 in 1886.[14] The gradual extension of democracy was rendered more effective by the growth of political organizations and of the press.

Political news and discussion had become very popular and fashionable by the last third of the nineteenth century. Disraeli

and Gladstone were, apart from Queen Victoria, the best-known
figures in the country; Salisbury and Chamberlain would not be
far behind. Apart from the plethora of Conservative and Liberal
Party institutions throughout the country, there also developed the
local 'Parliament' or 'House of Commons' – independent debating
societies run on the same lines as Parliament, with a 'Government'
and 'Opposition', motions and bills. The first of these to be founded
on a formal basis was established at Liverpool in 1860. By 1883,
when an article on these societies appeared in the *Nineteenth Century*,
over a hundred towns had them and their total membership was
over 35 000. They were an important aid to education, and
occasionally gave an initial push to a member who went on to attain
national political standing.[15]

The spread of party organizations throughout the country worked
together with changes in the electoral system to formalize and
centralize parliamentary politics.[16] The traditional informal
methods of electoral control, exercised by a landlord or an
employer, were losing influence. As comparatively few workers had
received the vote in 1832, and the pre-1832 'ancient right' electors
gradually decreased after that year, the political influence of
industrial employers had declined. The new franchise of 1867–8
seemed to open up extensive opportunities for employers'
influence. But these were hindered by the vast size of the new urban
vote, and the coming of the secret ballot in 1872. 'The 1868 election
was ... the only one', it has been said, 'which might be called an
employers' election.'[17] After 1872 political patronage was still
practised, until its overt manifestations were suppressed by the
Corrupt and Illegal Practices Act in 1883 and the virtual ending of
the small-borough constituencies in 1885. But after the secret ballot
came in, the effects of bribery could no longer be monitored at
the polls, and so penalties could no longer be administered to
deceitful electors. One of the effects of the ballot was that poll-
books (printed records of some elections, showing how named
electors gave their votes) could no longer be prepared and
published.

Attainment of the Secret Ballot

The continuance of electoral reform, both parliamentary and local, helped to stimulate the deep contemporary interest in politics. The 17 years from 1868 to 1885 were rich in electoral change. But three of the four most important reforms of this kind in the period were passed only at the end, in 1883–5 (the previous one being the ballot, in 1872); and the process of reform continued to advance democracy piecemeal rather than adopting it at one fell swoop.

Gladstone's first ministry of 1868–74 was more concerned with Irish matters, and with educational and other social reforms, than with electoral change, and it passed more local electoral reform than parliamentary. The Municipal Franchise Act of 1869 granted the vote in English and Welsh local council elections to all compound ratepayers after one year's residence, unmarried women receiving it on the same terms as men.[18] In Scotland the vote in local elections was given to women on a similar basis in 1881. The Education Acts of 1870 and 1872 established systems of a similar kind for elections to the new School Boards, and the cumulative voting method (whereby votes were accumulated on some candidates, others dropping out in consequence) was adopted in these cases. Women could stand for election to School Boards, but not for municipal and county councils until 1907. Apart from these measures of enfranchisement, and the introduction of some degree of proportional representation in School Board elections through the cumulative voting system, there was only one electoral initiative by this government, though it did apply to the national ground of Parliament as well as to local elections. This was the adoption of the secret ballot in parliamentary and municipal elections – the final victorious end of a 40-year campaign, achieved in 1872 after bills had failed in 1870 and 1871.

Francis Henry Berkeley, who died in 1870, had continued to move for the ballot in the Commons in 1866 and 1867, but lost in the former year by 197 votes to 110 and in the latter by 161 to 112.[19] Both the Reform Union and the Reform League had demanded the ballot, but as these organizations died out (in the case of the latter) or sank into relative obscurity (in the case of the former), the ballot managed to remain a leading democratic cause. This was largely because of energetic activity by the Ballot Society in the late 1860s. But in spite of its efforts, there was little obvious popular support for its aim.

The ballot was opposed by Disraeli, Gladstone, and other leading figures in both parties, until this pattern was broken when

Gladstone's new government decided, immediately after its formation, to move for the introduction of secret voting. When this change of heart occurred, 'Gladstone and his colleagues were not responding to a powerful extra-parliamentary demand for the ballot – such a demand did not exist.'[20] The ballot was still widely opposed as a means of secreting personal behaviour, and consequently (against the arguments which condemned the undemocratic influence encouraged by open voting) denounced with facile relish as 'un-English' and 'unmanly'.

The strength of the argument in favour of the ballot lay in its connection with the wider field of bribery and corruption, and the increased concern with these matters caused (on dubious grounds) by the newly expanded franchise. The menace of corruption was imagined to be growing with the increase of the electorate, whereas much enlarged numbers might more realistically have been seen as militating against such a menace. John Bright, who joined the new government, put his weighty support behind the ballot. He had written to Edmond Beales, President of the Reform League, in August 1867:

> The concession of a wide franchise is most incomplete as long as the security of the ballot is denied ... The more wide the suffrage, the more there are of men in humble circumstances who are admitted to the exercise of political rights, the more clearly is it necessary that the shelter of the ballot should be granted. I am confident [that] it would lessen expenses at elections, and greatly diminish corruption, and destroy the odious system of intimidation which now so extensively prevails, and that it would make the House of Commons a more complete representative of the opinions and wishes of the electoral body.[21]

Exposed examples of bribery and intimidation in the general election of 1868 gave grounds for the new-found support of leading Liberals for the ballot.[22] Henry Austin Bruce, the Home Secretary, was given the job of preparing the country for the first ministerial ballot bill, and announced his conversion to secret voting in January 1869. He still preferred, he said, demonstrated manliness, fearlessness, and openness in voting. But the intimidation which had occurred in the recent contests had persuaded him that the ballot was the lesser of two evils: better have secret voting with its humiliating aspects than the coercion and injustice of intimidation. Such an attitude reflected a growing acceptance, if not a very enthusiastic one, of the merits of more democratic voting, free from the control of patrons. In similarly tentative vein, the Queen's Speech in February 1869 (the customary announcement of intended government policy in the ensuing parliamentary session) said that a Select Committee should investigate the conduct of parliamentary and municipal elections and (in terms which sound almost sarcastic) 'consider whether it may be possible to provide any further guarantees for their tranquillity, purity, and freedom'. A Commons Select Committee on Parliamentary and Municipal Elections was duly appointed on 16 March. On the same day a radical MP, Edward Leatham – who was apparently succeeding Berkeley as leading back-bench advocate of the ballot in the Commons – carried a motion that the Committee should investigate different types of secret ballot which were now operated in some countries and states (especially Victoria and South Australia, which had used secret voting since 1856). The Committee was chaired by the Whig Marquess of Hartington and otherwise consisted of ten Liberals and ten Conservatives; eight of the Liberals, but none of the Conservatives, were in favour of the ballot.[23]

The Committee decided that it could not conclude its business in the 1869 session, and was therefore reappointed at the start of the next session in February 1870. At its final meeting on 15 March the Committee adopted its official report. The Conservative members of the Committee did not succeed in excluding from the report the recommendation of a secret ballot which had appeared in Hartington's draft report, though they did succeed in excluding the abolition of public nomination of candidates. Nevertheless, the latter provision, together with the ballot and some other reforms, appeared in Hartington's Parliamentary Elections Bill, which was approved by the Cabinet in May 1870. Although voting would be made secret by the bill, a judicial 'scrutiny' would be allowed if an election judge agreed that there were sufficient grounds to doubt the legality of a vote. A scrutiny could investigate the elector in such a case, because of numbers attached to the ballot papers. The secrecy of voting was to be, and, in fact, remains, limited by this means of trying to ensure that the law was observed.

The Select Committee had given full consideration to municipal elections. But only parliamentary elections were covered in the bill of 1870; municipal contests were to be dealt with in a later measure.[24] The adoption of secret voting as government policy was a new and most important step, not only in regard to the prospects of obtaining the ballot, but in showing more official support than hitherto for the more radical approach to Parliamentary Reform represented by the People's Charter and subsequent related motions. In 1870, with government acceptance of such an important radical desire as the ballot, the ministerial and radical strands in Parliamentary Reform appeared to have come effectively together – a development which would please the radicals in the Liberal Party more than the Whigs.

The ballot bill of 1870 failed to make sufficient progress in the Commons against the pressure of competing business, and it fell by the wayside. Its successor, the Elections (Parliamentary and Municipal) Bill of 1871, was more comprehensive as it included municipal contests and made provision to charge compulsory election expenses to the rates. W. E. Forster, Vice-President of the Council, assumed responsibility for the bill in the Commons. The debates were much fuller than in 1870 on the question. Gladstone justified his conversion to the ballot by saying that, while the sturdy honesty of open voting might be affordable to persons of private means, it was scarcely appropriate to 'the station of life to which probably now a majority of our town voters belong'.[25] The bill passed the Commons on 8 August. Two days later in the Lords, despite the efforts of the bill's advocates to appeal to the House by stressing the unwholesome electoral influence of trade union officials, the measure was summarily rejected by 97 votes to 48 on the motion of Lord Shaftesbury.[26]

The third government effort, however, brought success. The complexity of the arguments for and against the ballot, and the difficulty of reaching a coherent viewpoint when the effects of the new franchise were still uncertain, maintained general public apathy on the question. Shaftesbury chose to interpret public silence as meaning consent, and declared in January 1872 that he also felt compelled to accept the ballot.[27] The Government's determination to pass the measure, in a situation where there was little coherent opposition, was the one firm and decisive element in a mass of confused opinions which otherwise might have held off a settlement for many years.

A new bill was approved by the Cabinet on 22 January 1872. The measure included provisions for the ballot, and for abolition of public nomination of candidates, in both parliamentary and municipal elections. In the debates on the bill in the Commons, there remained some Liberal differences, Henry Fawcett and Sir William Harcourt being in favour of making the ballot voluntary rather than compulsory. But Liberals rallied solidly behind ministers in the third division, when the bill passed by 274 to 216 against unanimous Conservative opposition. The Marquess of Salisbury (the former Viscount Cranborne), in an interesting demonstration of his growing efforts to boost the House of Lords' resistance to the Commons, said that the Lords should reject the bill again in order to vindicate their position as 'a vital and independent part of the constitutional structure':

> If we listen to the Liberals we should accept all important Bills which had passed the House of Commons by a large majority. But that in effect would be to efface the House of Lords ... The plan which I prefer is frankly to acknowledge that the nation is our Master, though the House of Commons is not; and to yield our own opinion only when the judgment of the nation has been challenged at the polls, and decidedly expressed.[28]

Salisbury's determination to oppose the Ballot Bill was part of his broader anxiety to maintain a distinct place in government for the hereditary aristocracy, even if ultimately this could only be done by bowing to democracy and acknowledging that aristocrats were its servants ('the nation is our Master'). It was vital that the House of Lords should not be relegated to a position similar to that of the monarchy, and become a mere rubber-stamp for House of Commons legislation – especially when (as had been the case since 1830) there was usually a Liberal majority in the Lower House. Party interest and class interest guided Salisbury's initiatives in this respect, and political and social changes in the 1880s and 1890s enabled him to succeed more than he had believed possible in vindicating these interests.

Lord Carnarvon supported Salisbury in wanting to resist the ballot but, as in 1867, they represented a minority view among Conservative politicians. The Duke of Richmond and Lord Cairns, who were responsible for leading the Conservative majority in the Upper House, doubted whether rejection of the bill would help the Lords' interests in the fierce constitutional battle which was bound to follow such an action. As in the Irish Church struggle with the same government in 1869, they preferred to maintain their constitutional powers through diplomacy rather than risk losing them through adamant confrontation. Encouraged by the desires of Fawcett and Harcourt among the Liberals, Richmond and most Conservative peers (fully backed by Disraeli, the party leader) proposed to amend the bill by, among other alterations, making secret voting optional.

When the second reading was debated by the Lords on 10 June, Earl Grey proposed to reject the bill as being too narrow an answer to the country's electoral needs: franchise, distribution of seats, and methods of voting should be reviewed as a whole and not piecemeal. It was unwise, he maintained, to introduce the secret ballot without knowing the future electoral conditions in which it would be applied:

> And there is also this important objection to dealing with this question singly – that by doing so, by making one change in the representation this year, another next year, and another the year after, you may be gradually led into making such a total alteration in the whole character of our government, as would meet with your most determined resistance if it were proposed to you at once.[29]

Salisbury, in his speech opposing the bill, said that the future of Ireland under the ballot concerned him most. Secret voting, he believed, would return to the Commons a large body of MPs who wanted to separate Ireland from the United Kingdom.[30] He was soon proved right. In the 1874 election, in which the ballot was used, a majority of the MPs returned from Ireland were of Home Rule opinions, though it could hardly be claimed that the ballot was an essential prerequisite to this result. But Richmond was supported by the majority of Conservative peers in his advocacy of an optional ballot and in his decision to abstain from the division on the second reading. As a result, the second reading passed by 86 votes to 56.

In committee on 17 June, the Lords carried Richmond's amendment for a scrutiny of ballot papers by a majority of 29, and his amendment for optional secrecy of voting (which permitted, as an alternative, the marking of the ballot paper in front of election officials and agents) by a majority of 16. Other amendments were also inserted, including one (adopted by a majority of 63) to pass the bill as an experiment which should be fully reconsidered after eight years. After applying this substantial transformation, which was most unwelcome to Gladstone and his Government, the Lords passed the third reading after a brief debate on 21 June.

On 26 June the Cabinet decided to recommend that the Commons should accept scrutiny of votes – provided this proposal were amended to conform with the restrictions on scrutiny in the bill of 1870 – and two other Lords' amendments (extending polling hours, and banning the use of schools as polling stations). But Cabinet also decided to advise that the other Lords' amendments – including optional ballot and limiting of the Act to eight years' duration – should be rejected. The Commons rejected an optional ballot by 302 votes to 234 after a debate on 27 June. On 28 June, W. E. Forster advised that a closely limited scrutiny should be accepted for the sake of passing the bill, and argued that a scrutiny thus restricted would not damage the essential secrecy of the vote. But another Liberal, Henry James, argued to the contrary and obtained the support of 136 MPs (mostly radicals) in a division. In this division, however, the government easily carried a closely restricted scrutiny by a majority of 245 (382 votes to 137).

On 28 June, the Commons rejected three more Lords' amendments, but two of these (which prohibited the use of schools as polling stations, and extended polling hours) were thrown out against the government's advice. Two further Lords' amendments were rejected on 1 July, including the one limiting the Act to eight years, which was defeated by 246 to 165. In this debate Gladstone did not mince his words regarding the Lords' treatment of the bill:

> The House [of Commons] has spent weary months both this year and last year upon maturing this Bill with care and consideration in all its details, and the fact that in 'another place' it has only been found necessary to spend a few hours in pulling to pieces that which we have done, really is and can be no argument why we should blot out from our recollections the nature and character of our own labours.[31]

The Conservative majority in the Lords seemed likely to insist on an optional ballot, and a crisis between the two Houses seemed to be near. The crucial debate was held in the Lords on 8 July, amidst great excitement. 'Not since the 1838 division on Grote's motion', it has been said, 'had the ballot been the subject of such intense political interest.'[32] The outcome was a government victory over this amendment, obtained through the moderation of some Conservative peers. Seventeen Tories voted with the government, and many abstained, to produce a result of 157 to 138 against the optional ballot. On 12 July, however, the Commons reluctantly yielded to two amendments on which the Conservative peers were insisting, despite the Commons rejection. These included restriction of the Act to eight years. The measure received the Royal Assent on 18 July, but it remained subject to periodic renewal until its provisions were made permanent by the Representation of the People Act of 1918.

The introduction of the secret ballot was a large advance for democracy, as it enabled electors to vote as they themselves decided, without finding it tempting or prudent to submit to the pressure of landlord or employer influence. In the prevailing social and political circumstances, honest voting needed the support of secret voting. Calls to demonstrate manly honesty in open voting were bound to fall flat when there might be great material pressure to vote dishonestly (that is, against one's own conscience) when the voting took place openly. Secret voting was therefore an essential feature of democracy, except in the unlikely event of society becoming so disinterested and perfect that votes could be given openly without the hint of any attempt to influence them.

But the coming of the ballot was far from achieving its wider objective of ending electoral corruption. Intimidation greatly lessened, because this most direct form of influence was the least likely to be effective when the abused elector could still decide for himself when giving his secret vote. But bribery continued, perhaps in the belief that an elector who received a bribe would feel 'morally' bound to vote in the way intended by the person from whom he took his money or patronage.[33] Thus electoral corruption continued strongly for some years, being still widespread in the general election of 1880,[34] and not sharply receding until the passage of the stiff Corrupt and Illegal Practices Bill in 1883 and dis-franchisement of the small boroughs (where bribery flourished most) in 1885.

Another enactment in 1872 amalgamated the laws against corrupt practice in parliamentary and municipal elections, but did not extend those laws. Apart from this and the other Acts already mentioned, the only other measure relating to the franchise passed by the first Gladstone Government (and dealt with more extensively below) was the restoration to electors of the right to compound for the payment of rates, by an Act of 1869. This had the effect of increasing the voters in the general election of 1874 to a number approximating to that which had been originally expected to vote in the 1868 contest.

Women's Suffrage, the County Vote, and Proportional Representation

As one long-lasting electoral campaign, that for the ballot, was laid to rest, another was taking its place, and, indeed, exceeded it in longevity. If the ballot campaign had lasted for nearly 40 years, the campaign for women's suffrage was to last for over 50. J. S. Mill's unsuccessful motion of 1867 commenced a long line of similar failures for women's right to vote in parliamentary elections, although there was some alleviation in that the right of female voting in local elections received successive extensions. Except on one occasion, in 1870, a favourable division on a women's parliamentary suffrage bill or resolution was not obtained until 1897. During the years from 1867 to 1897, there were 12 unfavourable divisions and several other occasions when a bill was frustrated, being displaced by government business or 'talked out'. It was only in February 1897 that the first glimmer of success since 1870 appeared when Ferdinand Faithfull Begg, a Conservative MP for a Glasgow division, obtained a majority of 71 for the second reading of his women's suffrage bill. His measure got no further, however, as the committee stage was not attained. After this the results of parliamentary efforts became less one-sided in terms of success. Also from 1897 there developed more efficient and extensive extra-parliamentary organization, the National Union of Women's Suffrage Societies being formed in 1897 and the Women's Social and Political Union in 1903.

During the 1870s no such developments seemed near. In May

1870 Jacob Bright, brother of the more famous (and anti-women's suffrage) John, obtained a majority of 33 for the second reading of his Women's Disabilities Removal Bill. But thereafter there was failure on the second reading for seven similar bills up to June 1878. To cap the tale of fruitlessness in the 1870s, a resolution in favour of women's suffrage, introduced in March 1879 by Leonard Courtney (a radical MP), also met with defeat.[35]

Also urged from 1872 in the Commons, on an annual basis up to 1879, was household and lodging suffrage for the counties on the same basis as the boroughs.[36] George Otto Trevelyan, a radical MP who had resigned his office as a junior minister in 1870, first moved a resolution to effect this reform on 26 April 1872, but was defeated by 148 votes to 70. He introduced a private member's bill in 1873, 1874, and 1875. The bill was withdrawn without a division in the first year, and defeated on second reading by majorities of 114 and 102 in the second and third years respectively. Every year from 1876 to 1879, Trevelyan moved resolutions for the same reform, and was defeated by majorities of 99, 56, 52, and 65 in the successive years.[37] There was a lengthy debate on each occasion. Robert Lowe and other former Adullamites among the Liberals joined most Conservatives in opposition to the motions. But most of the leading Liberals showed signs of yielding to the proposals, and the opposition to them was not very determined.

Gladstone's first ministry did not take up this reform as part of its business, perhaps believing that the passage of the ballot would be quite enough for Whig political interests (and, consequently, the general interests of Liberal Party unity) to swallow at that juncture. But in 1872 Gladstone stated in the debate on the first of Trevelyan's motions:

> I have not disguised my opinion on the present condition of the county franchise, which cannot very long continue. I do not think it is possible, under present circumstances, to maintain for a lengthened period that broad line of demarcation between the county franchise and the borough franchise which at present exists.[38]

Thenceforth, Gladstone voted for Trevelyan's motions. In 1877 the Marquess of Hartington, the official leader of the Liberal Party, first gave positive support to the reform when he said in the debate:

'the extension of the franchise was by almost universal consent a question of time, and of time only.'[39]

The question became more pressing as it was arousing support in the country, being promoted especially by the very active National Agricultural Labourers' Union, formed in 1873 and calling for better conditions amid growing rural depression. This union did not, however, usually go so far as to support the call for manhood suffrage which was made by Northumberland coal-miners for a few years up to 1874.[40]

It was expected that such an important reform as county household suffrage would be made the subject of government legislation, and that party concerns about its impact would have to be assuaged by a large accompanying redistribution of seats. Conservatives (and some Liberals) disliked the idea of embarking on such an extensive reform, and it seemed that it would have to await the return of another Liberal Government.

Continued concern about the frustration of electors by the difficulty and complexity of the registration system led to an attempt by the Liberal Government, after the failure of more extensive bills by private members in 1871 and 1872, to pass a modest measure in 1873. The chief objects of this bill were to simplify the process of revising the lists of electors and to establish a common register for both parliamentary and municipal voters. The bill passed the Commons, but not the Lords. In 1878, however, a bill was passed by the succeeding Conservative Government (one of only two electoral reforms which it carried) enacting the proposal of 1873 for a common register of voters in parliamentary and municipal elections.[41]

Unsuccessful over registration reform, Gladstone's first ministry did clear up the chaos over compounding for rate payments which had been caused by the Reform Act of 1867 for England and Wales (compounding did not exist under Scots law). That Act, with the object of enfranchising about half a million males, had abolished compounding for rates through making payment through a landlord. But strong protests, including threats of violence, had resulted on account of the increased expense which the reform imposed on tenants. As a result, compounding was allowed to continue (even being introduced for the first time in some towns); and although this had effects on the electoral register in 1868, the principle of personal ratepaying was by no means always insisted on as a condition of voting in that year's general election. Tenants who compounded were accepted as voters in some constituencies in that election, but refused in others: 'the number of persons enfranchised in 1868 depended to a large extent, in many of the boroughs, upon the political activities of the lawyers, and the attitude of the overseers and revising barristers.'[42] Disraeli's Government of 1868 had not attempted to make a legal adjustment in the matter, which was left in utter confusion. Order was re-established in 1869 by the quiet legislative restoration of compounding, accompanied by the provision that the names of all male compound householders should appear on the electoral lists. After this the residence requirement, and in a few constituencies the limited vote, were the only restrictions on male household suffrage in the boroughs.

As well as county household suffrage and women's suffrage, the cause of proportional representation was sometimes quite prominent in the 1870s. J. S. Mill's initiative on this subject in the debates on the 1867 Reform Bill had failed, like his initiative on women's suffrage. But, as in the latter case, there was determination to increase support for the question. Through the initiative of the Reform League, a Representative Reform Association advocating proportional representation had been formed in 1868. A combination of middle- and working-class radicals supported the association. Thomas Hare was president, George Howell secretary, and leading supporters included J. S. Mill, Henry Fawcett, Leonard Courtney, George Holyoake, Edmond Beales, George Odger, Charles Bradlaugh, and Randall Cremer. The main result of the Association's activities was the introduction of an abortive bill in the Commons in 1872 by Walter Morrison (Liberal MP for Plymouth, treasurer and main financial benefactor of the Association), providing for proportional representation in England and Wales. The bill proposed to establish 69 constituencies, returning between three and 16 MPs each. Any candidate who obtained the required quota of votes (calculated by dividing the number of votes given by the number of MPs for the constituency) would be elected. Surplus votes (additional to the number required to give a candidate the quota) would be transferred to the elector's next choice of candidate.

The plan was, in essence, that known later as the 'single transferable vote', which was to emerge as the favourite scheme of

most advocates of proportional representation in Britain. But the
bill won the support of only 26 MPs, 154 voting against. The
Association declined, and died out in 1874. Howell was no longer
showing much interest in it, and Morrison had become tired of
being 'in my sole person the association'.[43]

There was no further association with these aims in view until
the Proportional Representation Society was founded in 1884,
advocating the single transferable vote system. In the intervening
years, however, the issue retained considerable life. The merits of
the single transferable vote had to be argued against those of 'the
second ballot' – the holding of a second poll when no candidate
got more than half the votes at the first – which was advocated by
Sir Charles Dilke. In the Commons from 1873 to 1878 the question
of proportionality kept a tenuous hold in debates, through the
annual discussion of unsuccessful bills which proposed to introduce
the cumulative vote in the election of aldermen by town councils.
This matter might not have seemed to be of first-rate democratic
importance, but it provided one of the recurrent flickers of
parliamentary interest in electoral change during the not very
promising years of Disraeli's second ministry. These municipal
reform bills attracted some Conservative support as well as Liberal,
several of the measures being introduced by Conservative MPs.[44]
In 1875 Dilke moved for an enquiry into 'the various methods of
bringing about a juster system of political power, with a view of
securing a more complete representation of the people'. But he
was opposed by both Disraeli and Gladstone, and was defeated by
190 votes to 120.[45] In 1878 an Irish Home Rule MP, R. P.
Blennerhassett, moved unsuccessfully that (in order, as he made
clear, to prevent the interests of property and education from being
submerged by the rise of lower-class representation):

> it is desirable that the whole electoral body should be enabled to
> enjoy that direct representation which is at present confined to
> majorities; that no effectual security exists for the due represen-
> tation of minorities; and that, as far as possible, all opinions should
> have an opportunity of being represented in direct proportion to
> the number of electors by whom they are held.[46]

In 1879 Blennerhassett also unsuccessfully moved an amendment
to Trevelyan's annual county franchise motion, by proposing to

add to it: 'and to provide, as far as possible, for the fair representation of minorities'. His main concern, he again stated (in a restrained version of Lowe's expressions of 1866), was the importance of ensuring that, among the alleged populist political tendencies, the representative system would give a substantial voice to the propertied and the educated.

During Disraeli's Government of 1874–80, the Conservatives had no pressing need to consider adopting county household suffrage or a redistribution of seats. The political conditions were not those of 1867–8, when the Conservatives were in office with a minority, or of 1884–5, when they were in opposition. The Conservatives obtained a sound majority in the 1874 election, and, in consequence, political interest did not encourage Disraeli to initiate major electoral reforms which would have risked a party split. Stalemate, therefore, had been reached on these questions. Conservatives for the most part did not wish to introduce large electoral changes. Liberals did introduce them, but without much hope of surmounting the Conservative majority and getting them through.

Only two electoral reforms were carried during this ministry, the Registration Bill of 1878 (already mentioned) and the Elections and Corrupt Practices Bill of 1879. The latter put into effect two of the recommendations of a Select Committee of the Commons, appointed in 1875 and chaired by Robert Lowe. Two judges rather than one would henceforth adjudicate on election petitions, and no election would be declared void unless both judges agreed.[47] The very small scale of these changes indicated that yet another chance had been lost to make decisive inroads on illegal electoral corruption. This large matter, and the even larger matters of franchise extension and redistribution of seats, awaited the much more positive electoral reforming attitudes of the new government that took office in 1880, following defeat at the polls for Disraeli's ministry.

Gladstone's Second Government and Reform

The Liberal Party returned to office after obtaining a large majority in the general election of April 1880. After some uncertainty as to who would become premier, Gladstone (who had retired as party leader in 1875) was reappointed to take the role. Two of the electoral reforms of this ministry were already expected – firm measures to deal with corruption, and county household suffrage. As regards the former, widespread bribery in the 1880 election was alleged to be 'responsible for the carrying through in 1883 of a draconian limitation of expenses which ensured that the next general election would be just over one-quarter as expensive as the election of 1880'.[48] But this effect probably also owed a lot to the wholesale removal of small borough representation in the Redistribution Act of 1885.

The early 1880s were a time of both encouragement and frustration for the rise of democracy. Whig aristocrats were suspicious of the intention to carry anti-bribery, county household suffrage, and Irish land measures. Gladstone's liberal appointment of Whigs (and very sparing appointment of radicals) to his new Cabinet was probably intended to diminish this looming difficulty for Liberal Party unity. However, the radical Joseph Chamberlain, who was given what was then the least prestigious cabinet office of President of the Board of Trade, would, within a few years, campaign for social, land, and Church reforms which alarmed Whigs as much as Tories. From 1883 his speeches and articles intensified the upper-class fears of a dangerous trend, which had already been aroused by some of the reforms of Gladstone's first ministry, as well as by the formation of the heavily radical National Liberal Federation, by the economic decline of landed estates through agricultural depression, and by the approaching policy of county household franchise.

After Chamberlain took up the cause of making the Liberal Party more democratic and populist, such tendencies were also partially displayed in regard to his own party by the young Conservative Lord Randolph Churchill, to the embarrassment of Lord Salisbury.[49] The widening support for Conservatism by the mid-1880s was shown by the spread of suburban 'villa' Toryism or 'terrace' Toryism. Growing middle- and working-class support for Conservatism, feeding on imperialism and (in a short time) on opposition to Irish Home Rule, was seen most visibly in the vast numbers who joined the Primrose League, founded by Churchill and Drummond Wolff in 1883 in commemoration of Disraeli. Women were admitted as 'dames' in the following year, and by 1900 there were 2300 branches (or 'habitations') and 1 250 000 members of this quasi-mediaeval but, in reality, very contemporary body.[50]

The growth of middle-class and even working-class Conservatism led Salisbury to realize the party value, in many parts of the country, of single-member constituencies of roughly equal size. Like Peel and Disraeli before him, Salisbury as a leading Conservative became more liberal in political approach. He became ready to accept a redistribution scheme based on single-member constituencies in exchange for conceding county household suffrage – about which he was very apprehensive.[51] Hitherto, the Reform Acts had seen each party acting by itself in its own electoral interests. The reforms of 1884–5, on the other hand, found each party compromising with the other's aims, and working with the other party, in order to achieve its own objectives.

Obstructions faced Gladstone in trying to put a Parliamentary Reform programme through in the course of his second ministry. This was because of Conservative resistance, especially that of the 'Fourth Party', a Tory ginger-group in the Commons led by Churchill. This group, and the Conservative Opposition as a whole, was able to capitalize on the difficulties caused by Irish disturbances and by the struggles of the atheist Charles Bradlaugh to take his seat in the House. In these circumstances it was not really surprising that a government bill for county household suffrage, though widely promised by Liberal candidates in 1880, was introduced only in 1884.[52] Nor was it entirely surprising that an effort of 1881 to pass a firm measure against bribery only succeeded in 1883, when it had been presented in three successive sessions, like the Ballot Bill 11 years before. It was this anti-corruption measure which was the first of a trio of important electoral reforms in the fruitful triennium of 1883–5.

Elimination of Corrupt Electoral Practice?

Dealing with electoral corruption was one of the leading priorities of the second Gladstone Government. Before eight Royal Commission reports into practices at the recent general election had become available, the Queen's Speech on 6 January 1881 announced that there would be the introduction of a bill for eliminating the corrupt practices 'of which, in a number of towns, there were lamentable examples at the last General Election'.[53]

On the following day a Parliamentary Elections (Corrupt and Illegal Practices) Bill was brought into the Commons by the Attorney-General, Sir Henry James. Basing his justification for the measure on the evidence of corruption which had emerged in the recent trials of election petitions, James gave details of the two main aims of the bill – to reduce election expenditure and to establish really severe penalties for corrupt practice. Under the first heading, a parliamentary candidate should not usually spend more than £1000 for every 5000 voters. Moreover, the number of agents and assistants whom he might employ would be strictly limited, so that a large increase in voluntary party workers was likely if the bill succeeded. Under the second heading, there would be much heavier penalties than previously for bribery, treating, intimidation, impersonation, and some other related practices. The punishment for being found guilty of taking part in these corrupt practices would be two years' imprisonment (perhaps with hard labour), a fine of £500, and loss of voting rights for ten years. If the person found guilty was a parliamentary candidate, he would be banned for life from representing the constituency in which the offences occurred. Some comparatively minor illegal practices would be punishable by a fine of £100, and a public house should not be used as a candidate's committee rooms.[54]

There was little opposition to the bill from the Conservatives. In fact, as has been said, 'there was a great deal of co-operation between the front benches in the Commons to get the bill through. A broad consensus obtained that something effective had to be done both to check corruption and to reduce costs.'[55] There would have been high hopes of passing the bill smoothly had it not been for the obstructive tactics of the Irish Home Rule MPs. Though these were met by new rules for closing debates, this was not before they had succeeded in retarding the government's parliamentary schedule. The second reading of the bill could not be moved, as planned, on 17 February 1881, and it was deferred until 3 March. But the second reading had still not been moved by 11 July. Sir Henry James then moved that the order for the reading be discharged, as it could no longer be hoped to carry the bill that session. He made a fairly firm statement that the measure would be reintroduced early in the 1882 session.

The bill brought into the Commons in 1882 was basically the

same as its predecessor, though the number of clauses had grown from 59 to 62. Irish concerns were at the root of a second failure in 1882, for prolonged debates on the Irish Crimes Bill in June absorbed the time which had been intended to deal with the Corrupt and Illegal Practices Bill in committee of the Commons. On 28 July Sir Henry James moved for, and was granted, discharge of the order for a committee.

It was arranged that a third attempt at legislation on electoral corruption would be given priority over all other bills in the 1883 session. Given a first reading in the Commons on 16 February that year, the new measure again contrived to be somewhat longer than the last. Despite government hopes of greater speed, the bill was not discussed again until 4 June. Matters then took on some swiftness: the second reading was agreed to without a division, and the bill went to committee on 7 June. But it stayed there for the next month on account of prolonged criticism, largely from Home Rulers, but also from many back-bench Conservatives and some back-bench Liberals. The debates in committee, where many amendments were added, ended on 13 July. Having finally got through the Commons after three sessions of effort, the bill passed all its stages in the Lords in August, and the Royal Assent was given on the 25th of that month.

The Act differed in some details from the original bill of 1881. Persons found guilty of corrupt practice by an election court would be imprisoned for a year and fined £200. Candidates found personally guilty of corruption would, in addition, suffer permanent exclusion from standing in the constituency where the offences had occurred and would, for seven years, lose voting rights, all public and judicial offices, and the right to sit in the Commons. Lesser punishments were imposed for the minor 'illegal practices'. Altogether, the measure was formidable: it was 'by far the most stringent ever passed in Britain against electoral malpractices'.[56]

The paid employment of election officials was strictly limited by the Act, so it became more important to candidates than before to find voluntary helpers. In that very politically-conscious age, these were usually available in abundance – not least in the form of middle-class ladies who were keen to get away from the role of mere 'angel in the home'. Thus women could help to get the vote from others even if they could not give it themselves. Enthusiastic help came from both male and female members of the numerous associations which were affiliated to, or sympathetic to, a political party. In the case of the Conservatives, for example, help came from members of the Primrose League, which was founded in the year that the Corrupt and Illegal Practices Bill was passed though it did not affiliate to the party until 1914. Thus the democratic benefits of that measure were very widespread. They included not only more freedom to vote according to conscience and inclination, but the spread of political activity among wider sections of the people.

Clearly the new Act meant business. But how far did it achieve it on its own? It is impossible to be certain on the question, but it would seem likely that post-1883 corruption would have been greater than it was had not the suppression of most of the smaller boroughs (traditionally the most easily bribable constituencies, because of their small electorates) taken place under the Redistribution Act of 1885.[57] Practices which had been of material benefit for so long and to so many people would hardly have disappeared as rapidly as they did, even after the stringent Act of 1883, if their most fruitful and productive constituencies had remained in being. The widespread, though by no means universal, disappearance of electoral corruption should therefore be seen as the result of two Acts, not merely one – the Parliamentary Elections (Corrupt and Illegal Practices) Act of 1883 and the Distribution of Seats Act of 1885. After both measures, the total official expenditure in the general election of November 1885 was only a quarter of the amount spent in the contest of 1880.[58]

The last Royal Commission on a British election sat at Worcester after the 1906 contest and discovered that about 500 electors there remained willing to sell their votes for small sums. Some of these admitted that 'for upwards of thirty years they had been accustomed to rewards for their votes'.[59] The petering out of such minority practices in the country meant that voting was increasingly carried out in accordance with choice and conscience, thus becoming more of a democratic exercise. The Acts of 1883 and 1885 brought about a major change which the introduction of the secret ballot had not been able to achieve.

The Reforms of 1884–5

The momentous parliamentary reforms of 1884–5 began with a County Franchise Bill which was in keeping with the previous attempts to equalize the voting qualifications in boroughs and counties. This bill, although not opposed by the Conservatives in the Commons, pleased only the majority of Liberals who introduced it, and it was rejected by the alarmed aristocracy in the Lords. Private inter-party negotiations produced a consensus settlement. This provided for passage of the bill, accompanied, as compensation, by passage of a measure for the thorough redistribution of seats. A full-scale redistribution – which would tend to separate industrial from agricultural elements in the counties, and middle-class suburbs from working-class in the towns – would give more electoral confidence to both Conservatives and Whigs who feared a radical take-over on account of the 1883 Act.[60]

County household enfranchisement seemed a natural pro-gression from the 1867–8 Reform Acts. This was partly because many dwellers in county constituencies were industrial workers who, unlike many of the workers living in towns, did not have the vote; while, at the same time, agricultural labourers dwelling in county constituencies could not vote though labourers living in rural boroughs perhaps could. The situation was thoroughly anomalous, and the line between borough and county franchise seemed both artificial and unjust.

County household suffrage was commended by 153 of the successful Liberal candidates in the 1880 election. Only a few Liberals, such as Lowe (newly created Viscount Sherbrooke) and G. J. Goschen, were clearly against this reform.[61] The likelihood of a bill being introduced by the new government and passed in the House of Commons therefore appeared strong. But the ministry's problems and preoccupations, and the expectation that a parliamentary dissolution and a general election should shortly follow a Reform Act, delayed the attempt until 1884. The introduction of the Corrupt Practices Bill in 1883 might have pleased the radicals by appearing as an earnest of ministerial intentions in regard to Parliamentary Reform in general. On the other hand, it was likely to stiffen the resistance of Whig peers who saw their traditional means of influence removed by the measure – and who, moreover, had to put up with the exuberant rhetoric of

Joseph Chamberlain, a radical in the Cabinet, who said in 1883 that the aristocracy were a useless class 'who toil not neither do they spin'.[62]

In the autumn of 1883 and the succeeding winter, many large meetings were arranged by Chamberlain and other radicals to demand county household suffrage. In January 1884 a deputation representing all trade unions in the United Kingdom urged Gladstone to introduce this reform.[63] A bill to give the counties the same electoral qualifications as the boroughs was introduced in the Commons by Gladstone on 28 February 1884. Thus began a Reform struggle which resembled that of 1831–2 in length, but not in breadth or intensity.

Some Whigs were reluctant to support the bill, because of the much-extended suffrage it would bring to Ireland and because of its likely detrimental effects on landlord influence in general. Gladstone anticipated that there would be strong opposition in the Lords, and hoped to obtain large majorities in the Commons in order to strengthen himself against the Upper House. The bill extended the borough household occupation and lodger franchises to the counties; reduced the rateable value franchise in the counties; and abolished the Chandos ('tenants-at-will') provision introduced in the 1832 Act. It retained, however, the freeholder, copyholder, and leaseholder qualifications in counties.[64]

For more radical eddies which disturbed the familiar pool of franchise and distribution argument, there was no success at this time. A revival of interest in urging the transferable vote, under the stimulus of the new Proportional Representation Society founded in January 1884 (with Sir John Lubbock, an able but eccentric Liberal MP, as president), produced considerable discussion of this issue in debates on the Franchise Bill. But nothing resulted, and in consequence Leonard Courtney resigned his junior post in the government.[65] The now equally well-established cause of women's suffrage was also unsuccessful. An amendment to this reform by William Woodall (a Liberal MP) that 'words [in the bill] importing the masculine gender include women' was defeated on 12 June by 273 votes to 137. A bill introduced by Woodall for the same purpose in November did not get to a second reading.

The Franchise (or 'Representation of the People') Bill sailed through the Commons on 26 June 1884, arousing no clear Conservative opposition to the principle of the reform, avoiding any division on its readings, and with hardly any alteration since its introduction. In the Lords, however, the bill was rejected on 8 July, on the motion of Earl Cairns, by 205 to 146. Nearly all the Whig peers had in the end supported the government. The Conservative peers' objection was not to the principle of the measure, but to the ministry's failure to couple it with a redistribution of seats which would make the Commons more representative of the people.[66] Salisbury and his Conservative colleagues emphasized a need for popular acceptance of the measure which bore some resemblance to Salisbury's wider proposal that popular referendums should be held on major reforms.[67]

In fact, Lord Salisbury, the reserved aristocrat, was perforce becoming something of a populist. His transformation was shown particularly by his attitude to Parliamentary Reform at this juncture. He had left a Conservative ministry rather than agree with its Reform intentions in 1867, but now he was adopting intentions not dissimilar to Disraeli's at that time. Relentless changes in economy and society, and the general trend of political concession from the 1820s to claims arising from these changes, had left him with no real alternative. By the 1880s, the secret ballot and stiff legislation against corruption on the one hand, and the formation of the Primrose League on the other, had greatly speeded the movement of the Conservative Party on to a lower and wider social level. This entailed the abandonment of much of the old aristocratic control. But at the same time it opened up new opportunities for the expansion of the party, which were accentuated by the popularity of imperialism and the Liberal split over Irish Home Rule in 1886. Salisbury, a natural right-winger, was not the most obvious person to seize the new opportunities, but he did not flinch from doing so. During the next decade or so he seemed to become reconciled to the middle- and working-class world in which his party increasingly moved in the quest to survive as a major political institution. His reward was that by 1900, his party – though it was to become damagingly divided within a few years – was showing impressive strength, breadth, and unity.[68]

The reasons of the Conservative peers for rejecting the Franchise Bill were stated in a declaration of 1 July 1884:

> ... this House, while prepared to concur in a well-considered and complete scheme for the extension of the franchise, does

not think it right to assent to the Second Reading of a Bill having for its object a fundamental change in the constitution of the electoral body of the United Kingdom, but which is not accompanied by provisions for so apportioning the right to return Members as to insure a true and fair representation of the people, or by any adequate security in the proposals of the Government that the present Bill shall not come into operation except as part of an entire scheme.[69]

Stalemate seemed to have been reached with the Lords' rejection of the franchise measure on 8 July. Gladstone simply announced that the bill would be reintroduced in an autumn session. Brought back into the Commons on 24 October, the bill passed its second reading on 7 November. The second reading debate in the Lords was scheduled for 18 November. But, the day before this, Gladstone in the Commons and his colleague Earl Granville in the Lords struck out on a new and unprecedented path regarding parliamentary (or rather extra-parliamentary) arrangement of electoral reform.

The new departure arose from the government's willingness, in return for the speedy passage of the Franchise Bill, 'to make the provisions of Redistribution the subject of friendly communication with the leaders of the Opposition'.[70] Re-entering the Lords on 13 November 1884, the Franchise Bill was not finally passed by that House until 5 December. The enactment added over two million men to the United Kingdom electorate, which now totalled over five and a half millions. All male householders who met the residence requirement now had the vote. Chamberlain, on 5 January at Birmingham, felt that he could congratulate the country on 'a revolution which has been peacefully and silently accomplished. The centre of power has been shifted, and the old order is giving place to the new.'[71]

The old order, however, was having a considerable say in the settlement. Agreement between Conservative leaders and government leaders was an essential preliminary to the Lords' acceptance of county franchise. Gladstone and Salisbury, together with Dilke, Northcote, and others, consulted about the crucial redistribution details at 10 Downing Street, from 19–27 November. Grappling with numerous boundary questions, they produced an agreed settlement which still forms the general basis of constituency

arrangements at the present day. The deal was concluded at
Salisbury's London house in Arlington Street, and hence was known
as the Arlington Street Compact.

Arriving thus at crucial electoral transformations behind the
closed doors of statesmen's houses – though the changes would of
course have to be confirmed by Parliament – brought to its highest
pitch the tendency for Parliamentary Reform to be initiated and
decided by politicians rather than by the multitude. In the Arlington
Street Compact the common interest of both main parties in using
Parliamentary Reform for their own benefit had indeed come to
maturity – the leaders of both not acting separately, as hitherto,
but meeting to agree on compromise changes with mutual
advantage in mind.

However, popular agitation on the issue, though much less than
in either 1831–2 or 1866–7, was by no means absent. While its effect
on the politicians is difficult to gauge, it may be hazarded that this
was less than in 1866–7, and much less than in 1831–2. Renewed
agitation arose in support of allowing the Franchise Bill to pass,
and condemned the Lords for rejecting it in July. A great many
public meetings of protest were held, and a new People's League
for the Abolition of the Hereditary Legislature was able to form
over 50 branches.[72] But there was not the widespread organization
which had characterized previous Reform agitations. The National
Agricultural Labourers' Union continued in existence, demanding
county household suffrage, but there was no Reform League,
Chartist movement, or National Political Union. The largest
combined Parliamentary Reform of the nineteenth century was
put through without major campaigning organized on a nationwide
basis.

The conditions on which the Franchise Bill would be allowed
through were drawn up in the private conclaves of political leaders.
'Never before', it has been said, 'had the details of a measure yet
to be introduced in Parliament been discussed between the leaders
of the major parties beforehand.'[73] The settlement was being
arranged by gentlemen's agreement, or perhaps more obviously
by managerial strategy.

The kernel of the settlement was that the Conservative leaders
adopted a traditional radical aim by moving considerably towards
equal electoral districts. This has often been seen as success for
another Chartist Point. But it was only this in the sense of reaching

greater approximation to the point, by no means of fully attaining it. After the Redistribution Act there remained some very large differences in constituency size, though these were much less frequent than before. The Conservative leaders also supported single-member constituencies, a development which pleased radicals but dismayed Whigs, and therefore contributed to growing divisions among Liberals. The Whigs were alarmed because two-member constituencies encouraged a facade of Liberal unity by allowing a Whig and a radical to run in harness, while single-member constituencies were likely to allow radical representation to swamp Whig. The position of the Whigs in the increasingly radicalized Liberal Party was becoming more and more uncomfortable. This tendency was heightened by the appearance of Chamberlain's *Radical Programme* in January 1885; and it rose to a peak, which led to disruption of the Liberal Party, after Gladstone was revealed as a convert to Irish Home Rule at the end of 1885 and introduced a bill to effect it in 1886.

The electoral scheme led to the first Parliamentary Reform Act to incorporate the entire United Kingdom in one single measure. The scheme gave Scotland 12 more seats, and allowed Ireland to keep all its representation (a controversial point, in view of the steep decline in Ireland's population since the 1840s). The older university constituencies, the City of London, and a majority (27) of the boroughs which had populations between 50 000 and 165 000, would return two members. Otherwise, the Conservative principle of single-member districts was applied. Through disfranchisement and raising the number of seats in the Commons by two, a total of 154 seats was available for redistribution. Disfranchisement took place on the time-honoured principle of suppressing small-borough seats. Boroughs with fewer than 15 000 inhabitants lost all their representation, and those with between 15 000 and 50 000 lost one of their two seats. Four more seats were provided by disfranchising two boroughs for corruption; two more were removed from the City of London, and two thinly populated counties lost one seat each. The three-member constituencies and the limited vote system were abolished. Apart from the 12 seats assigned to Scotland (mainly to urban areas), the redistribution of the remaining 142 seats was as follows: 39 seats to London boroughs, 34 to other English boroughs, 64 seats to English counties, and five to Wales (four to counties, and one to Swansea and its environs).[74]

The general shift of representation, as regards both geographical area and commercial interest, was greater than in 1832 or 1867–8. Comparative areas of representation now bore a shape much more suited to a country which had already taken some steps towards becoming a parliamentary democracy (but which, of course, needed to take many more). 'In general', it has been noted, 'the policy of granting full representation to the thickly populated industrial centers was followed':

> The metropolitan boroughs received thirty-nine new members, and the manufacturing towns of the North-West eighteen. The large towns, such as Manchester, Sheffield, Birmingham, and Liverpool, were given from three to six new seats apiece. The industrial county divisions were likewise favoured; Lancashire received fifteen new members and the West Riding thirteen ... All of the counties were cut up into one-seat constituencies, and the same system was also applied to the new boroughs, as well as to the large towns. Liverpool was thus divided into nine separate districts, and Tower Hamlets into seven ... In the South-west, on the other hand, thirty-three borough seats were disfranchised so that even with the seven new county members there was a net loss of twenty-six seats ... The counties of the southern seaboard, instead of returning half of the House of Commons as in unreformed days, were represented after 1885 by little more than a sixth.[75]

The changes dissatisfied a sizeable number of politicians, but on the whole, the marked shifts struck a reasonable balance for the time and gained the support of a majority of both parties. [76]

A bill incorporating the redistribution and single-member schemes was brought into the Commons on 1 December 1884, four days before the Franchise Bill became an Act of Parliament. There was then a parliamentary recess from 6 December to 19 February. In the protracted committee stage of the bill in March and April 1885,[77] an unsuccessful amendment for proportional representation obtained only 31 votes in favour; another unsuccessful one, introduced by James Bryce, for the abolition of university seats, obtained only 79 votes in favour.[78] The Redistribution (or Distribution of Seats) Bill passed its third, and final, reading in the Commons on 11 May. It was considered in the Lords for some three weeks from 15 May, and on 8 June passed that Chamber.

When the bill received the Royal Assent on 25 June, Salisbury, the prime mover behind the new Act, had been Prime Minister for two days. This ministerial change came about through the formation of a minority Conservative Government, after the resignation of Gladstone's ministry following a narrow defeat on a Budget amendment on 8 June. Within a few months the series of turbulent events began, centring on the Home Rule question, which gave Salisbury a majority in 1886 and brought political domination to his party for most of the next 19 years.

The main enactments of 1883–5 greatly encouraged the advance of democracy by clamping down on bribery, extending household suffrage to the counties, and creating more equal electoral districts. They finally dissolved the grasp of the traditional landed political class on a vast number of seats in the Commons. As has been noted: 'the reforms of 1884–5 did what those of 1832 and 1867 did not do; they broke the numerical hold of the landed élite in the House of Commons.'[79] They also consolidated the reputations of the Liberal and Conservative Parties as initiators and executors of Parliamentary Reform.

But the more radical agendas for Reform remained unfulfilled. The ratio between the largest and smallest constituencies had been greatly reduced by the 1885 Act (from 150:1 to 8:1);[80] but it remained unacceptably high to any democratic eye. The newly extended franchise had given the vote to about two-thirds of adult males. But this was very far from being a democratic suffrage. Many males, and all females, were still excluded, and for the enfranchised males there was a formidable residence requirement which prevented about a million people, otherwise qualified, from voting every year. In Scotland another barrier was the requirement of personal payment of rates, which disqualified some 60 000 people annually. A Registration Act of 1885 did little to diminish the vulnerability of voters to the machinations of party agents in the registering process. The plural vote continued undiminished in its university and business forms, and probably increased after 1885 on account of the new constituency divisions. Proportional representation remained far from being adopted.[81]

The role of the mainly hereditary and wholly non-elective House of Lords and its continuing power of veto were much debated after the Upper House had rejected the Franchise Bill in July 1884. A constitutional crisis and a Liberal attempt to end or reduce the Lords' veto power might have ensued, but were avoided by the inter-party agreement and did not occur for another 24 years. But relations between the two Houses, at times when a Liberal majority in the Commons was pitted against a Conservative majority in the Lords, were by no means smooth in the meantime. The Liberal split over Home Rule in 1886 had the effect of greatly strengthening the Conservative majority in the Upper House. This sharpened the conflicts between the Houses over policy when the Liberals were in power, and led to the notably democratic step of greatly curtailing the Lords' veto power in 1911.

Reform of the Lords, like abolition of plural voting and adoption of women's suffrage, had not appeared among the Six Points of the People's Charter. One of the claims which had so appeared, payment of MPs – a matter of considerable democratic concern because of its expected effect on broadening the social composition of the Commons – was not moved in the 1885 debates and, like reform of the Lords' veto, did not come about until 1911.

Altogether, despite the crucial changes of the Franchise and Redistribution Acts (or the collective Third Reform Act, as they are usually known), a pure and unalloyed system of parliamentary democracy was still very far from being attained – and indeed remains unattained over 100 years later. Campaigns for the various further moves towards a democratic system – to establish manhood suffrage, women's suffrage, payment of MPs and proportional representation, to abolish plural voting and reform the Lords, perhaps even to remove all official power from the monarchy – were, in varying degrees and proportions, among radical desires and Conservative fears in the late nineteenth and the early twentieth century.

Notes

1. Margot Finn, *After Chartism: Class and Nation in English Radical Politics, 1848–74* (Cambridge, 1993), pp. 309–10.
2. F. M. Leventhal, *Respectable Radical: George Howell and Victorian Working Class Politics* (London, 1971), pp. 93–117; R. Harrison, *Before the Socialists: Studies in Labour and Politics, 1861–81* (London, 1965), pp. 190–4.

3. F. M. Leventhal, op. cit., p. 128.
4. Ibid., pp. 128–32.
5. W. B. Gwyn, *Democracy and the Cost of Politics in Britain* (London, 1962), pp. 150–2.
6. Leventhal, pp. 135–6; Jenifer Hart, *Proportional Representation: Critics of the British electoral System, 1820–1945* (Oxford, 1992), pp. 62–5.
7. A. Hawkins, *British Party Politics, 1852–86* (Basingstoke, 1998), pp. 133–4. Cf. ibid., pp. 136–7, 270.
8. E. J. Feuchtwanger, *Disraeli, Democracy and the Tory Party: Conservative Leadership and Organization after the Second Reform Bill* (Oxford, 1968), pp. xiii, 127–30; H. J. Hanham, *Elections and Party Management: Politics in the Time of Disraeli and Gladstone* (London, 1959), pp. 96–108.
9. J. Vincent, *The Formation of the Liberal Party, 1857–68* (London, 1966), pp. 92–3.
10. M. Ostrogorski, *Democracy and the Organization of Political Parties* (vol. I, ed. Seymour M. Lipset, Chicago, 1964; 1st edn 1902), pp. xxx, lvii, 80–91, 166–8, 186–9.
11. See supporting information in H. J. Hanham, op. cit., pp. 135–6; J. Lawrence, 'The dynamics of urban politics, 1867–1914', in J. Lawrence and M. Taylor (eds), *Party, State and Society: Electoral Behaviour in Britain since 1820* (Aldershot, 1997), pp. 93–4.
12. Hanham, p. 133.
13. Ibid., pp. 109–12.
14. J. Vincent, op. cit., p. 65 (see also p. 58 ff.).
15. Hanham, p. 104; J. W. Davis, '"The uplifting game": Nonconformity and the working class in South Lambeth, 1884–1903' (D. Phil. thesis, University of Sussex, 1992).
16. A. Hawkins, *British Party Politics, 1852–86*, pp. 136–7. Cf. J. Lawrence, op. cit., pp. 80–1.
17. Vincent, pp. 104–5.
18. Hawkins, p. 137.
19. Bruce L. Kinzer, *The Ballot Question in Nineteenth-Century English Politics* (New York, 1982), pp. 88, 90.
20. Ibid., p. 93, see also pp. 107–11. Cf. C. O'Leary, *The Elimination of Corrupt Practices in British Elections, 1868–1911* (Oxford, 1962), p. 58.
21. Quoted B. L. Kinzer, op. cit., p. 95.
22. Seymour, p. 429.
23. Kinzer, pp. 104–15; C. O'Leary, op. cit., pp. 59–66.
24. Kinzer, pp. 127–39.
25. Ibid., p. 161.
26. Ibid., pp. 176–85; O'Leary, pp. 71–80.
27. Kinzer, p. 201.
28. Quoted ibid., p. 206.
29. Quoted ibid., p. 221.
30. Ibid., p. 225.
31. Quoted ibid., p. 236 (and see also pp. 225–43).
32. Ibid., p. 240.
33. Ibid., pp. 245–6; O'Leary, pp. 155–7; Seymour, pp. 433–41.

34. T. Lloyd, *The General Election of 1880* (Oxford, 1968), pp. 125–33; O'Leary, pp. 134–56.
35. Constance Rover, *Women's Suffrage and Party Politics in Britain, 1866–1914* (London, 1967), pp. 218–20.
36. Seymour, pp. 298–9, 333–4; O. F. Christie, *The Transition to Democracy, 1867–1914* (London, 1934), p. 131.
37. *Hansard's Parliamentary Debates*, 3rd series, vol. 210, cols 1884–1920 (26 Apr. 1872); 217, 806–54, 919 (23 July 1873); 219, 206–64 (13 May 1874); 225, 1061–1124 (7 July 1875); 229, 1442–94 (1 June 1876); 235, 488–588 (29 June 1877); 238, 159–258 (22 Feb. 1878); 244, 137–255 (4 Mar. 1879).
38. Ibid., 210, col. 1920.
39. Ibid., 235, cols 577–8.
40. E. F. Biagini, *Liberty, Retrenchment and Reform: Popular Liberalism in the Age of Gladstone, 1860–80* (Cambridge, 1992), pp. 287–97.
41. Seymour, pp. 373–9.
42. Ibid., p. 356 (and see pp. 352–8).
43. Jenifer Hart, *Proportional Representation: Critics of the British Electoral System, 1820–1945* (Oxford, 1992), pp. 62–72.
44. Ibid., pp. 73, 77.
45. Ibid., p. 80.
46. Quoted ibid., p. 81.
47. O'Leary, pp. 106–8.
48. Ibid., p. 157.
49. R. Shannon, *The Age of Salisbury, 1881–1902: Unionism and Empire* (London, 1996), pp. 169–73. See Salisbury's article on 'Disintegration' in *Quarterly Review* (October 1883), reprinted in P. Smith (ed.), *Lord Salisbury on Politics: A Selection from his Articles in the Quarterly Review, 1860–83* (Cambridge, 1972), pp. 335–76.
50. Shannon, pp. 114–22; M. Pugh, *The Tories and the People, 1880–1935* (Oxford, 1985), pp. 13–18 and *passim*; Hawkins, *British Party Politics, 1852–86*, p. 271.
51. Shannon, pp. 58–9, 62–5.
52. P. Marsh, *The Discipline of Popular Government: Lord Salisbury's Domestic Statecraft, 1881–1902* (Hassocks, 1978), p. 35.
53. O'Leary, p. 159; Hanham, *Elections and Party Management*, p. 267 (and see pp. 262–83); W. B. Gwyn, *Democracy and the Cost of Politics*, p. 51 and ff.; R. Shannon, *The Age of Salisbury, 1881–1902: Unionism and Empire* (London, 1996), p. 76.
54. O'Leary, pp. 159–61.
55. Shannon, *The Age of Salisbury*, p. 77.
56. O'Leary, p. 175 (and see pp. 169–78).
57. Cf. Seymour, pp. 447–8; Hanham, p. 281.
58. O'Leary, p. 231. Cf. Feuchtwanger, *Disraeli, Democracy and the Tory Party*, p. 158.
59. O'Leary, p. 221; Hanham, pp. 282–3. Cf. Ostrogorski, pp. 217–20; Gwyn, p. 55.
60. Seymour, p. 469; J. Parry, *The Rise and Fall of Liberal Government in Victorian Britain* (London, 1993), pp. 280–1.

61. E. J. Feuchtwanger, *Democracy and Empire: Britain, 1865–1914* (London, 1985), p. 147. Cf. Feuchtwanger, *Disraeli, Democracy and the Tory Party*, pp. 162–5.

62. Quoted Feuchtwanger, *Disraeli, Democracy and the Tory Party*, p. 167.

63. A. Jones, *The Politics of Reform, 1884* (Cambridge, 1972), p. 3.

64. Ibid., p. 5; Seymour, p. 465.

65. Jenifer Hart, pp. 100–19, 122–3; J. Parry, op. cit., pp. 283–4.

66. On the Conservative desire for redistribution, see Seymour, pp. 493–503. See also R. Shannon, *Gladstone: Heroic Minister, 1865–98* (London, 1999), pp. 334–44; W. A. Hayes, *The Background and Passage of the Third Reform Act* (New York, 1982), pp. 82–202.

67. Corinne C. Weston, 'Salisbury and the Lords, 1868–95', *Historical Journal*, XXV (1982), p. 106; D. Cannadine, *The Decline and Fall of the British Aristocracy* (New Haven, Conn., 1990), pp. 43–5.

68. P. Marsh, op. cit., p. 40; P. Smith, op. cit., pp. 93–4; R. Shannon, *Age of Salisbury*, pp. 60–2, 109–10; J. Lawrence and M. Taylor (eds), *Party, State and Society: Electoral Behaviour in Britain since 1820* (Aldershot, 1997), pp. 81–2.

69. Quoted Jones, pp. 6–7.

70. Ibid., p. 8.

71. O. F. Christie, op. cit., p. 141.

72. D. Cannadine, op. cit., pp. 41–3.

73. Jones, p. 8. Cf. P. Marsh, op. cit., p. 43.

74. Seymour, pp. 507–9, 540; W. A. Hayes, pp. 203–75.

75. Seymour, pp. 509–13.

76. Cf. Mary E. J. Chadwick, 'The role of redistribution in the making of the Third Reform Act', *Historical Journal*, XIX (1976), pp. 678–9; Seymour, pp. 513–18.

77. See Hayes, pp. 223–35.

78. Seymour, pp. 510–11.

79. W. C. Lubenow, quoted Hawkins, *British Party Politics, 1852–86*, p.285.

80. J. P. D. Dunbabin, 'Some implications of the 1885 British shift towards single-member constituencies: a note', *English Historical Review*, CIX (1994), p. 90n.; D. E. Butler, *The Electoral System in Britain, 1918–51* (Oxford, 1953), p. 205.

81. E. H. H. Green, 'An age of transition: an introductory essay', in E. H. H. Green (ed.), *An Age of Transition: British Politics, 1880–1914* (Edinburgh, 1997), p. 11; J. P. D. Dunbabin, op. cit., p. 90; N. Blewett, 'The franchise in the United Kingdom, 1885–1918', *Past and Present*, XXXII (1965), pp. 34–9; D. Tanner, 'The parliamentary electoral system, the "fourth" Reform Act and the rise of Labour in England and Wales', *Bulletin of the Institute of Historical Research*, LVI (1983), pp. 205–6, 218; J. Lawrence and M. Taylor, op. cit., p. 88; Shannon, *Age of Salisbury*, p. 96.

5 Whither Democracy?: 1885–1905

Introduction

The enfranchisement of 1884, based on household occupancy, was virtually the last one requiring a property qualification for the vote. The next enfranchisement, in 1918, was based on a simple age qualification, although there were some important exceptions to it. In this respect, together with the fact that it was the first to enfranchise women, the 1918 enfranchisement represented a dramatic leap towards a system of parliamentary democracy. But it did not fully attain such a system, on account of continuing inequalities in the voting provisions, the continuing power of a hereditary Chamber to reject bills on a temporary basis, and other questions. The difference between the democratic achievements of 1884–5 and those of 1918 was greater than the difference between any other two Parliamentary Reform measures. In this connection it may be noted that the period of time between the Redistribution Act of 1885 and the Representation of the People Act (or 'fourth Reform Act') in 1918 was two years less than that between the more similar Reform Acts of 1832 and 1867. Therefore, it can be argued, the gradual attainment of democracy was accelerating. There was growing pressure to build on previous achievements in order to reach higher levels of popular participation in the electoral system.

However, acceleration was little in evidence in the 20 years covered by the present chapter. Between 1885 and 1905 there was no Act of Parliamentary Reform. After 1885 there remained subjects of current debate which, it was urged, needed to be adopted by statute if a fully democratic parliamentary system were to be established – manhood suffrage, women's suffrage, payment of members, proportional representation, abolition of the plural vote and of election charges to candidates, removal of the veto power of the House of Lords (and possibly, though this was now comparatively little mentioned, removal of the veto power of the unelected head of State). The first of these to be attained after 1885, payment of members, did not come until 1911. Of the remaining points, there was a very substantial restriction of the Lords' veto power (also in 1911), and the adoption of manhood suffrage and a large degree of women's suffrage in 1918. In the latter year, also, the requirement that election charges be paid by the candidate was terminated. Women's enfranchisement on the same level as men's came ten years later. But the plural vote, whose abolition was urged by the Liberal Government before 1914, lasted until as late as 1948 (probably a reflection of the predominant political complexion of governments in the intervening period). The House of Lords retains, at the time of writing, a veto power which was further restricted in 1949; though the composition of the Upper Chamber was greatly changed in November 1999, and further changes are under consideration. The monarchy retains the official power to veto bills, though (in practical terms) on the understanding that it will continue not to be used. Proportional representation has not been introduced in the British Parliament, but was adopted on a restricted basis in the Northern Ireland Assembly (from 1973), and in the Scottish Parliament and the Welsh Assembly which were established by legislation in 1998.

The acceleration of democracy was much more pronounced in the 13 years after 1905 than it was in the 20 years before. Tangible democratic advance was not entirely absent during these 20 years. But it took place only in the sphere of local government, where the aspiration towards democracy was encouraged by statutory changes at a time when it could make no further inroads into the parliamentary system. County councils were established on an elective basis in 1888–9, and urban district, rural district, and parish councils in 1894. But the Lords insisted on important changes in the bills before they were passed. Women ratepayers, as well as men, were able to vote in the county, parish, rural district, and urban district council elections, and could become elected members of the three latter councils, but not (as yet) the county or borough ones. The new councils and their committees removed the former unrivalled role of the lords lieutenant and magistrates in the multifarious aspects of county administration. The new elective bodies had the effect of greatly broadening the representative nature of local government, which had commenced with the introduction of elective municipal councils, and boards of guardians under the New Poor Law, in the 1830s.

Against these substantial democratic reforms in local government, and a further reform (the Qualification of Women Act) of 1907 which permitted women to be elected to borough and county councils, the parliamentary electoral system remained unchanged from 1885 to 1911. Matters which had been discussed in the debates on the franchise measure in 1884, but had not been adopted in the enactment, remained unsuccessful for a long time after it. George Howell, now MP for Bethnal Green North-East, had no success with a bill, which he introduced in every session from 1886 to 1895, calling for manhood suffrage (on condition of only three months' residence) and the abolition of plural voting;[1] though the demand for 'one man one vote' was included in the Liberal Party's Newcastle Programme of 1891. Motions in 1884, 1886, and 1888 by another radical MP, Henry Labouchere, calling for removal of hereditary peers from the House of Lords, were similarly unsuccessful, although they sometimes obtained over 150 votes in favour.

The question of women's suffrage began to languish after 1885 as a parliamentary issue, compared with the hopeful interest shown in it in the Lower House in the 1870s and early 1880s. Although women's suffrage bills were introduced on nine occasions in the Commons, and twice in the Lords, from 1885 to 1897, few of these measures made any parliamentary progress, and all of them failed. There was no motion for women's suffrage in the Commons in the years 1898–1903. Proportional representation also languished in some respects after its failure in 1885. The Proportional Representation Society engaged in no very striking activity between 1888 and 1905, though it began to revive in the latter year. But Sir John Lubbock, Leonard Courtney and others remained very active in this cause.[2]

The sterile fortunes of all these democratic causes in Parliament were not necessarily experienced outside it during these two decades – though none aroused great popular excitement or upheaval which might have brought telling pressure on Parliament. Reform of the Lords, abolition of plural voting, and payment of members were adopted as parts of the Newcastle Programme drawn up by the National Liberal Federation in 1891; and the women's suffrage cause considerably strengthened its organization from 1897, when the National Union of Women's Suffrage Societies was formed. Although largely outlawed as subjects of serious parliamentary attention (and indeed as subjects of prominent popular demand) during this period, they stubbornly kept their places as candidates for parliamentary treatment at a future time when Parliament should turn a more encouraging face towards them.

Politics and Electoral Reform Questions, 1886–95

As was the case previously in the development of a more democratic system, the demand for electoral reform has to be seen against a background of change in party politics, as the two continuously interacted. The most important change in party politics affecting the years from 1885 to 1903 was the Liberal division over Irish Home Rule in 1886, and there was a further important division of Liberal opinion (though it did not cause another schism) over the question of support for the Boer War between 1899 and 1902. From 1903 the most important change for the next decade was division among Conservatives and their Liberal Unionist allies over Tariff Reform. Also important, especially for its potential, was the foundation in 1900 of the Labour Representation Committee, which formed an electoral pact with the Liberals in 1903 (lasting until 1917), and took the name Labour Party in 1906 after returning 29 MPs (mostly under the provisions of the pact) at the general election in January that year.

The Irish Home Rule issue brought to a head the growing discontents of the beleaguered Whig aristocrats in the increasingly radical and anti-landlord Liberal Party. Gladstone's decision to take up Home Rule had the effect of driving most Whigs (together with Chamberlainite radicals) into defecting from the Liberal majority and allying (as Liberal Unionists) with the Conservatives. The party rift over Home Rule weakened the Liberals, and conversely strengthened the Conservatives, until Chamberlain's Tariff Reform demand from 1903 had the reverse effect, weakening the Conservatives and strengthening the Liberals. Even if the growth of middle-class Toryism and a considerable degree of working-class Toryism (extensive in a few areas, notably Birmingham, Liverpool, and Glasgow) had continued to strengthen the Conservatives as they were doing by 1885,[3] they would not have achieved the dramatic breakthrough to 19 years of Conservative domination which was caused most directly by the Home Rule crisis in 1886.

The Conservative domination from 1886 to 1905 did little to aid the advance of democracy. The demands for manhood suffrage, payment of members, and restriction of the veto power of the Lords, were not currently advocated among Conservatives. It was only in 1909 that some Conservatives began reluctantly to support payment of MPs, as an alternative to a trade union political levy which was bestowed on the Labour Party.[4] Lord Salisbury and his chief party agent, R. W. Middleton, believed that manhood suffrage would mean electoral disaster for the Conservative Party, and that Conservative electoral security would be threatened if the proportion of adult males registered as voters rose above 60 per cent.[5] There was Conservative minority support, however, including that of Salisbury and his nephew, A. J. Balfour, for a restricted women's suffrage provision, based on household suffrage and not including married women.

The Conservative domination in these years – broken only by a Liberal Government with a small majority from 1892–5 – deterred the emergence of important democratic recommendations from the Commons. Even if the Commons had produced more of these, the Lords would have been confident in resisting them as the Whig defection in 1886 gave more backing to the Conservative majority in the Upper House. The sharpest demonstration of this bolstered Conservative domination in the Lords was the massive rejection of the Liberals' second Home Rule Bill in 1893 by 419 votes to 41. But this was not the only occasion when the Lords greatly irritated the current Liberal Government by rejecting or altering its measures.[6] Gladstone was threatening the Lords with a 'peers versus people' general election before he resigned the premiership in 1894. This was presumably his reply to Salisbury's referendal theory, which called for similar action in the Conservative interest against crucial Liberal measures. But the Liberal reply in this electoral form did not materialize until the general elections of 1910 followed the Lords' rejection of Lloyd George's 'People's Budget' in 1909. Gladstone's successor as Liberal premier in 1894, Lord Rosebery, also threatened action against the Lords. But the general election of 1895 brought no redress for the Liberals as it returned a large

Conservative majority.

The Conservatives, however, were conscious of becoming a more broadly based party in social terms, and they did not want to appear exclusively as defenders of aristocratic interests. As has recently been said:

> The Conservatives' caution is explicable in terms of their desire not to allow their party, or their party's dominance of the House of Lords, to appear as open instruments of class or sectional interest. They were concerned that a naked display of self-interest by the Lords would undermine the institution's legitimacy and provoke Radical attacks.[7]

The Conservatives, in fact, chose their grounds of defence carefully and selectively, sometimes yielding in order to allow reforms to be enacted, and sometimes resisting in full force. The concessions to reform made by Salisbury and other leading Conservatives did not always please their followers, and on several occasions the leaders aroused bitter disappointment in their own landowning class.[8] 'Some aristocrats were tempted ... to "lash out" in defence of titled wealth, status and power, and it was this temptation that Salisbury sought to control, on the grounds that in the long run the interests of his class were best served by a patient war of manoeuvre rather than head-on confrontations.'[9] 'A patient war of manoeuvre' might be sensible in terms of party survival and prosperity, but it permitted some sharp blows to landowners – not only the Liberal budget of 1894 which introduced death duties on estates, but the Conservatives' own Local Government Act of 1888 and Irish Land Acts of 1896 and 1903, the two latter measures providing favourable conditions for the purchase of parts of estates by the tenant farmers.[10]

Another reason for a sometimes liberal approach to policy by Salisbury was that, between 1886 and 1892, he depended on alliance with the Liberal Unionists for a majority in the Commons. The interests of Conservative and Whig aristocrats – now in political alliance – had to be combined with the egregious radical reforming urges of their incongruous colleague, Joseph Chamberlain. There were shades here of the occasional Disraelian alliance of Conservatives and radicals, of which Salisbury himself had formerly been so damning.[11] The adhesion of Chamberlain, John Bright, and a number of other radicals to the anti-Home Rule cause had largely transferred the aristocratic-radical battle from the Liberal to the Conservative side. It was one of Salisbury's aims to neutralize this potential strife by giving some encouragement to Chamberlain's reforming desires. Without some radical adhesion and the threat of Irish Home Rule, Salisbury's second government (1886–92) would probably have been much more lacking in reform than it actually was.

Chamberlainite wishes were behind the two major reforms of the 1886–92 ministry – C. T. Ritchie's Local Government Acts introducing elective county councils in England and Wales in 1888–9 and in Scotland in 1889, followed by the introduction of free elementary education in 1891. Ritchie's democratic measures were strongly disliked by many Tories, but Lord Randolph Churchill described them in 1892 as 'really a fine piece of work and the best thing the Government had done'.[12] Another Conservative, Henry Chaplin, reluctantly acquiesced in these reforms, but felt that by so doing, he was 'putting an extinguisher upon too many of the class with which he had associated himself – the country gentlemen of England'.[13]

The establishment of county councils encouraged more representation of the middle classes, and eventually of the working classes, just as the local council reforms of the 1830s had done in the boroughs. The role of aristocrats in county government by no means disappeared in the new regime of the councils, and they tended to retain a hold in rural areas when they lost it in industrial districts. In the early county elections many members of landed families stood and were returned. But their old position was rapidly eroded, and by about 1900 their presence in the councils had clearly diminished.[14] The Proportional Representation Society, at a general meeting of its members in 1888, decided to send a deputation to government ministers, urging that the reform advocated by the Society be adopted for elections to the proposed county councils. Lubbock and Courtney argued for proportional representation in the debates on the county councils bill. But an amendment by Lubbock was rejected by 372 votes to 94, and he withdrew another amendment on account of government opposition.[15] Over county council elections, proportional representation got no further than it did in regard to parliamentary elections in 1884 and 1885. There were various other opportunities for the proportional representation case to be heard. It was raised unsuccessfully in connection with the system of electing parish councillors under the Local Government Act of 1894, in order (as argued by A. J. Balfour) to give more weight to the educated minority of voters. Proportional representation was also advocated by W. E. H. Lecky in 1896, in connection with possible forms of election in Ireland, as a means of strengthening the political power of the educated minority and combating what he saw as the threat of democracy to liberty. The reform was also recommended by Courtney and Lubbock in 1899 in connection with the election of the new borough councils in London, which were established in that year. It was advocated (up to a point) by Moisei Ostrogorski in 1902 as a means of stemming the power of party organizations and undermining the 'party list' of candidates by strengthening the electoral prospects of minorities.[16]

After 1885, the vote for women in parliamentary elections was probably the most continuously discussed of all the outstanding democratic questions until it was gained at last in 1918. But within this 33-year period it was much more prominent at some times than at others. For 20 years after 1885 the question was little more than a background issue, sometimes debated in Parliament and party assemblies, and sometimes having resolutions passed in its favour, but not being any closer to success in 1905 than it had been in 1885. In this respect it was in good democratic company: similar abortive delays and lack of positive outcomes were the fate of manhood suffrage, the elimination of plural voting, and the restriction of the powers of the Lords.

Among the obstacles to the progress of female suffrage were the argument that the main legal injustices towards women were now being corrected by parliamentary action, and the persistent view that women's attributes did not include adequate powers of judgement for giving a vote.[17] Samuel Smith, a Liberal MP, wrote in an anti-suffrage pamphlet of April 1891:

Let any one investigate the ordinary reading and intellectual pabulum of maid-servants, shop and factory girls, working men's wives, etc. These will constitute nine-tenths of the ultimate female electors. I make bold to say that he will not find one in twenty even reads a political speech or article, or has the slightest knowledge or concern for the staple questions that occupy Parliament

... The mass of women do not have, and never will have, the opportunities that men, even the roughest, have to study politics. Men usually work together, frequent clubs or public houses, and discuss the events of the day. Women cannot undertake this without destroying their domestic life. A good wife and mother cannot leave her home to attend clubs and public meetings, and if she does she will soon cease to be a good wife and mother ... most men rapidly and easily take to politics, most women will never do so, because the Creator has made them different.[18]

A further obstacle was a division of opinion as to whether the vote should be claimed for all adult women, or only for single women, on the same property qualifications on which it was held by men. Lydia Becker (who died in 1890) and Millicent Garrett Fawcett held that the vote should be claimed only for single women. But in 1899 the *avant-garde* Women's Franchise League was formed to urge that all women, married as well as single, should be enfranchised.[19]

Finally, the situation in Parliament held out little hope for women's suffrage, as both major parties were divided on the subject. In the 1890s there were some signs of hope from both parties, on a minor scale, for women's political advance. There was further progress in regard to local government when a Liberal ministry allowed women to become members of the parish, rural district, and urban district councils established in 1894. But the enabling of women to sit as members of borough and county councils did not come until the passage of an Act in 1907, after six previous bills on the subject had failed since 1889. In regard to the women's vote in parliamentary elections, Liberal support seemed to become weaker in the 1890s while Conservative backing (for a restricted enfranchisement) seemed to be growing. In the annual conferences of the National Union of Conservative and Unionist Associations, resolutions for limited women's suffrage were carried on several occasions in the later 1880s and early 1890s. Salisbury was pleased with these resolutions.[20] There was no debate in the Commons on the subject in the later 1880s, but several back-bench Conservative members, such as Sir Albert Rollit and Ferdinand Faithfull Begg, introduced women's household suffrage bills from 1891 to 1897. In 1897 the second reading of Begg's bill was carried by 230 votes to 159, but no further progress was made with it. A bill introduced in the Lords in 1897 and resolutions tabled in the Commons in 1899, 1900, and 1901 were not taken to a debate.[21]

The next parliamentary debate on the question was not until March 1904, when a resolution by a Liberal MP, Sir Charles McLaren (nephew of John Bright), passed by 182 votes to 68. The Liberal leadership was divided over women's suffrage, but the majority of Liberal MPs favoured it. There were marked differences between Liberals on the issue, even between Liberal women. It was not until the mid-1890s that the Women's Liberal Federation, founded in 1887, adopted female suffrage as one of its policies. This caused the secession of a minority of members to form another body, the Women's National Liberal Federation; and it was only in 1902 that the Women's Liberal Federation began to refuse its endorsement to parliamentary candidates who did not declare that they favoured women's suffrage. The National Liberal Federation passed resolutions for the abolition of plural voting and for minor electoral change (such as reducing the residence period for voters) from 1888 to 1901, but did not introduce and carry a resolution for women's suffrage until 1905. In these circumstances it was not surprising that many campaigners for women's suffrage became attached to one of the new socialist political organizations, including the Independent Labour Party which was founded in 1893. In the ILP, as in all other parties, there were differing views on the question, but the group contained strong advocates such as Richard and Emmeline Pankhurst and Keir Hardie.[22]

At the opening of the twentieth century there was no sign of a government attempt to legislate for female suffrage. When parliamentary efforts on the question revived in 1904, in the form of a resolution or a bill, they came as before only from the back benches. At this time, also, the beleaguered women's movement had to try and fight off attempts by its opponents to portray it as part of the 'new woman' concept of the 1890s, which questioned the restrictions of marriage and advocated the libertarian benefits of free love.[23] Amidst this wave of *fin-de-siècle* anarchy, it could be difficult to insist that the women's suffrage movement was thoroughly respectable, indeed, almost conventional – wanting a mere extension of the male suffrage demand and representing the revival, by the literal kin of Cobden and Bright, of the Anti-Corn Law League in a feminist guise. On the other hand, the wider feminists, champions of the 'new woman', were far from regarding the women's suffrage societies as part of their own movement. Dora Marsden, editor of the *Freewoman*, saw even the militant Women's Social and Political Union, founded by the Pankhurst family at Manchester in 1903, as antithetical to her wider feminism. The new society did not 'fight for the full humanity and the economic, social and sexual freedom of women', but merely 'asked for a trifling political adjustment – the vote!'[24] Many suffragists, however, did see their campaign as an essential part of the wider struggle for female independence.

The last three years of the nineteenth century were not an encouraging time for women's suffrage. There was, it is true, an important advance in organization. In 1897 a Combined Committee, existing since 1895, was re-formed as the executive committee of a new federal body, the National Union of Women's Suffrage Societies (NUWSS), of which Millicent Fawcett became president.[25] The aim of the NUWSS was to obtain the suffrage for women 'as it is, and may be given, to men'.[26] But this development in the country was not paralleled by parliamentary activity: no bill for female suffrage was brought into the Commons in the seven years from 1898 to 1904. It has been noted that the campaigners 'badly needed new impetus by the turn of the century'.[27]

Politics and Electoral Reform Questions, 1895–1905

Following an interlude of Liberal government from 1892 to 1895, a Coalition of Conservatives and Liberal Unionists took office after obtaining a majority of 152 seats in the general election of July 1895. This government remained in power for the next ten years, sustained by another large majority (of 134) which was gained in the general election of October 1900. During this time, as has been seen, the cause of women's suffrage made little progress, though there were signs of revival by 1905. Manhood suffrage and abolition of plural voting also failed to make any progress, and – not surprisingly in view of the Conservative Party's defence of the House of Lords, in which lay much of its strength – the power and composition of the Upper House were not currently under threat. The division of the country into mostly one-member constituencies in 1885 had considerably increased the opportunities for plural voting, and it was calculated in 1888 that there were well over half a million duplicate votes in an electorate of more than five and a half millions. Such a proportion could appreciably influence the result of a general election. The Liberal leaders believed, and Gladstone publicly claimed, that most of the plural voting benefited their opponents. But parliamentary efforts by Liberals in 1891 and 1892 to establish 'one man one vote' were defeated by Conservative opposition.[28]

There was also no government move in this period to adopt State payment of either a salary to MPs or the charges made to candidates by returning officers at elections. However, although State payment of MPs did not come until 1911, there were some important political changes in this period which gave more weight to this significant aspect of democratic advance. These developments were especially concerned with the growing desire, by the 1880s and 1890s, to return more working-class MPs, which was spurred on especially by the adoption of a wider franchise and more equal electoral districts in 1884–5. The electoral changes of the 1880s, together with greater radical weight in the Liberal Party after the split of 1886 and the formation of socialist groups aiming at parliamentary represent-ation for themselves, commenced a more favourable era for the concept of State payment of MPs. Although it had been one of the Chartist Points, this claim had never aroused much support in Parliament. In 1870, for example, a proposal to introduce payment of members by a radical MP, Peter Angelo Taylor, had been opposed by Gladstone and received only 24 votes in its favour (and 211 against).[29]

By the end of the 1880s, political changes were bringing about a notable change in this situation, and Gladstone's attitude to payment of members became rather more favourable. In July 1888, the first respectable Commons vote in favour of this reform (135 for, 192 against) was obtained when Charles Fenwick, a Liberal MP who had been a coalminer, introduced a resolution for it. Fenwick's resolution was defeated again, by 227 to 162, in March 1892. But an identical resolution by another Liberal MP, W. Allen, was carried in 1893 by 276 to 229, and obtained the significant adherence of the government. The Chancellor of the Exchequer, Sir William Harcourt, said that the resolution 'should be carried out as soon as practical, when we have at our disposal the time and the money which are necessary'. But these commodities must have eluded the government, for two years later nothing had been done. Allen then introduced his resolution again and carried it by 18 votes.[30]

The growing pressure to return working-class MPs independently of either main party (signified especially by the foundation of the Independent Labour Party in 1893), put more emphasis on the question of State payment of MPs. This was because of demands on trade union funds to maintain Labour members (whether or not they were affiliated to the Liberal Party), and the desire of trade unions to relieve themselves of such payments by shifting them on to the taxpayer.[31] Membership of trade unions increased vastly towards the end of the nineteenth century, reaching a total of some two millions by 1900 – a figure which doubled by 1914. The unions therefore seemed increasingly able, on account of rising subscription receipts, to provide the money to maintain Labour members in Parliament; and the supporters of Labour represent-ation became more and more desirous of obtaining the necessary funds from the unions. It was calculated that 'the large unions alone, with their membership of a million, could provide £30 000 [per annum] to finance 50 Labour candidates at £600 apiece, and [thereby] to force forward the long deferred legislation for payment of members and election expenses.'[32]

It was some years before a permanent fund for this purpose was established with the agreement of the Trade Union Congress. A policy to raise a fund, agreed at the 1893 annual Congress, failed through lack of contributions; and a proposal to raise another fund was defeated at the 1896 Congress. The 1899 Congress decided to hold a special conference, consisting of members of trade unions and of socialist and co-operative societies, to draw up a scheme to promote independent Labour membership of the House of Commons. This famous conference, held in London in February 1900, established the Labour Representation Committee (LRC), which in 1906, after the general election of January that year, adopted the title of Labour Party. The LRC's funds arising from membership were initially small, and the new organization was reluctant to allocate money for the maintenance of MPs. Keir Hardie, who was returned as one of the two LRC members in the election of October 1900, was only maintained as an MP by means of a private subscription.[33] The LRC's first annual conference in 1901 defeated proposals to create a Labour Members' Maintenance Fund.

However, after the Taff Vale Judgement, given by the House of

Lords that year, against the financial interests of the trade unions, the funds of the unions appeared vulnerable and there was more enthusiasm to affiliate to the LRC as a means of promoting the unions politically. Consequently the LRC began to enjoy a large increase in membership, and the additional monetary resources that this entailed. This was reflected in a change of policy regarding the maintenance of MPs. Whereas the 1901 LRC conference had declined to establish a Maintenance Fund, the 1902 conference at Birmingham resolved to commence one – and, moreover, to try and meet returning officers' charges for Labour candidates at elections. It was hoped that this policy would increase the number of Labour MPs; and that these would, among other benefits, swell the demand for State payment of MPs and, through success in this aim, transfer the burden of maintenance from the LRC to the State. Money was, in fact, being given by the LRC in the hope that it would be so effective in realizing its aims that the need for it would be eliminated. The democratic concerns of the new Labour Party, however, were far from being limited to agitation for State payment of its MPs. Members of the LRC generally held the same democratic aims as radical Liberals. They certainly wanted manhood suffrage. Most of them also wanted female suffrage, provided it was combined with men's in the aim of giving the vote to all adults.[34]

Only two LRC candidates were returned in the general election of October 1900. But in 1903 the electoral prospects of the new party were greatly enhanced through the formation of a pact with the Liberals, according to which neither party would oppose the other in some seats in England and Wales. The Liberal landslide victory in the next general election, in January 1906, rendered the pact superfluous to Liberal fortunes for the time being (and raised up a rival to oppose and overtake the Liberals in the not too distant future). But the pact proved a useful aid to the Liberals in the more difficult elections of January and December 1910. For the LRC the pact had a much more positive significance. It was one of the crucial turning-points in the Labour movement's political fortunes, enabling Labour to boost the number of its MPs strikingly, to a figure of 26 in England and Wales (another three were returned for Scottish constituencies, where the pact did not run). Thus the 1903 agreement proved to be a valuable encouragement to a party which held similar democratic aims to those of the Liberals.

The year 1903 was also important to democracy on account of

developments in the women's suffrage movement. In that year not only did the NUWSS, now six years old, commence a more active and expanding phase, but a dose of 'gingering up' began to be administered by Emmeline Pankhurst and her daughters, Christabel and Sylvia. This was done through the initiation of what eventually became a more aggressive and violent strain ('physical force' rather than 'moral force', in an appropriate reversion to Chartist terminology) in their new organization founded in Manchester, the Women's Social and Political Union (WSPU).[35]

For about two years there was little difference in the somnolent suffrage scene. The Pankhursts in their new organization occupied themselves for some time with fairly quiet propaganda among working women. In June 1905 a bill for restricted women's suffrage (the first on the subject for eight years) was introduced by Bamford Slack, a Liberal MP. The bill, supported by both the NUWSS and the WSPU, was talked out in the Commons.[36] But the Pankhursts decided to adopt more vigorous methods. This turn of events followed a Liberal election meeting in Manchester in October 1905. At this meeting Christabel Pankhurst and her close associate, Annie Kenney, asked Sir Edward Grey whether a Liberal Government would give women the vote. Obtaining no answer, they pressed their question and were ejected from the hall. After addressing a protest meeting in the street and allegedly assaulting policemen, they were arrested and imprisoned. The ensuing publicity was seen as being of great value by Emmeline Pankhurst, who masterminded from that time the 'suffragette' agitation, one of the strident and often violent ingredients in society which marked the disturbed years before the First World War.[37] Through the development of demonstrations and attacks on property by the suffragettes, a British democratic movement acquired a significant degree of popular activism for the first time since the Reform League in 1865–7 – and, unlike the latter, the suffragettes took to pursuing deliberate destruction. In distinction from the direct 'physical' force which accumulated as the suffragettes took to breaking windows, burning empty houses and mail in postboxes, and digging up the greens of golf courses, the more patient NUWSS (known as the 'suffragists') persisted in a more moderate or 'constitutional' course.

Thus the relatively quiet process of democratic discussion and advance through party assembly, parliamentary debate and ministerial conclave, which had taken place since the 1860s, was now varied once more by demonstrations on the streets, together with a greater degree of violent sensationalism than ever before. Women's suffrage was pushing itself to the forefront of the democratic demands when the Unionists' differences over Tariff Reform engulfed them and a decade of Liberal government commenced in December 1905.

Notes

1. F. M. Leventhal, *Respectable Radical: George Howell and Victorian Working Class Politics* (London, 1971), p. 207.
2. Jenifer Hart, *Proportional Representation* (Oxford, 1992), p. 126.
3. B. Coleman, *Conservatism and the Conservative Party in Nineteenth-Century Britain* (London, 1988), pp. 185–6, 201–2.
4. E. H. H. Green, *The Crisis of Conservatism: The Politics, Economics and Ideology of the British Conservative Party, 1880–1914* (London, 1996), p. 295.
5. Ibid., pp. 125–6.
6. D. Cannadine, *The Decline and Fall of the British Aristocracy* (New Haven, Conn., 1990), pp. 43–5.
7. E. H. H. Green, op. cit., p. 93.
8. Ibid., pp. 94–5.
9. Ibid., p. 94.
10. O. F. Christie, *The Transition to Democracy, 1867–1914* (London, 1934), pp. 171–2.
11. I. Machin, *Disraeli* (London, 1995), p. 97.
12. O. F. Christie, op. cit., pp. 167–70.
13. Quoted ibid., p. 169. On this Act, see also E. J. Feuchtwanger, *Democracy and Empire, 1865–1914* (London, 1985), pp. 199–200; M. Pugh, *State and Society: British Political and Social History, 1870–1992* (London, 1994), p. 48.
14. Christie, p. 170; D. Cannadine, op. cit., pp. 158–61; E. H. H. Green, 'An age of transition: an introductory essay', in E. H. H. Green (ed.), *An Age of Transition: British Politics, 1880–1914* (Edinburgh, 1997), p. 12; P. Marsh, *The Discipline of Popular Government: Lord Salisbury's Domestic Statecraft, 1881–1902* (Hassocks, 1978), p. 127.
15. Jenifer Hart, op. cit., pp. 129–31.
16. Ibid., pp. 132–40.
17. B. Harrison, *Separate Spheres: The Opposition to Women's Suffrage in Britain* (London 1978), pp. 70–1, 114.
18. Quoted Jane Lewis (ed.), *Before the Vote was Won: Arguments For and Against Women's Suffrage* (London, 1987), pp. 429–30.
19. Jill Liddington and Jill Norris, *One Hand Tied Behind Us: The Rise of the Women's Suffrage Movement* (London, 1978), pp. 73, 76; Barbara Caine, *English Feminism, 1780–1980* (Oxford, 1997), pp. 121–2.

20. R. Shannon, *The Age of Salisbury, 1881–1902* (London, 1996), p. 120.
21. Constance Rover, *Women's Suffrage and Party Politics in Britain, 1866–1914* (London, 1967), p. 221.
22. M. Pugh, 'The limits of liberalism: Liberals and women's suffrage, 1867–1914', in E. F. Biagini (ed.), *Citizenship and Community: Liberals, Radicals and Collective Identities in the British Isles, 1865–1931* (Cambridge, 1996), pp. 48–9, 57–64; M. Pugh, *State and Society*, p. 25; B. Harrison, *Separate Spheres*, pp. 27, 39; Barbara Caine, op. cit., p. 131; Jane Lewis, op. cit., pp. 409–17 ('an appeal against female suffrage', June 1889, by Mrs Humphrey Ward and about 100 others); Liddington and Norris, op. cit., pp. 127–8 and ff.
23. Caine, pp. 133–44.
24. Ibid., p. 145.
25. Leslie P. Hume, *The National Union of Women's Suffrage Societies, 1897–1914* (New York, 1982), pp. 4–6, 14, 20–3.
26. D. Morgan, *Suffragists and Liberals: The Politics of Woman Suffrage in England* (Oxford, 1975), p. 17.
27. Lewis, p. 10.
28. M. Barker, *Gladstone and Radicalism: The Reconstruction of Liberal Policy in Britain, 1885–94* (Hassocks, 1975), pp. 212–13, 216–17.
29. W. B. Gwyn, *Democracy and the Cost of Politics in Britain* (London, 1962), p. 206.
30. Ibid., pp. 206–12; O. F. Christie, *Transition to Democracy*, p. 296.
31. W. B. Gwyn, op. cit., pp. 152–4.
32. Ibid., p. 159.
33. Ibid., p. 160.
34. D. Morgan, op. cit., p. 34.
35. Ibid., pp. 34–5; Sandra S. Holton, *Feminism and Democracy: Women's Suffrage and Reform Politics in Britain, 1900–18* (Cambridge, 1986), pp. 29–52; L. Barrow and I. Bullock, *Democratic Ideas and the British Labour Movement, 1880–1914* (Cambridge, 1996), pp. 154–5; Ulrike Jordan and Jutta Schwarzkopf, 'Reform politics, gender relations and women's social role in circum-1900 Britain', in Ulrike Jordan and W. Kaiser (eds), *Political Reform in Britain, 1886–1996* (Bochum, 1997), pp. 111–29.
36. A. Rosen, *Rise Up, Women!: The Militant Campaign of the Women's Social and Political Union, 1903–14* (London, 1974; reprinted Aldershot, 1993), pp. 36–7.
37. Ibid., pp. 50–71.

6 Women's Participation Takes the Lead, 1905–1

Introduction

When the Liberals took office again in December 1905, after ten years in opposition, they could not avoid constitutional questions regarding the extension of democracy. Some of the specific issues facing them were ones they had encountered in their last ministry, notably the issue of the House of Lords in relation to a Liberal Government and its policies. This was given additional point by the huge Conservative and Liberal Unionist majority in the Upper House, facing what became, in the general election of January 1906, a huge Liberal majority in the Lower. Lacking the reassuring accompaniment of a big Conservative majority in the Commons, such as had been returned in the two preceding general elections, the big Conservative majority in the Lords was openly given a party role in challenge to the new government by Balfour, the Conservative leader. In this Balfour echoed Lord Salisbury, his deceased uncle and predecessor in the premiership, who had suggested other means of trying to frustrate important Liberal policies. Balfour no doubt saw a strong challenge by a Conservative Lords to a Liberal Commons as a promising means of restoring the morale of his party after its severe splits over Tariff Reform. The road to 1911 and reduction of the Lords' veto power by decision of the Commons was soon opened up by repeated clashes over legislation between the two Houses.

Other democratic issues faced the new government, not least women's suffrage, recently forced to the front by the new militancy of the Women's Social and Political Union. This seemed to represent not simply an intensification of political agitation but the threat of a more liberal culture, which alarmed many in Edwardian Britain:

... both politicians and the press viewed heckling by women as a radical departure from normal mores, particularly as photographs of well-dressed women being thrown out of meetings by burly male stewards were shocking to a public accustomed to Victorian forms of chivalry.[1]

Failing to obtain a positive response to their claims from the new government, the suffragettes maintained a persistent activity against the authorities which was exuberant and noisy and involved numerous attacks on private property.[2] This brought them a great deal of notoriety, but also resistance from an exasperated government and public, and when the First World War broke out in 1914 their demand was still unrealized.[3]

Like the Chartists, whose example of fearless campaigning they revered and emulated, the suffragettes were given to splitting into factions. In February 1908 they organized a 'Women's Parliament' which bore resemblances to the Chartist Conventions, and in June that year they held an enormous Hyde Park rally which was modelled on the Reform League demonstrations of 1866 and 1867. Unlike the Chartists, however, they never obtained a great deal of working-class support, and they could never wholly escape the appearance of a relatively privileged and wealthy group of trouble-makers without much consistent popular backing.

The new element of excitement injected by the suffragettes into the movement for the women's vote distinguished them from the more cautious (but more unified) suffragists who formed the National Union of Women's Suffrage Societies (NUWSS). The suffragists were themselves stirred up by the suffragettes to take a more active and public role. But the suffragists shunned and condemned the more violent suffragette methods, and the alliance between the two bodies dissolved by 1909.[4] In 1908, campaigners for the female vote were confronted with the first women's organization opposed to their claim, the Women's National Anti-Suffrage League, which soon had many branches. This obtained the support of a Men's Committee for Opposing Female Suffrage. The men's and women's anti-suffrage organizations combined in 1910 to form the National League for Opposing Woman Suffrage. In that year a separate Scottish National Anti-Suffrage League also made its appearance.[5]

Among the varied points of the National Liberal Federation's

Newcastle Programme of 1891, State payment of MPs was, apart from restriction of the Lords' veto, to be the only measure of democratic advance carried in Parliament in the years of Liberal government from 1905 to 1915. Both of these reforms were effected in 1911. Manhood suffrage and abolition of plural voting, which had also figured in the Newcastle Programme, were the subjects of unsuccessful legislative efforts during this period. Surprisingly, the cause of manhood suffrage at this time showed an almost complete lack of the force which now marked women's suffrage. This has been ascribed partly to inadequate trade union interest and support, and partly to the related fact that (in contrast to the suffragettes) 'the unenfranchised men tended to include the least organised, least politically conscious and least articulate sections of the population.'[6]

Among the various political questions, proportional representation attracted considerable attention again during this period. The Proportional Representation Society (PRS), which had declined into inanition since its peak of activity at the time of the Reform Bills of 1884 and 1885, was refounded in 1905 by Leonard Courtney. The type of reform which it advocated, in the aim of giving more representation to minorities, attracted some support in all parties – whether this was motivated by the hope of immediate party gains or by broader considerations. The Labour Party showed more support for the question than any of its rivals. But there was considerable opposition even in this struggling minority party, and it did not become committed to the reform. Efforts by the PRS to obtain the passage of a Municipal Reform Bill, adopting the transferable vote in local elections, were not successful up to 1914. But bills for this purpose were debated in Parliament, and passed the House of Lords in 1908 and 1914, although they failed in the Commons. Bills of 1912 and 1913 to introduce proportional representation into parliamentary elections made very little progress in the Commons. Nevertheless, it has been noted, between 1910 and 1914 proportional representation 'was treated far more seriously than it had been in the 1880s'.[7] It was in these years, indeed, that proportional representation won its first legislative success after 55 years – only to see, by a supreme stroke of irony, the fruits of triumph snatched from it because the legislation was not put into effect. This was after proportional representation was adopted for elections to the Irish Senate, and to some seats in the

Irish House of Commons, under the third Home Rule Bill of 1912, which was finally enacted in 1914 but then suspended because of the war.[8]

Electoral and Constitutional Questions, 1906–10

Between 1906 and 1910, before it again went to the country in a general election, the government did not give high priority to matters of electoral reform. A comprehensive government plan of franchise reform does not appear to have been prepared until 1911.[9] This delay was probably a reflection of the growing government interest in passing social welfare reforms – an area in which they made considerable progress because the Lords looked much more kindly on them than on land, education, temperance, and plural voting measures, which were blocked by the Upper House. Partly, also, the delay probably owed something to Liberal fears that an enlarged franchise might benefit the Labour Party. This factor might also explain the delay of State payment of MPs until 1911, a time when Labour support had become much more important to the government.[10]

Finally, differences within the government over women's suffrage, and the complicated links of this issue with the desires and prospects of the different political parties, frustrated any hopes that the Liberal ministry would soon introduce a measure for female enfranchisement. While a majority of members of the Commons was in favour of votes for women, all the parties were divided over it.[11] Those Conservatives (60 to 80 MPs) who wanted women's suffrage favoured a restricted measure to enfranchise householders, many of whom they hoped would vote for them. Those Liberals who favoured the women's vote (including most Liberal MPs and two-thirds of the Cabinet) wanted it as part of a wider adult suffrage extension which would include the unenfranchised males. So too did a narrow majority at the Labour Party conference in 1906, which rejected a plea by Keir Hardie to support woman householder enfranchisement.[12]

These differences were sometimes marked among leaders of the respective parties. Asquith, who was against women's suffrage, thought differently from Lloyd George on the issue; Ramsay MacDonald (opposed to the reform) differed from Keir Hardie;

and Austen and Joseph Chamberlain (opposed) differed from Balfour. The cause of female enfranchisement seemed to take a step backward when the discouraging Asquith succeeded the moderately favourable Campbell-Bannerman as Prime Minister in 1908. Asquith did indicate that an amendment for women's suffrage might be inserted by the Commons in a government electoral reform bill, and that the government would not oppose this. But apart from the much more negative instances of the passage of a Public Meetings Bill to curb political militancy in December 1908, and government authorization, from September 1909, of the forcible feeding of suffragettes who went on hunger strike in prison, there was no ministerial intervention to try and resolve the women's suffrage issue.

In the absence of such intervention there was no more parliamentary encouragement for the women's franchise cause than the continuing series of unsuccessful moves by backbenchers. In 1906, debates on the second reading of an Adult Suffrage Bill introduced by Sir Charles Dilke, and on a resolution moved by Keir Hardie, were talked out. In 1907 the same fate befell the second reading debate on a bill to enfranchise women householders brought in by a Liberal MP, Willoughby Dickinson. The second reading of a similar bill introduced by another Liberal, Henry Stanger, in 1908, was carried by 273 votes to 94; the bill was then referred to the consideration of a Committee of the Whole House, but made no further progress. An Adult Suffrage Bill, brought in by the Liberal Geoffrey Howard in 1909, passed its second reading by 35 votes, but this measure also progressed no further after being referred to a Committee of the Whole House.[13]

Even if a franchise measure had passed the Commons, it might (especially if it was an adult suffrage bill) have been quashed by the Lords. After the Liberal landslide victory in January 1906, Balfour, the Conservative leader, declared that the Unionists had a similarly impregnable majority in the Lords, implying that this would be used to frustrate the government. Whether in office or out of it, the Unionists would 'continue to control the destinies of this great empire'.[14] From 1906 to 1909 the Upper House, encouraged by Liberal by-election losses, destroyed or rejected ten government bills, especially land and education measures, and including one to abolish plural voting. This measure, the Plural Voting Bill of 1906, was thrown out on the grounds that any alteration to the franchise should be accompanied by redistribution.[15] In these years, on the other hand, the Lords allowed government reforms to pass which benefited trade unions or extended social welfare (including the introduction of old age pensions).[16] In effect, the Lords were trying to outdo the government in appealing to sections of the population. In view of the large rise in Unionist seats in the general election of January 1910, and the general popular indifference towards the restriction of the Lords' veto power in 1911, it seems that their strategy was not very far from success – though obviously it did fail in the end. The battle with the government over what reforms to allow through was a double-edged fight, as many electors who were pleased by the adoption of old age pensions or trade union legislation would have been antagonized by the rejection of educational, land, or temperance reform. Clear electoral lines of battle between the Unionists and the government were, therefore, not at all simple to draw up. An important factor which aided the Unionists was fear and uncertainty among many about the reforms, especially Irish Home Rule and Welsh disestablishment, which were likely to be carried when the Lords could no longer block them.

Franchise reform was not clearly among the measures which could be expected to pass in the course of time after the Lords' veto had been controlled. Party attitudes to the suffrage question remained complex, and the government was unlikely to respond clearly when it remained subject to the provocation of suffragette militancy. Asquith informed a delegation of 60 Liberal MPs in May 1908 that the government would permit a women's suffrage amendment to be inserted, if the Commons so decided, in an intended measure for electoral reform.[17] But nothing was done to introduce this supposedly intended measure until 1912.

Confronted by the Lords' blocking of some of their policies during their first two years in office, the Liberal ministers began to show an exasperation similar to Gladstone's after the rejection of his second Home Rule Bill by the peers in 1893. This time, an official warning of government action was issued. On 26 June 1907, a resolution of the premier, Campbell-Bannerman, was passed in the Commons by 432 votes to 147. The resolution declared:

> That, in order to give effect to the will of the people as expressed
> by their elected representatives, it is necessary that the power of

the other House to alter or reject Bills passed by this House, should be so restricted by law as to secure that within the limits of a single Parliament the final decision of the Commons shall prevail.[18]

In other words, the government might take action to ensure that all bills passed by the Commons would become law within the period of a Parliament. The Lords appointed a committee to consider reforming the composition of their Chamber, but otherwise the warning of the Lower House seems to have passed them by. Further casualties of their continuing policy of defiance in 1908 were another Education Bill (following failed ones in 1906 and 1907) and a Licensing Bill.

In the following year, the government more clearly turned on the Upper House and commenced retaliation against it. Lloyd George's celebrated budget of 1909 sought to raise money for defence and social reform (more specifically, for both Dreadnoughts and old age pensions), and in attempting to do this, it squeezed the landlord as a substitute for the government's frustrated attempt to pass land legislation. In view of continuing agricultural depression and the consequent devaluation of landed estates, the land taxes, supertax, and increased death duties and income tax imposed by the 1909 budget seemed pointed and fearsome indeed. Strong allegations of 'social engineering' raised against the government did not seem entirely unjustified.[19] The landed aristocracy had been subject to deleterious economic pressure for many years on account of the decline of agricultural production, and the government now seemed to be piling Pelion on their Ossa.

The budget had probably not been intended to cause a constitutional crisis and the restriction of the Lords' powers, but these were the effects it produced. The Conservative and Liberal Unionist majority in the Lords seized the chance to try and force a general election which, after the encouragement of several Conservative by-election gains in 1908, they hoped would put them back in power.[20] In what turned out to be a startling blunder, as regarded the maintenance of their own powers, they ignored a precedent of well over 200 years and threw out a finance bill – namely, the budget – on 30 November 1909 by 350 votes to 75. A general election on the budget issue in January 1910 was marked by vivid verbal attacks on the Lords by Lloyd George, resembling Joseph Chamberlain's onslaughts in the early 1880s.

The Unionist strategy did not succeed. The Liberals were returned to power again, though they had a much reduced majority which depended on the support of the Home Rule and Labour Parties. Thereafter the Lords passed the contentious budget in April 1910 without a division.[21] But the government was moving on to a wider, associated question, seeking to strengthen itself and its flagging electoral fortunes by adopting a democratic policy of restricting the Lords' veto. The King's Speech at the opening of Parliament on 21 February 1910 stated: 'Proposals will be laid before you ... to define the relations between the Houses of Parliament, so as to secure the undivided authority of the House of Commons over finance and its predominance in legislation.'[22]

This was the fundamental purpose of the Parliament Bill, which was based on resolutions adopted by the Commons on 14 April. The resolutions declared that the House of Lords should not be able to reject or amend a money bill; that it should not be able to block for more than three parliamentary sessions (and not more than two years) any other bill passed by the Commons; and that the length of a Parliament should be limited to no more than five years, rather than the existing seven.[23] The main question involved, the restriction of the Lords' veto, was of far greater constitutional moment than the dispute over the budget. It brought into play an important democratic issue of wide and general application – whether or not a hereditary, unelected Chamber should have the authority to reject the policies of the people's elected representatives.

Electoral and Constitutional Questions, 1910–14

The domestic concerns of the government in the four or five years before the First World War were so congested and tangled that there is an air of unreality about the concurrent international problems, and a feeling of surprise when a war situation suddenly emerged to dwarf all the internal contentions. During these years, electoral and constitutional issues were as pronounced as trade union and Irish ones, and, like them, they were mostly still seeking solutions when the war broke out.

Of the pre-war domestic questions, the constitutional issue of the relative powers of the Houses of Parliament was the only one to reach a comparatively clear-cut solution, and even this was not something that democrats were likely to regard as final. The conflict over powers between the two Houses, which had been spurred on by the 1909 budget issue, came to a head when the Commons adopted the government resolutions to restrict the Lords' veto (and reduce the maximum length of a Parliament) on 14 April 1910. A Parliament Bill based on these resolutions was then introduced. Asquith, the Prime Minister, indicated the alternative reactions the bill might arouse, almost suggesting that there might be a resemblance to the political crisis of 1831–2 – which, like the current situation, had heralded a new constitutional departure. The Lords could simply accept the government's plan to restrict their veto power, and in this case there would be no constitutional crisis. If they did not accept it, the government would either resign – in which case a Unionist ministry would have to try and govern amidst all the turbulence of the Irish situation – or they would appeal to the country in another election. Asquith said that a dissolution would only occur if (as in 1832) the government obtained assurances that its plan would pass in a new Parliament – that is, if the King agreed to create enough Liberal, Home Rule, and Labour peers (about 500 might be needed) to get the bill through the Lords. The King gave this assurance privately to Asquith before another dissolution late in 1910.[24]

There were no further parliamentary proceedings on the bill until a prolonged effort had been made – on the prompting of the new King, George V – to reach an agreed solution of the difficulties. On some dates between 17 May and 10 November a Constitutional Conference took place between the party leaders. A variety of solutions to the inter-House conflict was discussed, including Lloyd George's idea of a National Coalition Government.[25] In the previous March a committee of the Lords had resolved, on a motion of the Liberal Earl of Rosebery, that the Upper Chamber should be reconstituted in a somewhat different form, without the right of all hereditary peers to be part of it.

The Constitutional Conference broke up without reaching agreement on 10 November 1910; the question of Irish Home Rule had proved the main stumbling block in the fruitless attempt to reach conciliatory solutions to current disagreements. The Cabinet thereupon decided to dissolve Parliament on 28 November and hold a general election on the issue of the Lords' powers. Before the dissolution, a resolution of Lord Rosebery was carried without a division in the Upper House. This proposed that the Lords should consist of representatives chosen by the hereditary peers from their own number, together with additional members (some being nominated by the Crown and some holding certain State offices). The Lords also adopted proposals of the Marquess of Lansdowne, Unionist leader in the Upper House, for a reduction of their powers. They would abandon the right to reject or amend money bills. They would also submit bills which were disputed between the Houses for settlement by a joint committee of Lords and Commons, provided (in a revival of Salisbury's theory) that especially important matters should be decided by referendum.[26] But the Liberals still suspected that a referendum provision would be applied mainly against Liberal measures. Ministers were, in any case, now set on passing their Parliament Bill and thereby reducing the Lords' veto power, before any change in the composition of the Upper House took place.

The second general election of 1910, taking place in December, was again disappointing for the Liberal Government. The electorate refused, as a whole, to treat the Parliament Bill with the enthusiasm which the ministers believed it merited. Perhaps this indicated that many voters were really expressing themselves against measures such as Irish Home Rule, which depended on reduction of the Lords' veto power for their passage. The election result was very similar to that of the preceding January. The ministers obtained a majority over the Conservatives and Liberal Unionists (soon to be amalgamated as one party), and popular endorsement for their Parliament Bill; but it was practically the case that this was only because of their alliance with the Home Rule and Labour parties.

After the government's re-election, the first reading of the Parliament Bill passed the Commons on 21 February 1911, and the second reading (by 368 votes to 243) on 2 March. After 14 days in Committee, the bill's third reading passed by 362 to 241 on 15 May, and the measure went to the Lords.[27]

The majority in the Upper House would naturally have preferred another solution to the constitutional problem than the stark proposals of the Parliament Bill. They wanted to except from the operation of the bill any reform which was judged to be of great constitutional importance by submitting it to a referendum. Accordingly, they inserted amendments that any bill affecting the existence of the Crown or the Protestant Succession, establishing a national Parliament or Council in Ireland, Scotland, Wales, or England, or dealing with other matters judged to be of great constitutional gravity, should not be passed by the Lords before a referendum had been held. A joint committee of the Houses would decide whether a bill was of such a nature as to justify a referendum on it. However, Asquith announced the King's agreement, given before the election, to create enough peers to get the Parliament Bill through the Lords. This gave the Commons enough encouragement to reject the Lords' amendments, and they did this by 8 August – with the exception of one which removed from the operation of the Parliament Bill any measure to extend the duration of Parliament.

On the crucial matter of whether the Lords should pass the Parliament Bill or not, Lansdowne advised his Unionist followers to abstain in order to let the bill through and avoid drastic changes in the Upper House. A number of former opponents, indeed, decided to vote for the bill. But Lord Halsbury, the former Conservative Lord Chancellor, and a substantial number of others formed a group of 'die-hards' who were determined to resist to the last; and so the Parliament Bill, true to form, resembled the 1832 Reform Bill by passing only after die-hard opposition had been voted down. The final vote (on third reading) on 10 August, after two days of fraught debate in exceptionally hot weather, was 131 to 114 in favour of the bill.

The defeated die-hards lamented that they had been 'stabbed in the back by their friends', but a large and humiliating creation of peers had been avoided. The Lords emerged from the crisis with their composition unchanged but their power greatly reduced. The bill, which became law on 18 August, prevented the Upper House from rejecting a money bill passed by the Commons; allowed it to reject any other bill, passed in the Lower House, for no more than three successive parliamentary sessions; and reduced the maximum length of a Parliament from seven to five years.[28] A fundamental achievement had been gained towards the attainment of democracy.

Nevertheless, the Parliament Act promised more than has been subsequently achieved in the direction of full parliamentary democracy. For the Act began by stating that the Second Chamber would, in the near future, be reconstructed on a popular instead of a hereditary basis.[29] The frequent creation of life peers since 1958, and the virtual cessation for many years of the creation of hereditary peers, seemed to begin to meet this intention. But the recommendations of various commissions bore little fruit. Radical changes have at last been made, in November 1999, but complete fulfilment of the intention of 1911 is still awaited.

The Act of 1911 did not set out, clearly and systematically, to establish a Second Chamber reflecting an increasingly democratic country. Rather it seemed to be trying to control an immediate, unsatisfactory situation in which an Upper House, with a large majority strongly opposed to the large majority in the Lower, was frequently rejecting or greatly altering the Lower House's bills. From this viewpoint, it might be possible to subscribe to the statement that the Act reduced the legal rights of the Upper House 'little below the authority actually exerted by it before 1892'.[30] The Act, however, was a lot more important than this statement implies, because it permanently reduced the constitutional powers of the peers, regardless of whether these powers had always been used as fully as they might have been.

Despite all the implied emphasis on passing reforms by statute which lay behind the Parliament Act, the other democratic measure of 1911 was implemented on 7 August (only 11 days before the Parliament Bill became law) not by statute, but by means of a supplementary financial estimate. This followed a resolution of the Commons, and the ensuing provision was that a salary of £400 a year, but no pensions or travelling expenses, would be paid to MPs from the Treasury. The method of introduction was strongly criticized for 'furtiveness' by the Opposition.[31]

The timing of the payment indicated that the reform was affected by the Osborne Judgement of 1909, which had the effect of reducing contributions to trade union funds and hence the amounts available from union coffers to support Labour MPs. Half of the Labour members had in fact lost the £200 annual maintenance payments they had been receiving from this source.[32] Although they disliked State payment of MPs, Conservatives regarded this as preferable to reversal of the Osborne Judgement by law (which came about, however, in 1913). The introduction of official payment of MPs had important democratic implications, as it encouraged the appearance of candidates in parliamentary elections from a wider social spectrum. It was also the realization of another Chartist Point, leaving only manhood suffrage (and the forgotten claim for annual Parliaments) still unattained.

Unlike the carriage of restrictions on the Lords' veto and the payment of MPs, the women's suffrage question, which made a greater impact on public attention than either of these matters, remained unresolved in the years before the First World War. The fundamental difficulty was uncertainty and division over the issue in the Liberal Government, exacerbated by the militant tactics of the suffragettes.[33] Herbert Gladstone, the Home Secretary, summarized this situation in September 1909:

> it is simply a delusion to think that a Government divided on a question by root differences can deal with it as a Government. All these militant tactics, at any rate in their later developments, are not only lost labour, but now are most seriously putting obstacles in the way of a solution. I am afraid the outlook is thoroughly bad ... Honestly, I believe the great majority of both political parties are willing and ready to co-operate for the solution of this question. But no one will lift a finger now because of these absurd tactics, which are intensely exasperating without being effective.[34]

There were also other factors against a settlement: the opposition of most Conservatives to female suffrage, and the indifference of the Irish Home Rule Party to this question compared with the interests of their own leading objective.

In this unpromising situation, some half-hearted legislative efforts were made which, even if they had succeeded, could hardly have been expected to provide a final settlement of the women's electoral question. After their successful passage of the Parliament Act and the National Insurance Act in 1911 – neither of which momentous turning-points created much of a vital spark amongst the public – the government could have done with adopting another large reform which might have seemed likelier to bring them electoral dividends. The passage of manhood suffrage and women's suffrage might well have given them the elusive public triumph, but they failed to carry the former and remained disunited over the latter. Their failure to satisfy Liberal women campaigners for the vote meant that they lost the support of many thousands of these.[35]

In the summer of 1909 the suffragettes had commenced using violent methods. These grew over most of the time between then and the outbreak of war, and took place all over Britain. In September 1909 the government commenced the forcible feeding of suffragettes who went on hunger strike while undergoing terms of imprisonment. Public revulsion against this practice was so great that the 'Cat and Mouse Bill' was eventually passed in April 1913. This measure, whose official title was the Prisoners' Temporary Discharge for Ill Health Bill, was adopted so that hunger-striking suffragettes would not die in State detention, but would be released and allowed to recover before being re-arrested. At this time the suffragette campaign had reached a particularly high pitch. In February 1913 Mrs Emmeline Pankhurst, who had recently declared that 'the argument of the broken pane [of glass] is the most valuable argument in modern politics', orchestrated an arson and window-smashing campaign in London and throughout Britain. Appearing in court for these activities, she referred to a recent speech which had said that women suffragists had not so far managed to arouse the popular fervour shown in the Hyde Park riots in 1866. She obviously regarded this statement as a call to arms and a justification of her new destructive tactic. In April she was given a lengthy term of penal servitude for shouldering responsibility for various events, including the blowing up of an empty house which was under construction for Lloyd George. In June another prominent suffragette, Emily Davison, who had been involved in this incident, tried to seize the reins of the King's horse as it was running in the Derby, and died as a result.

Early in 1910 there had commenced a prolonged, but unsuccessful effort to obtain an agreed inter-party solution to the women's suffrage issue. A Conciliation Committee was formed in February that year, with Lord Lytton as chairman and H. N. Brailsford as secretary, and a large membership comprising 25 Liberal MPs, 17 Conservative, six Irish Home Rule, and six Labour. The committee decided to sponsor a private member's measure, known as a Conciliation Bill or 'a bill to extend the parliamentary franchise to women occupiers'. Women who had a household qualification, according to the provisions for men in the 1884 Reform Act, would be given the vote. Married women would not be excluded, but a husband and wife could not both qualify for the franchise in respect of the same property. In social terms, the

effects of the bill would differ from one part of the country to
another, but most of those who qualified were, it was believed, likely
to be middle or upper class. The total enfranchised would be only
about a million, or one woman in 13.[36] These provisions were
adopted in order to win Conservative backing, but they lost much
Liberal and Labour support. The WSPU, the NUWSS, and other
suffrage societies gave official support to the measure. But a solution
based on such a narrow compromise could only be a temporary
satisfaction to them, a means of opening the way to fuller
enfranchisement.

Three unsuccessful attempts were made (in 1910, 1911, and
1912) to pass the Conciliation Bill. On 12 July 1910 the bill,
introduced by D. J. Shackleton, a Labour MP, passed its second
reading by 299 votes to 189. But, it has been stated, 'the vote was
essentially an affirmation of support for the principle of women's
suffrage, rather than for the particular measure.'[37] The Cabinet,
after debating the matter in three meetings, had decided not to
allow further time for the bill that session; and, a few minutes after
the bill's success on second reading, the Commons voted by 320 to
175 to refer it to a Committee of the Whole House. This meant, in
effect, that the bill was extinguished.[38]

On 5 May 1911 a second and revised Conciliation Bill, introduced
by Sir George Kemp (a Liberal MP), passed the second reading by
255 to 89.[39] But on 29 May Lloyd George announced that the
government had decided that further time would not be allowed
for the bill that session, as government measures would otherwise
be jeopardized. In November, finally fulfilling long-held intentions,
Asquith stated that the ministry would introduce a suffrage bill in
the next session. This would provide for manhood suffrage, and
would permit amendments to be moved which would extend the
bill to include the enfranchisement of women on a basis equivalent
to manhood suffrage. Such amendments would, if carried, become
parts of the bill.

But the suffragette leaders viewed such a measure as being likely
to disrupt the suffragist majority in the Commons by alienating
Conservatives and some Liberals. As supporters of the Conciliation
Bill, the suffragette leaders were dismayed by a statement by Lloyd
George before a vast crowd on 24 November 1911 that the 'unfair'
Conciliation Bill had been 'torpedoed' by the government's
decision to introduce its own measure.[40] A third Conciliation Bill,

introduced by a Conservative MP (J. T. Agg-Gardner), did indeed fail by 14 votes to pass its second reading in March 1912 – though not only government lukewarmness towards the bill, but the recent intensification of suffragette violence might have been largely responsible for this.

The government's own promised manhood suffrage measure, the Franchise and Registration Bill, was given a first reading on 18 June 1912 and passed its second on 12 July. After the ensuing parliamentary recess it was debated in Committee of the Commons on 23 and 24 January 1913. On 13 January Mrs Emmeline Pankhurst was at length persuaded by moderate suffragists to suspend militant action until amendments to include women's suffrage in the bill had been dealt with.[41] Nevertheless, Mrs Pankhurst was certain that the amendments would be defeated, and she was proved correct in a sense. On 23 January in the Commons, Bonar Law, the Conservative leader, asked the Speaker, James Lowther (later Lord Ullswater), whether the insertion of amendments for women's suffrage would so change the character of the Franchise Bill that it would have to be withdrawn and reintroduced after revision. Lowther did not reply immediately, but after reflection he 'came to the conclusion that the insertion of any of the proposed three alternative qualifications by which women would be qualified to vote, would bring about such a change in the Bill as to completely alter its general purport and intention and convert it into a new Bill'.[42] On 23 or 24 January he informed some cabinet ministers privately that he would rule that the nature of the bill would be so changed by the amendments that it would have to be withdrawn. Many years later he wrote: 'I am satisfied that, however unexpected, it [my judgement] was correct.'[43] Asquith, indeed, told King George V that such a ruling was 'wholly unexpected', and furthermore that it was 'entirely wrong and impossible to reconcile with what took place in the case of previous Franchise Bills'.[44] However, as Asquith also told the King, there was 'no right of appeal against a dictum of a Speaker in such matters';[45] and the bill was withdrawn after the Speaker had informed the Commons of his ruling on 27 January.[46]

The suffragettes immediately resumed and intensified their militant actions. Before the war another bill to abolish plural voting was introduced. This passed the Commons in both 1913 and 1914, but failed to get through the Lords in both sessions, and would not have become law under the Parliament Act until 1915. There was also discussion in the Commons of a private member's bill for women's suffrage, introduced by Willoughby Dickinson. This was defeated on second reading, in May 1913, by 47 votes. Also defeated, in the Lords in May 1914, was Lord Selborne's Women's Enfranchisement Bill, which was lost on second reading by 44 votes.[47] So far all the legislative activity concerning the women's vote had ended in nothing. Manhood suffrage had also been lost on account of its possible conjunction with women's suffrage in the same measure. The abolition of plural voting would have come about under the terms of the Parliament Act, but legislation for it was shelved because of the inter-party truce which was observed during the war. Ironically, although the removal of plural voting had come nearer to success than either manhood or womanhood suffrage, it was the only one of these three objectives which had not been enacted by the end of the war. It was indeed put off into the indefinite future, and not realized until 1948.

War and the Extension of Franchise, 1914–18

The demands of total war for over four years from August 1914 led to the passage of much temporary reform – nationalization of coal and railways, compulsory conscription, food rationing, and State intervention in other respects – which would have been thought scarcely possible before the war began. On the other hand, important reforms which had long been fought over and had reached parliamentary enactment before the war – Irish Home Rule and Welsh disestablishment – were suspended for the duration of the conflict. Unlike these matters, women's suffrage, manhood suffrage, and abolition of plural voting had failed to reach the statute book, but they too were initially suspended as legislative aims.

However, suffrage questions were kept alive during the war. This was not through continuance of the militancy of suffragettes but through a strategic reversal of tactics on their part. On the outbreak of war, Emmeline Pankhurst and her daughter Christabel turned abruptly from being thorns in the government's flesh to espousing the role of ardent patriots and champions of the war effort. The vote was now to be won, it was hoped, by patriotism rather than provocation. Christabel Pankhurst spoke of the need to defeat 'the German peril' in order to gain more rights for women: 'In the English-speaking countries under the British flag and the Stars and Stripes woman's influence is higher, she has a greater political radius, her political rights are far more extended than in any other part of the world.'[48] Equally important to the female suffrage cause as a demonstration of patriotism was the readiness of many women to aid the war effort by working in munitions factories and as auxiliaries to the armed forces. This sterling war-work was allegedly the main reason for giving women the vote in 1918. But the terms of the concession (giving the vote only to women over 30 years of age) undermined this reason. For a great many, perhaps most, of the women who engaged in war-work were under 30 and remained without the vote after 1918. Female suffrage, in a limited form, probably came before the end of the war in order to remove a difficult problem, which otherwise would have been likely to revive strongly and violently after the restoration of peace. It was important to exclude younger women, and retain plural voting, in order to obtain the support of the Conservatives in the wartime Coalition Government for a Franchise Bill.

Manhood suffrage and limited women's suffrage were introduced and carried as part of the domestic reconstruction which began to be an important part of government concerns in 1916. The question of manhood suffrage provided the catalyst for the adoption of partial women's suffrage. Manhood suffrage was bound up with the emotive question of giving the vote to soldiers, sailors, and airmen who were so nobly serving their country. An Act of 1915 extended the life of the existing Parliament from five to six years, and postponed a revision of the electoral register on the grounds that one composed in wartime would be unreliable. A measure of 1916, the Parliament and Local Elections Act, extended the existing Parliament again for a further eight months; and another Act of that year provided for a new register to be drawn up.

It was held by a growing number of politicians that there should also be an extension of the franchise and a redistribution of seats, arrived at by inter-party agreement. Arthur Henderson, the Labour leader in the Coalition, advocated both manhood suffrage and women's suffrage in a paper of May 1916 entitled 'Necessary Electoral Changes'. He suggested that a minimum voting age of 25 for women would be enough to satisfy the suffragist organiz-ations.

On 14 August 1916 Asquith, in a speech in the Commons on the Parliament and Local Elections Bill, implied that he was now turning, after habitual opposition, to support women's suffrage. Walter Long, Conservative President of the Local Government Board, soon afterwards also declared his conversion to the female vote. Asquith nevertheless ruled out the prospect of a bill for women's suffrage during the war.[49] However, by October 1916 the Cabinet had (on the suggestion of Walter Long) placed the whole vexatious question of franchise, registration, and constituency reform in the hands of an inter-party conference. The conference moved quickly to recommend sweeping franchise extensions, which were enacted by Parliament well before the end of the war.

The gathering was known as the Speaker's Conference, as it was chaired by the Speaker of the House of Commons, James Lowther. He had been regarded as a foe of women's suffrage on account of his ruling against amendments to the Franchise and Registration Bill in 1913. But he was now disposed to be more conciliatory, not least to try and prevent the revival of conflict over the women's vote after the war. As he later wrote:

> the war was acting as a strong cementing force, a Coalition Government was in power, and the time was perhaps opportune for an agreement if such a thing were possible. I felt very strongly that to renew these party and domestic polemics at the end of the war would bring discredit upon Great Britain.[50]

Apart from the chairman there were 34 other members of the conference: 13 Conservatives, 13 Liberals, four Irish Home Rulers, and four representing the Labour Party. All of these were MPs, except three of the Liberals and two of the Conservatives, who were peers.

The Conference worked hard to reach agreement, meeting 26 times between the start of proceedings on 12 October 1916 and their termination on 26 January 1917, and ploughing on through the government crisis of December 1916 which replaced an Asquith Coalition with a Lloyd George Coalition. Although three Conservatives who could not agree with the general tendency of discussion had resigned, the conference had reached much agreement on electoral reform before the government crisis took place. There was agreement on principles for redistributing seats and in favour of adopting proportional representation on an experimental basis in many boroughs, amounting to more than a third of the representation of Great Britain.[51] It was also agreed to recommend manhood suffrage on a residential qualification.

About mid-January, towards the end of its labours, the conference took the important step of voting, by 15 to six, in favour of female suffrage. It also rejected narrowly, by only 12 to ten, a proposal that women should have the vote on the same basis as men. In order to prevent a female majority in the electorate, the conference recommended giving the parliamentary franchise to women who were voters in local council elections or who were the wives of such voters. Parliament should adopt an age limit for women voters of either 30 or 35. Members of the conference apparently thought they were recommending the vote for only six million women, not the figure of nearly eight and a half million who got on to the register for the 1918 election. After these votes on women's suffrage, Lowther was able to inform the premier, Lloyd George, that the main recommendations had been prepared and would be confirmed in a final session on 26 January.[52]

The Speaker's Report was in Lloyd George's hands by 27 January 1917, and the premier described it in a speech as 'almost a miracle'.[53] But it was two months before the Cabinet decided (on 26 March) to support the introduction of a bill embodying the recommendations. Ministers did not feel compelled to act quickly, as there was the possibility of considerable Conservative opposition and, amidst the preoccupations of war, there was no great public cry for electoral reform. 'The Report might well have been shelved until peacetime as were so many other measures of reconstruction, had not certain leading politicians had good reason for taking it up.'[54]

On 28 March 1917, Asquith opened the Commons debate on the Speaker's Report by moving that a bill be introduced in accordance with its recommendations. Asquith was probably a reluctant and sceptical convert to the women's vote, but his clear public support of the reform was significant as coming from one who had been a noted opponent of it. The reasons he gave for his advocacy included women's remarkable war-work; the right of women to participate directly in matters of post-war reconstruction which would affect them; and the absence during the war of 'that detestable campaign which disfigured the annals of political agitation in this country'. No one, he said, 'can now contend that we are yielding to violence what we refused to concede to argument'.[55] The House approved the introduction of a bill by the huge majority of 341 votes to 62. Although the opposition was composed of Conservatives, 79 MPs from that party (outnumbering the opponents) voted in favour.[56] 'This division', it has been said, 'marked the real turning point in the Parliamentary progress of women's suffrage – thereafter, the outcome was never seriously in doubt.'[57]

There were other personal changes on the question, in addition to Asquith's. The Earl of Selborne wrote to the Marquess of Salisbury in August 1916, showing that he now advocated a fuller enfranchisement than previously:

> Personally I think it would be most unjust to women and danger-ous to the State to enfranchise the adult fighting men and no women ... On theory I would always enlarge the franchise by stages, but I think that the history of the war has settled the question for us. In my judgement the way that the men of our race have be-haved in this war has made adult manhood suffrage inevitable; we shall have to do in one stage what I should have preferred to do in several.[58]

Perhaps the outcome of the new Representation of the People Bill was 'never seriously in doubt'; but there was some opposition on partisan grounds on the back benches, while the leaders of all the parties were determined to carry an agreed solution based on the recommendations of the Speaker's Conference.

After a first reading of the bill in the Commons on 16 May, the second reading passed on 23 May by 329 votes to 40, the opposition (still wholly Conservative) having dwindled considerably. The public, not surprisingly, appears to have shown more interest in vital developments taking place in the war. This at least seems to have been assumed by the press, which gave only brief references to the measure despite its proposing an enfranchisement which was both enormous and original in comparison with the previous three Reform Acts. Clause Four of the bill gave the vote to women over 30 years of age, provided they were householders or wives of householders, occupiers of property worth at least £5 a year, or university graduates. This clause passed the Committee stage in the Commons by a resoundingly decisive 387 votes to 57 on 19 June 1917. The majority had a distinct inter-party appearance, as it consisted of 184 Liberals, 140 Conservatives, 33 Irish Home Rulers, and 30 Labour MPs. The minority was less inter-party, comprising 45 Conservatives and 12 Liberals, no Home Rulers and no Labour MPs. The transformation from the difficulties of women's suffrage bills in pre-war days was remarkable.[59] The limitations on female voting were adopted in order to prevent a female majority in the electorate. This was certainly achieved. The anticipated six million women voters, swelled to 8 479 156 by the time of the general election of December 1918, but there were still 12 913 166 men to counterbalance them.[60] The women's organizations were ready to acquiesce at this juncture in the higher minimum voting age for women, in order to get the reform through. Sylvia Pankhurst, supported by her mother and sister, was almost alone in wanting to hold out for equal suffrage.[61] The male vote was substantially increased by a provision which was an important democratic breakthrough in itself – abandoning the household requirement for the vote and giving it to men purely as individuals, provided they could meet a residence requirement of six months in the constituency. The residence requirement, in fact, regularly excluded about 5 per cent of men from voting in elections.[62]

These ground-breaking matters easily went through the Commons. Another one, proportional representation, was narrowly defeated in Committee by 150 to 143, the Conservatives voting 86–39 against it.[63] The electoral method of the alternative vote, however, passed the Commons by one vote on 9 August, and by a much wider margin in November – only to be dropped from the bill in the following February.[64]

Substantial redistribution of constituencies took place under the bill, aiming at providing equal one-member constituencies of some 70 000 electors each (with the exception of a few boroughs which remained undivided seats, each returning two members, until 1950). The new total of constituencies for the United Kingdom (still of course embracing the whole of Ireland with its 103 seats) was 707. A long-standing radical claim, the transfer of payment of the returning officer's expenses from the candidate to public funds, was finally met by the bill. These were henceforth to be paid from the local rates. However, as a precaution against 'freak' candidatures, a deposit of £150 would be required from each person standing in a parliamentary election. The deposit would be forfeited by candidates who obtained less than one-eighth of the total vote in the constituency. The bill also reduced the amount of election expenditure legally permitted to candidates, and provided that all the voting in a general election would henceforth take place on the same day.[65]

Plural voting was not ended by the bill, despite its having come so near to termination in 1914. It was kept on a strictly limited basis in order to retain majority Conservative support for suffrage extension. Only one extra vote could henceforth be used, for the possession of either business premises or a university degree.[66] Some 300 000 people had a second vote by this means, and this remained the position until abolition finally came in the Representation of the People Act of 1948. Another provision of the bill, arising from the tense wartime conditions in which it passed, was that conscientious objectors were disfranchised for five years from 1921 by a clause which was carried quite narrowly (by 209 votes to 171).[67]

The bill emerged from the Lower House after a third reading on 7 December. The Lords seemed likely to pass the measure because it was supported by the Conservative Party, and although some strong resistance might have been expected it did not materialize. The second reading was carried on 18 December, without opposition. In a prolonged and critical interchange in Committee on the question of conceding female suffrage, commencing on 8 January 1918, Lord Curzon (chairman of the League against Women's Suffrage) reluctantly abandoned his parliamentary opposition to the female vote. He began his speech by listing reasons for opposing women's suffrage, but then urged his fellow-objectors to abstain from voting in order to avoid a damaging clash with the Commons. Although this debate contained considerable condemnation of the damage inflicted by suffragettes before the war, the peers endorsed the female vote by 134 to 71.[68]

The main point at issue between the two Houses, it emerged in the Lords' debates, was not manhood or womanhood suffrage but proportional representation. The peers wanted to keep this in the bill, and to remove the alternative vote.[69] But the Commons had thrice defeated the experimental scheme for proportional representation which had been recommended by the Speaker's Conference. The Prime Minister, Lloyd George, had condemned proportional representation in January 1917, when he tellingly described it as 'a device for ... disintegrating parties'.[70] A critical period came at the end of the debates on the bill, in the opening days of February 1918. Amendments on proportional representation and the alternative vote were then 'shuttled rapidly back and forth between the two Houses'.[71] The Lords found that if they were not to risk the collapse of the whole bill, they would have to forgo an attempt to get the Commons to agree to experimental proportional representation at this juncture, and instead accept the government's offer of a Royal Commission on the question. This they did; and the Commons rejected an amended scheme for the alternative vote. The amended bill then passed, without any ingredient of proportional representation, after a final reading in the Lower House by 216 votes to nine on 5 February.

Thus the momentous Representation of the People Act of 1918 failed to go the extra mile and embrace the new departure of proportional representation in addition to those of manhood suffrage and limited women's suffrage. Subsequently, the Royal Commission's scheme was published on 13 April. It affected 99 MPs, who would be elected in 24 enlarged constituencies of three to seven members each. But the Commons rejected the scheme in May, so even this limited experiment with proportional representation was not adopted. However, the advocates of the system could take comfort in the thought that 'they had come nearer to success than at any time previously, and [that] the subject had had considerable publicity. They had not expected at the beginning of 1917 that there would be sixteen debates on it in the Commons and more controversy over [that and related questions] ... than over the rest of the bill put together.'[72] The British Parliament still remains, in 2000, without an element of proportional representation; but this form of election was partly operated in the Northern Ireland Parliament from 1921 to 1929, in the Northern Ireland Assembly from 1973, and in the new Scottish Parliament and Welsh Assembly from 1999.

The 'fourth Reform Act' of 1918 has not been paralleled since that time in the scope of its democratic changes. Many of the innovations, including the two major ones of manhood suffrage and the limited women's vote, were new departures. They were not simply extensions of what had gone before, as was the case with the Reform Acts of 1867–8 and 1884. A fairly credible system of representative parliamentary democracy, though limited in important respects, came into being in 1918. The extensions to it from that year to the end of the century have not been large, though important innovations and transformations occurred in 1999, and further change (in the House of Lords) appears likely in the near future.

Notes

1. A. Rosen, *Rise Up, Women!: The Militant Campaign of the Women's Social and Political Union, 1903–14* (London, 1974; reprinted Aldershot, 1993), pp. 54–5.
2. Ibid., pp. 55–123; Jill Liddington and Jill Norris, *One Hand Tied Behind Us: The Rise of the Women's Suffrage Movement* (London, 1978), pp. 208–30.
3. Cf. E. J. Feuchtwanger, *Democracy and Empire: Britain, 1865–1914* (London, 1985), pp. 330–6.
4. Leslie P. Hume, *The National Union of Women's Suffrage Societies, 1897–1914* (New York, 1982), pp. 28–59.
5. B. Harrison, *Separate Spheres: The Opposition to Women's Suffrage in Britain* (London, 1978), pp. 12, 52.
6. M. Pugh, *Electoral Reform in War and Peace, 1906–18* (London, 1978), p. 30.
7. Jenifer Hart, *Proportional Representation: Critics of the British Electoral System, 1820–1945* (Oxford, 1992), p. 162 (see also pp. 164–8).
8. M. Pugh, op. cit., pp. 5–14; Jenifer Hart, op. cit., pp. 145–77.
9. Pugh, p. 32.
10. W. B. Gwyn, *Democracy and the Cost of Politics in Britain* (London, 1962), pp. 213–17.
11. Barbara Caine, *English Feminism, 1780–1980* (Oxford, 1997), pp. 157–8.
12. D. Morgan, *Suffragists and Liberals: The Politics of Woman Suffrage in England* (Oxford, 1975), p. 44.
13. Constance Rover, *Women's Suffrage and Party Politics in Britain, 1866–1914* (London, 1967), pp. 221–2; Pugh, pp. 33–4.
14. D. Cannadine, *The Decline and Fall of the British Aristocracy* (New Haven, Conn., 1990), p. 46; Jane Ridley, 'The Unionist Opposition and the House of Lords, 1906–10', *Parliamentary History*, XI (1992), 252–3; Corinne C. Weston, 'The Liberal leadership and the Lords' veto, 1907–10', *Historical Journal*, XI (1968), 508–23.
15. N. Blewett, 'The franchise in the United Kingdom, 1885–1918', *Past and Present*, XXXII (1965), 53.
16. P. Rowland, *The Last Liberal Governments: The Promised Land, 1905–10* (London, 1968), pp. 76–169.
17. D. Morgan, op. cit., pp. 48–52.
18. Quoted A. Lawrence Lowell, *The Government of England* (2 vols., New York, 1917; first published 1908), vol. I, p. 423.

19. See the views of the Speaker of the Commons on this matter: Viscount Ullswater, *A Speaker's Commentaries* (2 vols., London, 1925), vol. II, pp. 103–4.
20. E. H. H. Green, *The Crisis of Conservatism: The Politics, Economics and Ideology of the British Conservative Party, 1880–1914* (London, 1996), p. 272.
21. For details of the budget and the constitutional crisis over it, see P. Rowland, op. cit., pp. 214–49.
22. Ibid., p. 285.
23. A. L. Lowell, op. cit., vol. I, p. 428.
24. Ibid., vol. I, pp. 428–9, 431.
25. Rowland, pp. 305–24; Corinne C. Weston, op. cit., 523–37.
26. Lowell, vol. I, pp. 429–30.
27. For the Parliament Bill in the Commons and Lords, see P. Rowland, *The Last Liberal Governments: Unfinished Business, 1911–14* (London, 1971), pp. 18–24, 44–8, 57–63.
28. Lowell, vol. I, pp. 430–3.
29. Ibid., vol. I, p. 432.
30. Ibid., vol. I, p. 433.
31. Ibid., vol. I, p. 434; W. B. Gwyn, *Democracy and the Cost of Politics in Britain* (London, 1962), pp. 167–9, 222–3.
32. C. O'Leary, *The Elimination of Corrupt Practices in British Elections, 1868–1911* (Oxford, 1962), pp. 215–16.
33. Cf. N. Blewett, op. cit., 54–6.
34. Quoted Rowland, *The Last Liberal Governments: The Promised Land*, pp. 353–4.
35. M. Pugh, 'The limits of liberalism: Liberals and women's suffrage, 1867–1914', in E. F. Biagini (ed.), *Citizenship and Community: Liberals, Radicals and Collective Identities in the British Isles, 1865–1931* (Cambridge, 1996), pp. 64–5.
36. A. Rosen, op. cit., pp. 118–23, 134–5; Leslie P. Hume, op. cit., pp. 67–74.
37. A. Rosen, p. 137.
38. Ibid., pp. 136–7; Morgan, pp. 68–9; M. Pugh, p. 35.
39. A. Rowland, op. cit., p. 37.
40. Rosen, p. 154. Cf. Morgan, pp. 82–3; Leslie P. Hume, p. 171.
41. Rosen, p. 186.
42. Ullswater, op. cit., vol. II, pp. 136–7.
43. Ibid., vol. II, p. 137.
44. Quoted Morgan, pp. 114–15.
45. Quoted ibid., p. 115.
46. Pugh, pp. 41–2; Hume, pp. 185–9.
47. Morgan, pp. 123–4; Pugh, p. 43.
48. Quoted Rosen, p. 250.
49. Pugh, pp. 57–66; Rosen, pp. 257–9.
50. Ullswater, vol. II, pp. 196–7.
51. Pugh, pp. 69–83; Hart, pp. 179–82; Ullswater, vol. II, pp. 197–8, 205.
52. Pugh, p. 86; Ullswater, vol. II, pp. 203–4.
53. Ullswater, vol. II, pp. 205.
54. Pugh, p. 87. Cf. Sandra S. Holton, *Feminism and Democracy: Women's Suffrage*

and Reform Politics in Britain, 1900–18 (Cambridge, 1986), pp. 145–50; D. H. Close, 'The collapse of resistance to democracy, 1911–28', *Historical Journal*, XX (1977), 900–2.

55. Quoted B. Harrison, op. cit., p. 207. Cf. Rosen, pp. 262–3.
56. Pugh, p. 97.
57. Rosen, p. 265.
58. Quoted J. Turner, *British Politics and the Great War: Coalition and Conflict, 1915–18* (New Haven, Conn., 1992), p. 120.
59. B. Harrison, op. cit., pp. 212–13; Pugh, p. 148.
60. Rosen, p. 265.
61. Pugh, p. 150.
62. A. J. P. Taylor, *English History, 1914–45* (Oxford, 1965), pp. 115–16.
63. Pugh, p. 109 (see also pp. 118–22, 132 for divisions in the Commons and the failure of substantial opposition to the bill to be mobilized).
64. Ibid., pp. 116, 123.
65. W. B. Gwyn, op. cit., pp. 28, 56.
66. A. J. P. Taylor, op. cit., p. 116.
67. Ibid.
68. Pugh, p. 153; Morgan, pp. 148–9; Harrison, pp. 216–18.
69. For the peers' reasons for wanting proportional representation in the Commons, see Pugh, p. 156.
70. Quoted ibid., p. 158. Cf. Hart, p. 184.
71. Pugh, p. 165; Hart, pp. 185–90.
72. Hart, pp. 185–99, where the different arguments in the debates are given.

7 Conclusion

The treatment in this book has shown that the fairly advanced stage of parliamentary democracy reached in Britain by 1918 had emerged slowly out of two main general tendencies. These may be summarized as public demand and party political interest.

Public demand for more political participation – especially the vote in parliamentary elections, but also, to a considerable extent, in municipal elections – had arisen from social changes and political stimuli. The social changes had occurred because of the effects of the Industrial Revolution, producing an enlarged and, in some ways, rather more cohesive middle class and working class. Both of these rising, and increasingly assertive, social classes felt inadequately represented, in differing degrees, in the political realm of parliamentary elections and returns and the effects these had on legislation.

Mainly middle-class objectives concerning commercial, social, and religious reforms often overlapped with aims of the working classes, but were sometimes distinct from them. The political efforts of the middle and working classes also sometimes worked in conjunction, and sometimes fairly separately. In 1830–2 there was a considerable degree of alliance (though far from a complete one) between middle- and working-class radicals in striving for political change. But in the Chartist era of the late 1830s and the 1840s, there was much more distinction between them, highlighted by the hostility between Chartism and the Anti-Corn Law League. When popular pressure for Parliamentary Reform appeared clearly again in the 1860s, middle- and working-class radicals were fairly closely allied. In the next period of considerable popular participation in Parliamentary Reform agitation (1906–14) there was a similar confluence between them, mainly because the leading electoral question of the time, votes for women, clearly affected both classes.

External political stimuli, of both an ideological and practical nature, which worked on these changes in society, came from the eighteenth-century American and French Revolutions. Political stimuli from within the country came from the inclinations of the Whig and Tory Parties (or sections of them) towards reform, and the confluence of these inclinations with the desire to increase their electoral support in the country. In the case of the first Reform Act it was the Whigs (or Liberals) who took the plunge towards substantial, though highly restricted, Parliamentary Reform. After a lengthy gap which another political force, the Chartists, tried unsuccessfully to fill, there were signs from 1848 that both parties were beginning to be interested in extending Parliamentary Reform beyond the provisions of the 1832 Act. In the 1850s both parties made unsuccessful legislative attempts in this direction, and when the second instalment of Reform Bills was passed in 1867–8, it was the Conservatives who introduced them.

Whereas the first two Reform Acts (1832 and 1867) were carried by one party opposed officially by the other, the 1884–5 Acts were carried by inter-party agreement. The two main parties co-operated in the details of the large-scale redistribution of seats which, it had been agreed, should accompany the extension of the franchise in the Third Reform Act of 1884. The next extension of the franchise and redistribution of seats, in 1918, was also achieved by inter-party agreement, under the additional pressure on this occasion of a wartime Coalition being in force.

Public demand, as expressed in popular agitation through societies, meetings, demonstrations, and radical newspapers, sometimes acted together with the interests of political parties, and sometimes against them. There was a fair degree of confluence between popular and party political pressures in the campaigns for the First and Second Reform Bills. But in an intermediary phase of agitation, conducted by the Chartists, the two elements of popular and party pressure were separated, as neither established political party showed any inclination to support the People's Charter. In the years from 1848 to 1864 the reverse tended to occur. Public agitation, while not absent, was relatively quiet while the political parties, first the Liberals and then the Conservatives, unsuccessfully introduced their own modest efforts at Parliamentary Reform.

Popular pressure was less in evidence in the campaign for the 1884 Reform Bill than it had been in 1830–2 and 1866–7, and in 1884–5 the matters at issue were resolved by inter-party discussions between opposing political leaders. The years from 1885 to 1905 were characterized by the comparative absence of both pronounced party pressure and pronounced popular pressure. The Conservatives did not think, on the whole, that their interests would be served by a further extension of the franchise. The Liberals, after losing most of their Whig wing in the Irish Home Rule crisis of 1886, were now radical-dominated and were readier to initiate populist reforms than ever before. But they were comparatively weak, and during the two decades from 1885 to 1905 only held office (with a small majority) from 1892 to 1895.

From 1905, public pressure revived in the form of the suffragette agitation for women's votes; but, largely because of its violence, it was at odds with the Liberal Government to a much greater degree than it won sympathy from it. The Liberals were much more attracted to the important democratic advance of heavily restricting the Lords' veto power, which was achieved in 1911. Even after this success, however, the Liberals were unable to secure manhood suffrage or abolition of plural voting before the First World War broke out.

The disappearance of suffragette action during the war, and the desire to prevent its renewal in the subsequent peace, brought revived official purposefulness over Parliamentary Reform. The continuing needs of wartime Coalition added their own positive influence to the situation; and the Representation of the People Bill (or Fourth Reform Bill) was carried in 1918 with wide inter-party agreement, granting at last manhood suffrage and a large degree of women's suffrage.

The British democratic achievement in 1918 seemed to come at an appropriate moment in view of the sudden advance made by democracy in much of Europe later in that year. The end of the First World War and the collapse of autocratic empires released the hope of making democracy triumph through the establishment of new states in Europe and further afield. The over-optimism behind these intentions soon began to be revealed. The history of the inter-war years showed how ill-founded were the hopes placed in widespread democracy and how persistent could be the attractions of despotic government. These developments were a salutary lesson to democrats, who perhaps assumed with too much facility that their preferred form of government would conquer the world – a lesson to democrats not only of that time, but of the present and the future. Whatever some recent suggestions about world trends and developments may have been,[1] democracy continues to be rivalled by forms of government which are arbitrary rather than participatory. Such rival forms might appear to be in recession at present, particularly because of momentous events in Eastern Europe a decade ago. But they continue in some countries, and their revival in others remains a clear possibility. The attainment, maintenance, and decay of democracy depend largely on changeable economic, social, and political circumstances; and it can by no means be assumed that the world, by the end of the twentieth century, has been made safe for democracy.

Britain had suddenly risen to quite a high place in the advance towards democracy by 1918. In terms of adopting manhood suffrage, she had lagged behind some other countries. France had had manhood suffrage since 1870, the United States had had white male suffrage since 1825. But women's suffrage was not implemented on a federal basis in the United States until 1920, although it had been adopted in a growing number of the Union's component territories and states since 1869. Although it was adopted in New Zealand in 1893 and Australia in 1902, women's suffrage had to wait much longer than in these countries (and longer than in Britain) until it was adopted in two countries which had been in the vanguard of democracy – in 1940 in Switzerland and 1944 in France.

The large British electoral extensions in 1918 still left a good deal of democratic reform to be achieved. It took a further ten years for the women's vote to be granted at the same age as men, by the second Representation of the People Act (or Equal Franchise Act) of 1928. Agitation for this purpose in the intervening decade was considerable.[2] While the Women's Social and Political Union ended in 1918, the National Union of Women's Suffrage Societies continued in being under a new name, the National Union of Societies for Equal Citizenship, and developed a wider range of objectives. Although women could sit in the Commons from 1918, they were not allowed to sit in the Lords (by hereditary right) until 1963, though they could become life peeresses from 1958.

After the Parliament Act of 1911, no further restriction on the right of the House of Lords to reject bills came about until the Parliament Act of 1949. Under this surprisingly cautious measure, two parliamentary sessions rather than three (and one year) became the maximum time allowed for delay by the Lords of a bill passed by the Commons. This provision still remains unaltered. The Upper House was considerably restructured in 1999, but pure parliamentary democracy continues to elude the country. It is not yet known whether the new House of Lords will contain any elective element, and the abolition of the official royal veto is not, so far as is known, being currently considered.

Despite all the reforming attention given to plural voting and the hopes invested in its abolition, party political conditions and interests were not conducive to its removal in 1918, or for many years afterwards. The abolition of the business and university vote did not occur until the third Representation of the People Bill was passed in 1948.

Proportional representation had been given a boost by the large amount of parliamentary attention bestowed on it in the electoral reform debates of 1917–18, and it formed part of the procedure for elections to the Northern Ireland Parliament from 1921 to 1929.[3] It was then withdrawn, however, though much later (in 1973) it was re-adopted as a component in the elections to a new Northern Irish Assembly. It was not adopted in Great Britain, in connection with parliamentary institutions, until 1998 when it became part of the electoral procedure for the Scottish Parliament and the Welsh Assembly.

At the present day, Britain is nearly a parliamentary democracy. But since the fundamental changes in 1918, she has advanced further towards this position in only a slow and piecemeal fashion, without the great disputes of the nineteenth and early twentieth centuries, but in a similarly cautious way. Moreover, there still remain obstacles (as mentioned above) to Britain's attaining a full state of parliamentary democracy.

If Britain is not completely a parliamentary democracy, neither is she a direct democracy in the sense of obtaining decisions directly from the people. In the use of such directly popular methods as referendum decisions, public initiatives for the passage or repeal of laws, and demands for the recall of unsatisfactory representatives, Britain lags far behind Switzerland and some of the American states. The referendum has been employed only three times in Britain, once (in 1975) in regard to membership of the European Common Market and twice in Scotland and Wales (in 1979 and 1997) in regard to devolution. If use of the referendum is still in its infancy in Britain, the public initiative for the passage or repeal of laws has not come into use at all, nor has the recall of representatives who are claimed to be unsatisfactory. These methods have long been part of the normal political procedure in Switzerland, and in increasing areas of the United States. They are an important reinforcement of the parliamentary role as a representative of, and respondent to, public wishes for political action.[4]

The computer age has brought suggestions that Parliament might be virtually by-passed by direct electronic appeals to the public on legislation, when the people are asked to respond to questions on this matter by clicking 'yes' or 'no' on the Internet. Possibilities for direct popular political decision would therefore appear to be opened up by computerization, and so no doubt in response would be the more traditional replies that only the expertise of elected representatives can make such decisions. Such a reply was made almost a century ago, in November 1906, by the executive committee of the Fabian Society. This body did not want democracy to 'find its consummation in a House of Commons where, without any discussion, divisions were taken by counting postcards received from the entire population on questions submitted to the people by referendum and initiative'.[5] Britain still has a virtually all-powerful, though now partially devolved, parliamentary system. She shows little desire to replace or supplement its processes by more direct democratic means, which might include another form of assembly. The revolutionary ideas and attitudes of the 1960s produced the concept of government by local assemblies alone. But such an idea obtained little support, and soon receded.

So Britain remains a parliamentary representative democracy, not a direct one except on the very rare occasions when a referendum has been held. It retains some non-democratic features, such as very restricted powers of veto by a non-elected Upper Chamber and the official possibility of a royal veto. Some advances towards democracy have been made since 1918, when the detailed treatment in this book ended, but a good deal more could be done to extend them further.

Notes

1. See F. Fukuyama, *The End of History and the Last Man* (Harmondsworth, 1992), especially pp. 12, 328–39.

2. Cheryl Law, *Suffrage and Power: The Women's Movement, 1918–28* (London, 1997).
3. Jenifer Hart, *Proportional Representation* (Oxford, 1992), pp. 205–10.
4. I. Budge, *The New Challenge of Direct Democracy* (Cambridge, 1996), p. 33. On the use of these methods in Switzerland and the USA, see Thomas E. Cronin, *Direct Democracy: The Politics of Initiative, Referendum and Recall* (Cambridge, Mass., 1989); J. Bryce, *Modern Democracies* (2 vols., London, 1921), vol. I, pp. 415–551, vol. II, pp. 367–475; A. V. Dicey, *Introduction to the Study of the Law of the Constitution* (9th edn, London, 1945; first published 1885), pp. 604–19; J. A. Hobson, *The Crisis of Liberalism: New Issues of Democracy* (London, 1909).
5. L. Barrow and I. Bullock, *Democratic Ideas and the British Labour Movement, 1880–1914* (Cambridge, 1996), p. 165.

Bibliography

(Place of publication of books is London unless otherwise stated.)

Adonis, A., *Making Aristocracy Work: The Peerage and the Political System in Britain, 1884–1914* (Oxford, 1993).

——, 'Lords and monarchy in late Victorian Britain', in Ulrike Jordan and W. Kaiser, eds, *Political Reform in Britain, 1886–1996* (Bochum, 1997), pp. 67–79.

Aspinall, A., *Politics and the Press, c.1780–1850* (1949).

Bagehot, W., *The English Constitution* (1993; first published 1867).

Ball, S., *The Conservative Party and British Politics, 1902–51* (1995).

Barker, M., *Gladstone and Radicalism: The Reconstruction of Liberal Policy in Britain, 1885–94* (Hassocks, 1975).

Barker, R., and Xenia Howard-Johnston, 'The politics and political ideas of Moisei Ostrogorski', *Political Studies*, XXIII (1975), 415–29.

Barrow, L., and I. Bullock, *Democratic Ideas and the British Labour Movement, 1880–1914* (Cambridge, 1996).

Bealey, F., and H. Pelling, *Labour and Politics, 1900–06* (1958).

Beckett, J. V., *The Aristocracy in England, 1660–1914* (Oxford, 1988).

Belchem, J., *Popular Radicalism in Nineteenth-Century Britain* (Basingstoke, 1996).

Bell, H. C., 'Palmerston and parliamentary representation', *Journal of Modern History*, IV (1932), 186–213.

Bentham, J., *Plan of Parliamentary Reform* (1827).

Bentley, M., *Politics without Democracy, 1815–1914: Perception and Preoccupation in British Government* (1984).

——, *The Climax of Liberal Politics: British Liberalism in Theory and Practice, 1868–1918* (1987).

——, and J. Stevenson, eds, *High and Low Politics in Modern Britain: Ten Studies* (Oxford, 1983).

Biagini, E. F., *Liberty, Retrenchment and Reform: Popular Liberalism in the Age of Gladstone, 1860–80* (Cambridge, 1992).

——, ed., *Citizenship and Community: Liberals, Radicals and Collective Identities in the British Isles, 1865–1931* (Cambridge, 1996).

——, and A. J. Reid, eds, *Currents of Radicalism: Popular Radicalism, Party Politics and Organized Labour, 1850–1914* (Cambridge, 1991).

Black, A., *Guilds and Civil Society in European Political Thought from the Twelfth Century to the Present* (1984).

——, *Political Thought in Europe, 1250–1450* (Cambridge, 1992).

Blake, R., *Disraeli* (1966).

Bibliography

Blewett, N., 'The franchise in the United Kingdom, 1885–1918', *Past and Present*, XXXII (1965), 27–56.
——, *The Peers, the Parties and the People: The General Elections of 1910* (1972).
Bogdanor, V., *The Monarchy and the Constitution* (Oxford, 1995).
Bolt, Christine, *The Women's Movement in the United States and Britain from the 1790s to the 1920s* (1993).
Bonjour, E., H. S. Offler and G. R. Potter, *A Short History of Switzerland* (Oxford, 1952).
Bourne, J. M., *Patronage and Society in Nineteenth-Century England* (1986).
Brash, J. I., ed., *Papers on Scottish Electoral Politics, 1832–54* (Scottish Historical Society, Edinburgh, 1974).
——, 'The new Scottish county electors in 1832: an occupational analysis', *Parliamentary History*, VII (1988), 98–121.
Briggs, A., *The Age of Improvement* (1959).
——, ed., *Chartist Studies* (1959).
Brock, M., *The Great Reform Act* (1973).
Bromhead, P. A., *The House of Lords and Contemporary Politics, 1911–57* (1958).
Bryce, J., *Modern Democracies* (2 vols, 1921).
Budge, I., *The New Challenge of Direct Democracy* (Cambridge, 1996).
Burroughs, P., 'The Northumberland elections of 1826', *Parliamentary History*, X (1991), 78–103.
Butler, D. E., *The Electoral System in Britain, 1918–51* (Oxford, 1953).
Caine, Barbara, *English Feminism, 1780–1980* (Oxford, 1997).
Cannadine, D., *The Decline and Fall of the British Aristocracy* (New Haven, Conn., 1990).
Cannon, J., *Parliamentary Reform, 1640–1832* (Cambridge, 1973).
Carstairs, A. M., *A Short History of Electoral Systems in Western Europe* (1980).
Chadwick, Mary E. J., 'The role of redistribution in the making of the Third Reform Act', *Historical Journal*, XIX (1976), 665–83.
Charlton, J., *The Chartists: The First National Workers' Movement* (1997).
Chase, M., 'Out of Radicalism: the mid–Victorian Freehold Land Movement', *English Historical Review*, CVI (1991), 319–45.
Christie, O. F., *The Transition from Aristocracy, 1832–67* (1927).
——, *The Transition to Democracy, 1867–1914* (1934).
Claeys, G., ed., *Political Writings of the 1790s* (8 vols, 1995).
Clark, J. C. D., *English Society, 1688–1832* (Cambridge, 1985).
——, *Revolution and Rebellion: State and Society in England in the Seventeenth and Eighteenth Centuries* (Cambridge, 1986).
Clarke, M. L., *George Grote, a Biography* (1962).
Clarke, P. F., 'Electoral sociology of modern Britain', *History*, LVII (1972), 31–55.
——, *Hope and Glory: Britain, 1900–90* (Harmondsworth, 1997).
Close, D. H., 'The collapse of resistance to democracy:

Conservatives, adult suffrage, and Second Chamber reform, 1911–28', *Historical Journal*, XX (1977), 893–918.

Cole, A., and P. Campbell, *French Electoral Systems and Elections since 1789* (Aldershot, 1989).

Coleman, B., *Conservatism and the Conservative Party in Nineteenth Century Britain* (1988).

Collini, S., *Public Moralists: Political Thought and Intellectual Life in Britain, 1850–90* (Oxford, 1991).

Conacher, J. B., *The Aberdeen Coalition, 1852–5* (Cambridge, 1968).

——, ed., *The Emergence of British Parliamentary Democracy in the Nineteenth Century* (New York, 1971).

Cornford, J., 'The transformation of Conservatism in the late nineteenth century', *Victorian Studies*, VII (1963), 35–66.

Cowling, M., *1867: Disraeli, Gladstone and Revolution* (Cambridge, 1967).

Cowman, Krista, '"We intend to show what our Lord has done for women": the Liverpool Church League for Women's Suffrage, 1913–18', in R. N. Swanson, ed., *Gender and Christian Religion* (*Studies in Church History*, XXXIV, 1998), pp. 475–86.

Cragoe, M., 'Welsh electioneering and the purpose of Parliament: "from radicalism to nationalism" reconsidered', *Parliamentary History*, special issue 5 (1998), 113–30.

Cromwell, Valerie, 'The losing of the initiative by the House of Commons, 1780–1914', *Transactions of the Royal Historical Society*, 5th series, XVII (1968), 1–23.

Cronin, T. E., *Direct Democracy: The Politics of Initiative, Referendum and Recall* (Cambridge, Mass., 1989).

Crook, D. P., *American Democracy in English Politics, 1815–50* (Oxford, 1965).

Davies, J. K., *Democracy and Classical Greece* (2nd edn, 1993; first published 1978).

Davis, J., and D. M. Tanner, 'The borough franchise after 1867', *Historical Research*, LXIX (1996), 306–27.

Davis, J. W., '"The uplifting game": Nonconformity and the working class in South Lambeth, 1884–1903' (D. Phil. thesis, University of Sussex, 1992).

——, 'Working-class make-believe: the South Lambeth Parliament (1887–90)', *Parliamentary History*, XII (1993), 249–58.

Davis, R. W., *Political Change and Continuity: A Buckinghamshire Study, 1760–1885* (Newton Abbot, 1972).

——, 'The Whigs and the idea of electoral deference: some further thoughts on the Great Reform Act', *Durham University Journal*, LXVII (1974), 79–91.

——, 'Deference and aristocracy in the time of the Great Reform Act', *American Historical Review*, LXXXI (1976), 532–9.

——, 'The mid-nineteenth century electoral structure', *Albion*, VIII (1976), 142–53.

——, ed., *The Origins of Modern Freedom in the West* (Cambridge, 1995).

De Gruchy, J. W., *Christianity and Democracy* (Cambridge, 1995).

Derry, J. W., *Politics in the Age of Fox, Pitt and Liverpool: Continuity and Transformation* (Basingstoke, 1990).

——, *Charles, Earl Grey: Aristocratic Reformer* (Oxford, 1992).

Dicey, A. V., *Introduction to the Study of the Law of the Constitution* (9th edn, 1945; first published 1885).

——, *Lectures on the Relation between Law and Public Opinion in England during the Nineteenth Century* (2nd edn reprinted, 1952; first published 1905).

Dickinson, H. T., *Liberty and Property: Political Ideology in Eighteenth-Century Britain* (1977).

——, *The Politics of the People in Eighteenth-Century Britain* (Basingstoke, 1994).

Dinwiddy, J. R., 'English radicals and the French Revolution, 1800–50', in F. Furet and Mona Ozouf, eds, *The French Revolution and the Creation of Modern Political Culture* (3 vols, Oxford, 1989), vol. III, pp. 447–66.

——, *Radicalism and Reform in Britain, 1780–1850* (1992).

Dunbabin, J. P. D., 'Some implications of the 1885 British shift towards single-member constituencies: a note', *English Historical Review*, CIX (1994), 89–100.

Dunn, J., ed., *Democracy: The Unfinished Journey, 508 BC to AD 1993* (Oxford, 1993).

Durham, M., 'Suffrage and after: feminism in the early twentieth century', in Mary Langan and B. Schwarz, eds, *Crises in the British State, 1880–1930* (1985), pp. 179–91.

Dyer, M., '"Mere detail and machinery": the Great Reform Act and the effects of redistribution on Scottish representation, 1832–68', *Scottish Historical Review*, LXII (1983), 17–34.

——, *Men of Property and Intelligence: The Scottish Electoral System Prior to 1884* (Aberdeen, 1996).

——, *Capable Citizens and Improvident Democrats: The Scottish Electoral System, 1884–1929* (Aberdeen, 1996).

Eastwood, D., *Government and Community in the English Provinces, 1700–1870* (Basingstoke, 1997).

——, 'Contesting the politics of deference: the rural electorate, 1820–60', in J. Lawrence and M. Taylor, eds, *Party, State and Society: Electoral Behaviour in Britain since 1820* (Aldershot, 1997), pp. 27–49.

Edsall, N. C., 'A failed national movement: the Parliamentary and Financial Reform Association, 1848–54', *Bulletin of the Institute of Historical Research*, XLIX (1976), 108–31.

——, *Richard Cobden: Independent Radical* (1986).

Ellens, J. P., *Religious Routes to Gladstonian Liberalism: The Church Rate Conflict in England and Wales, 1832–68* (Pennsylvania, 1994).

Ellis, H. A., 'Aristocratic influence and electoral independence: the Whig model of Parliamentary Reform, 1792–1832', *Journal of Modern History*, V (1979), supplement, 1255–61.

Epstein, J., *Radical Expression: Political Language, Ritual and Symbol in England, 1790–1850* (Oxford, 1994).

——, and Dorothy Thompson, eds, *The Chartist Experience: Studies in Working-Class Radicalism and Culture, 1830–60* (1982).

Evans, D. G., *A History of Wales, 1815–1906* (Cardiff, 1989).

Evans, E. J., *The Great Reform Act of 1832* (1983).

——, *Britain before the Reform Act: Politics and Society, 1815–32* (1989).

——, *The Forging of the Modern State: Early Industrial Britain, 1783–1870* (2nd edn, 1996; first published 1983).

Ferguson W., 'The Reform Act (Scotland) of 1832: intention and effect', *Scottish Historical Review*, XLV (1966), 105–14.

——, *Scotland, 1689 to the Present* (Edinburgh, 1968).

Feuchtwanger, E. J., *Disraeli, Democracy and the Tory Party: Conservative Leadership and Organization after the Second Reform Bill* (Oxford, 1968).

——, *Democracy and Empire: Britain, 1865–1914* (1985).

Fforde, M., *Conservatism and Collectivism, 1886–1914* (Edinburgh, 1990).

Finer, S. E., *The History of Government from the Earliest Times* (3 vols, Oxford, 1997).

Finlayson, G. B. A. M., 'The politics of municipal reform, 1835', *English Historical Review*, LXXXI (1966), 673–92.

Finley, M. I., *Democracy Ancient and Modern* (1973).

Finn, Margot, *After Chartism: Class and Nation in English Radical Politics, 1848–74* (Cambridge, 1993).

Fletcher, J. C., '"This zeal for lawlessness": A. V. Dicey, the Law of the Constitution, and the challenge of popular politics, 1885–1915', *Parliamentary History*, XVI (1997), 309–29.

Flick, C., *The Birmingham Political Union and the Movements for Reform in Britain, 1830–9* (Hamden, Conn., 1978).

Foster, J., *Class Struggle and the Industrial Revolution: Early Industrial Capitalism in three English Towns* (1974).

Francis, M., and Ina Zweiniger-Bargielowska, eds, *The Conservatives and British Society, 1880–1990* (Cardiff, 1996).

Fraser, D., 'The agitation for Parliamentary Reform', in J. T. Ward, ed., *Popular Movements, c. 1830–50* (1970), pp. 31–53.

——, *Urban Politics in Victorian England: The Structure of Politics in Victorian Cities* (Leicester, 1976).

——, ed., *Municipal Reform and the Industrial City* (Leicester, 1982).

Freeden, M., *Ideologies and Political Theory: A Conceptual Approach* (Oxford, 1996).

Fukuyama, F., *The End of History and the Last Man* (Harmondsworth, 1992).

Furet, F., and Mona Ozouf, eds, *The French Revolution and the Creation of Modern Political Culture* (3 vols, Oxford, 1989).

Gallagher, T. F., 'The second Reform movement, 1848–67', *Albion*, XII (1980), 147–63.

Garner, L., *Stepping Stones to Women's Liberty: Feminist Ideas in the*

Women's Suffrage Movement, 1900–18 (1984).

Garrard, J. A., *Leadership and Power in Victorian Industrial Towns, 1830–80* (Manchester, 1983).

Gash, N., *Politics in the Age of Peel: A Study in the Technique of Parliamentary Representation, 1830–50* (1953).

——, *Aristocracy and People: Britain, 1815–65* (1979).

Gauldie, Enid, *One Artful and Ambitious Individual: Alexander Riddoch (1745–1822), Provost of Dundee* (Abertay Historical Society, Dundee, 1989).

Golby, J. M., 'A great electioneer and his motives: the fourth duke of Newcastle', *Historical Journal*, VIII (1965), 201–18.

Goodway, D., *London Chartism, 1838–48* (Cambridge, 1982).

Green, E. H. H., *The Crisis of Conservatism: The Politics, Economics and Ideology of the British Conservative Party, 1880–1914* (1996).

——, ed., *An Age of Transition: British Politics, 1880–1914* (Edinburgh, 1997).

Gruchy, see de Gruchy

Gwyn, W. B., *Democracy and the Cost of Politics in Britain* (1962).

Hamer, D. A., *The Politics of Electoral Pressure: A Study in the History of Victorian Reform Agitations* (Hassocks, 1977).

Hanham, H. J., *Elections and Party Management: Politics in the Time of Disraeli and Gladstone* (1959).

——, *The Reformed Electoral System in Great Britain, 1832–1914* (Historical Association, 1968).

——, ed., *The Nineteenth Century Constitution: Documents and Commentary* (Cambridge, 1969).

Hansard's Parliamentary Debates, 3rd series.

Hare, T., *The Machinery of Representation* (1857).

——, *Treatise on the Election of Representatives, Parliamentary and Municipal* (1859).

Harling, P., *The Waning of 'Old Corruption': The Politics of Economical Reform in Britain, 1779–1846* (Oxford, 1996).

Harrison, B., *Drink and the Victorians: The Temperance Question in England, 1815–72* (1971).

——, *Separate Spheres: The Opposition to Women's Suffrage in Britain* (1978).

——, 'Women's suffrage at Westminster, 1866–1928', in M. Bentley and J. Stevenson, eds, *High and Low Politics in Modern Britain: Ten Studies* (Oxford, 1983).

——, *The Transformation of British Politics, 1860–1995* (Oxford, 1996).

Harrison, R., *Before the Socialists: Studies in Labour and Politics, 1861–81* (1965).

Hart, Jenifer, *Proportional Representation: Critics of the British Electoral System, 1820–1945* (Oxford, 1992).

Harvey, A. D., *Britain in the Early Nineteenth Century* (1978).

Harvie, C., *The Lights of Liberalism: University Liberals and the Challenge of Democracy, 1860–86* (1976).

Hawkins, A., *Parliament, Party, and the Art of Politics in Britain, 1855–9* (1987).

——, *British Party Politics, 1852–86* (Basingstoke, 1998).

Hay, D., and N. Rogers, *Eighteenth–Century English Society* (Oxford, 1997).

Hayes, W. A., *The Background and Passage of the Third Reform Act* (New York, 1982).

Heesom, A., '"Legitimate" versus "Illegitimate" influences: aristocratic electioneering in mid-Victorian Britain', *Parliamentary History*, VII (1988), 282–305.

Hempton, D., *Methodism and Politics in British Society, 1750–1850* (1984).

Henderson, Frances, 'Putney debates', *Oxford: The Journal of the Oxford Society*, XLIX (Nov. 1997), 58–60.

Hennock, E. P., 'The sociological premises of the First Reform Act: a critical note', *Victorian Studies*, XIV (1971), 321–37.

——, *Fit and Proper Persons: Ideal and Reality in Nineteenth-Century Urban Government* (1973).

Hill, B., *The Early Parties and Politics in Britain, 1688–1832* (Basingstoke, 1996).

Hill, Dilys M., *Democratic Theory and Local Government* (1974).

Himmelfarb, Gertrude, *Victorian Minds* (1968).

Hobson, J. A., *The Crisis of Liberalism: New Issues of Democracy* (1909).

——, *Democracy after the War* (1917).

Hollis, Patricia, *The Pauper Press: A Study of Working–Class Radicalism of the 1830s* (Oxford, 1970).

——, ed., *Pressure from Without in Early Victorian England* (1974).

——, *Ladies Elect: Women in English Local Government, 1865–1914* (Oxford, 1987).

Holton, Sandra S., *Feminism and Democracy: Women's Suffrage and Reform Politics in Britain, 1900–18* (Cambridge, 1986).

Hoppen, K. T., *Elections, Politics and Society in Ireland, 1832–85* (Oxford, 1984).

——, 'The franchise and electoral politics in England and Ireland, 1832–85', *History*, LX (1985), 202–17.

——, 'Roads to democracy: electioneering and corruption in nineteenth-century England and Ireland', *History*, LXXXI (1996), 553–71.

——, *The Mid-Victorian Generation, 1846–86* (Oxford, 1998).

Howe, A., *The Cotton Masters, 1830–60* (Oxford, 1984).

Huch, R. K., and P. A. Ziegler, *Joseph Hume: The People's MP* (American Philosophical Society, Philadelphia, 1985).

Hume, Leslie P., *The National Union of Women's Suffrage Societies, 1897–1914* (New York, 1982).

Hunt, Karen, *Equivocal Feminists: The Social Democratic Federation and the Woman Question, 1884–1911* (Cambridge, 1996).

Hutchison, I. G. C., *A Political History of Scotland, 1832–1924* (Edinburgh, 1986).

Jackson, J. M., ed., *The City of Dundee* (*Third Statistical Account of Scotland*, vol. XXV, Arbroath, 1979).

James, D., *Class and Politics in a Northern Industrial Town: Keighley, 1880–1914* (Keele, 1995).

James, R. R., *The British Revolution: British Politics, 1880–1939* (2 vols, Cambridge, 1976).

Jenkins, R., *Mr Balfour's Poodle: An Account of the Struggle between the House of Lords and the Government of Mr Asquith* (1954).

——, *Gladstone* (1995).

Jenkins, T. A., *The Liberal Ascendancy, 1830–86* (Basingstoke, 1994).

——, *Parliament, Party and Politics in Victorian Britain* (Manchester, 1996).

Jones, A., *The Politics of Reform, 1884* (Cambridge, 1972).

Jones, D. J. V., 'The Merthyr riots of 1831', *Welsh History Review*, III (1966–7), 173–205.

——, 'The Carmarthen riots of 1831', *Welsh History Review*, IV (1968–9), 129–42.

——, *Chartism and the Chartists* (1975).

——, 'Women and Chartism', *History*, LXVIII (1983), 1–21.

Jones, G. Stedman, *Languages of Class: Studies in English Working-Class History, 1832–1982* (Cambridge, 1983).

Jones, Grace A., 'Further thoughts on the franchise, 1885–1918', *Past and Present*, XXXIV (1966), 134–8.

Jones, G. W., *Borough Politics: A Study of the Wolverhampton Town Council, 1888–1964* (1969).

Jones, J. R., ed., *Liberty Secured?: Britain Before and After 1688* (Stanford, 1992).

Jordan, Ulrike, and W. Kaiser, eds, *Political Reform in Britain, 1886–1996: Themes, Ideas, Policies* (Veröffentlichungen Arbeitskreis, Deutsche England-Forschung, 37, Bochum, 1997).

Joyce, P., *Work, Society and Politics: The Culture of the Factory in Later Victorian England* (1982).

——, *Visions of the People: Industrial England and the Question of Class, 1840–1914* (Cambridge, 1991).

——, *Democratic Subjects: The Self and the Social in Nineteenth-Century England* (Cambridge, 1994).

Jupp, P., *British Politics on the Eve of Reform: The Duke of Wellington's Administration, 1828–30* (Basingstoke, 1998).

Kent, Susan, *Sex and Suffrage in Britain, 1866–1914* (Princeton, NJ, 1987).

Kinzer, B. L., *The Ballot Question in Nineteenth-Century English Politics* (New York, 1982).

Koditschek, T., *Class Formation and Urban Industrial Society: Bradford, 1750–1850* (Cambridge, 1990).

Koss, S., *The Rise and Fall of the Political Press in Britain* (2 vols, 1981, 1984).

Kuhn, W. M., *Democratic Royalism: The Transformation of the British Monarchy, 1861–1914* (Basingstoke, 1996).

Lang, S., *Parliamentary Reform, 1785–1928* (1999).

Langan, Mary, and B. Schwarz, eds, *Crises in the British State, 1880–*

1930 (1985).

Larsen, T., *Friends of Religious Equality: Nonconformist Politics in Mid-Victorian England* (Woodbridge, 1999).

Law, Cheryl, *Suffrage and Power: The Women's Movement, 1918–28* (1997).

Lawrence, J., 'Class and gender in the making of urban Toryism, 1880–1914', *English Historical Review*, CVIII (1993), 629–52.

———, 'The decline of English popular politics?', *Parliamentary History*, XIII (1994), 333–7.

———, 'The dynamics of urban politics, 1867–1914', in J. Lawrence and M. Taylor, *Party, State and Society: Electoral Behaviour in Britain since 1820* (Aldershot, 1996) pp. 79–105.

———, *Speaking for the People: Party, Language and Popular Politics in England, 1867–1914* (Cambridge, 1998).

———, and M. Taylor, eds, *Party, State and Society: Electoral Behaviour in Britain since 1820* (Aldershot, 1996).

Lecky, W. E. H., *Democracy and Liberty* (2 vols, 1896).

Lee, A. J., *The Origins of the Popular Press in England, 1855–1914* (1976).

Leneman, Leah, *A Guid Cause: The Women's Suffrage Movement in Scotland* (Aberdeen, 1991).

Leventhal, F. M., *Respectable Radical: George Howell and Victorian Working-Class Politics* (1971).

Lewis, Jane, ed., *Before the Vote was Won: Arguments For and Against Women's Suffrage* (1987).

Lewis, R., 'The Welsh radical tradition and the ideal of a democratic popular culture', in E. F. Biagini, ed., *Citizenship and Community: Liberals, Radicals and Collective Identities in the British Isles, 1865–1931* (Cambridge, 1996), pp. 325–40.

Liddington, Jill, and Jill Norris, *One Hand Tied Behind Us: The Rise of the Women's Suffrage Movement* (1978).

Lindsay, A. D., *The Essentials of Democracy* (1930).

Lloyd, T., *The General Election of 1880* (Oxford, 1968).

Lopatin, Nancy D., 'Political Unions and the Great Reform Act', *Parliamentary History*, X (1991), 105–23.

———, *Political Unions, Popular Politics and the Great Reform Act of 1832* (Basingstoke, 1998).

Lowell, A. Lawrence, *The Government of England* (2 vols, New York, 1917; first published 1908).

Lowther, J. W.: see Ullswater, Viscount

McCalmont's Parliamentary Poll Book: British Election Results, 1832–1918 (8th edn, ed. J. Vincent and M. Stenton, Brighton, 1971; first published 1879, 7th edn 1910).

McCord, N., *The Anti-Corn Law League* (1958).

———, 'Some difficulties of Parliamentary Reform', *Historical Journal*, X (1967), 376–90.

———, *British History, 1815–1906* (Oxford, 1991).

McWilliam, R., *Popular Politics in Nineteenth Century England* (1998).

Machin, G. I. T., *Politics and the Churches in Great Britain, 1832 to 1868* (Oxford, 1977).

——, 'George Julian Harney in Jersey, 1855–63: a Chartist "abroad"', *Bulletin of Société Jersiaise*, XXIII: 4 (1984), 478–95.

——, *Politics and the Churches in Great Britain, 1869 to 1921* (Oxford, 1987).

——, *Disraeli* (1995).

——, 'Disestablishment and Democracy, c. 1840–1930', in E. F. Biagini, ed., *Citizenship and Community: Liberals, Radicals and Collective Identities in the British Isles, 1865–1931* (Cambridge, 1996), pp. 120–47.

Maddox, G., *Religion and the Rise of Democracy* (1995).

Mallock, W. H., *The Limits of Pure Democracy* (1918).

Mandler, P., *Aristocratic Government in the Age of Reform: Whigs and Liberals, 1830–52* (Oxford, 1990).

Marsh, P., *The Discipline of Popular Government: Lord Salisbury's Domestic Statecraft, 1881–1902* (Hassocks, 1978).

——, *Joseph Chamberlain: Entrepreneur in Politics* (New Haven, Conn., 1994).

Masheder, R., *Dissent and Democracy: Their Mutual Relations and Common Objects* (1864).

Mather, F. C., ed., *Chartism and Society: An Anthology of Documents* (1980).

Matthew, H. C. G., *Gladstone, 1809–98* (Oxford, 1997).

Mayer, Annette, *The Growth of Democracy in Britain* (Access to History series, 1999).

Meadowcroft, J., and M. W. Taylor, 'Liberalism and the Referendum in British political thought', *Twentieth Century British History*, I (1990), 35–57.

Mill, J. S., *On Liberty* (1859).

——, *Considerations on Representative Government* (1861).

——, *Essays on Reform* (1867).

——, *Essay on the Subjection of Women* (1869).

Miller, Naomi C., 'John Cartwright and radical Parliamentary Reform, 1808–19', *English Historical Review*, LXXXIII (1968), 705–28.

Moore, D. C., 'The other face of Reform', *Victorian Studies*, V (1961–2), 7–34.

——, 'Concession or cure: the sociological premises of the First Reform Act', *Historical Journal*, IX (1966), 39–59.

——, *The Politics of Deference: A Study of the Mid-Nineteenth Century English Political System* (Hassocks, 1976).

Morgan, D., *Suffragists and Liberals: The Politics of Woman Suffrage in England* (Oxford, 1975).

Morgan, Jane, 'Denbighshire's *Annus Mirabilis*: the borough and county elections of 1868', *Welsh History Review*, VII: 1 (1974), 63–87.

Morgan, Kenneth O., *Wales in British Politics, 1868–1922* (3rd edn,

Cardiff, 1980; first published 1963).

——, *Rebirth of a Nation: Wales, 1880–1980* (Oxford, 1981).

Morris, H. L., *Parliamentary Franchise Reform in England, 1885–1918* (New York, 1921).

Morris, R. J., ed., *Class, Power and Social Structure in British Nineteenth-Century Towns* (Leicester, 1986).

——, *Class, Sect and Party – The Making of the British Middle Class: Leeds, 1820–50* (Manchester, 1990).

Morton, G., *Unionist-Nationalism: Governing Urban Scotland, 1830–60* (Scottish Historical Review Monographs, no. 6; East Linton, 1999).

Newbould, J. A., *Whiggery and Reform, 1830–41* (1990).

Nossiter, T. J., *Influence, Opinion and Political Idioms in Reformed England: Case Studies from the North East, 1832–74* (Brighton, 1975).

O'Brien, P. K., and R. Quinault, eds, *The Industrial Revolution and British Society* (Cambridge, 1993).

O'Gorman, F., 'Electoral deference in unreformed England, 1760–1832', *Journal of Modern History*, LVI (1984), 391–429.

——, *British Conservatism: Conservative Thought from Burke to Thatcher* (1986).

——, *Voters, Patrons and Parties: The Unreformed Electoral System in Hanoverian England, 1734–1832* (Oxford, 1989).

——, 'Campaigns, rituals and ceremonies: the social meaning of elections in England, 1780–1860', *Past and Present*, CXXXV (1992), 79–115.

——, *The Long Eighteenth Century: British Political and Social History, 1688–1832* (1997).

O'Leary, C., *The Elimination of Corrupt Practices in British Elections, 1868–1911* (Oxford, 1962).

Oldfield, T. H. B., *The Representative History of Great Britain and Ireland* (6 vols, 1816).

Olney, R., *Lincolnshire Politics, 1832–85* (Oxford, 1973).

Ostrogorski, M., *Democracy and the Organization of Political Parties* (2 vols: vol. I, ed. Seymour M. Lipset, Chicago, 1964; first published 1902).

Paine, T., *Rights of Man* (ed. H. Collins, Harmondsworth, 1969; first published 1791–2).

Parry, J., *Democracy and Religion: Gladstone and the Liberal Party, 1867–75* (Cambridge, 1986).

——, *The Rise and Fall of Liberal Government in Victorian Britain* (New Haven, Conn., 1993).

Parsinnen, T. M., 'Association, convention and anti-parliament in British radical politics, 1771–1848', *English Historical Review*, LXXXVIII (1973), 504–5.

Patterson, A. T., *Radical Leicester: A History of Leicester, 1780–1850* (Leicester, 1954).

Paul, Shona G., 'Dundee radical politics, 1834–50' (M. Phil. thesis,

University of Dundee, 1999).

Perry, K., *British Politics and the American Revolution* (Basingstoke, 1990).

Phillips, G. D., *The Diehards: Aristocratic Society and Politics in Edwardian England* (Cambridge, Mass., 1979).

——, 'Lord Willoughby de Broke and the politics of radical Toryism, 1909–14', *Journal of British Studies*, XX (1981), 205–24.

Phillips, J. A., *The Great Reform Bill in the Boroughs: English Electoral Behaviour, 1818–41* (Oxford, 1992).

——, and C. Wetherell, 'Parliamentary parties and municipal politics: 1835 and the party system', *Parliamentary History*, XIII (1994), 48–85.

Pickering, P. A., 'Chartism and the "trade of agitation" in early Victorian Britain', *History*, LXXVI (1991), 221–37.

——, *Chartism and the Chartists in Manchester and Salford* (Basingstoke, 1995).

Pinto-Duschinsky, M., *The Political Thought of Lord Salisbury, 1854–68* (1967).

Plamenatz, J., *Man and Society: Political and Social Theories from Machiavelli to Marx* (2 vols, 1992; first published 1963).

Pombeni, P., 'Starting in reason, ending in passion: Bryce, Lowell, Ostrogorski and the problem of democracy', *Historical Journal*, XXXVII (1994), 319–41.

Porter, B., *Britannia's Burden: The Political Evolution of Modern Britain, 1851–1990* (1994).

Prentice, A., *Historical Sketches and Personal Recollections of Manchester: The Progress of Public Opinion, 1792–1832* (3rd edn, 1970; first published 1851).

Prest, J., *Lord John Russell* (1972).

——, *Politics in the Age of Cobden* (1977).

——, *Liberty and Locality: Parliament, Permissive Legislation, and Ratepayers' Democracies in the Nineteenth Century* (Oxford, 1990).

Pugh, M., *Electoral Reform in War and Peace, 1906–18* (1978).

——, *Women's Suffrage in Britain, 1867–1928* (1980).

——, *The Tories and the People, 1880–1935* (Oxford, 1985).

——, *Women and the Women's Movement in Britain, 1914–59* (Basingstoke, 1992).

——, *The Making of Modern British Politics, 1867–1939* (2nd edn, Oxford, 1993; first published 1982).

——, *State and Society: British Political and Social History, 1870–1992* (1994).

——, 'The limits of liberalism: Liberals and women's suffrage, 1867–1914', in E. F. Biagini, ed., *Citizenship and Community: Liberals, Radicals and Collective Identities in the British Isles, 1865–1931* (Cambridge, 1996), pp. 45–65.

——, *The March of the Women: A Revisionist Analysis of the Campaign for Women's Suffrage* (Oxford, 2000)

Purvis, June, and Sandra Holton, eds, *Votes for Women* (1998).

Quinault, R., 'Lord Randolph Churchill and Tory democracy, 1880–
    5', *Historical Journal*, XXII (1979), 141–65.
——, '1848 and Parliamentary Reform', *Historical Journal*, XXXI
    (1988), 831–51.
——, 'The Industrial Revolution and Parliamentary Reform', in P.
    K. O'Brien and R. Quinault, eds, *The Industrial Revolution and
    British Society* (1993), pp. 183–202.
Ramsden, J., *The Age of Balfour and Baldwin, 1902–40* (1978).
Read, D., *Press and People, 1790–1850: Opinion in Three English Cities*
    (1961).
——, *The English Provinces, c. 1760–1960: A Study in Influence* (1964).
——, *England, 1868–1914: The Age of Urban Democracy* (1979).
Redford, A., *The History of Local Government in Manchester* (2 vols,
    1939–40).
Rees, R. D., 'Electioneering ideals current in South Wales, 1790–
    1832', *Welsh History Review*, II (1964–5), 233–50.
Ridley, Jane, 'The Unionist Opposition and the House of Lords,
    1906–10', *Parliamentary History*, XI (1992), 235–53.
Robbins, K., *John Bright* (1979).
——, *The Eclipse of a Great Power: Modern Britain, 1870–1975* (1983).
——, *Great Britain: Identities, Institutions, and the Idea of Britishness*
    (1998).
Roberts, A., *Salisbury: Victorian Titan* (1999).
Roberts, J. M., *The Pelican History of the World* (Harmondsworth,
    1980).
Robson, R., ed., *Ideas and Institutions of Victorian Britain* (1967).
Rose, J. Holland, *The Rise of Democracy* (1912; first published 1897).
Rosen, A., *Rise Up, Women!: The Militant Campaign of the Women's
    Social and Political Union, 1903–14* (1974; reprinted Aldershot,
    1993).
Rover, Constance, *Women's Suffrage and Party Politics in Britain, 1866–
    1914* (1967).
Rowland, P., *The Last Liberal Governments: The Promised Land, 1905–
    10* (1968).
——, *The Last Liberal Governments: Unfinished Business, 1911–14*
    (1971).
Royle, E., *Chartism* (3rd edn, 1996; first published 1980).
—— and J. Walvin, *English Radicals and Reformers, 1760–1848*
    (Brighton, 1982).
Rubinstein, W. D. 'The end of "Old Corruption" in Britain, 1780–
    1860', *Past and Present*, CI (1983), 55–86.
——, *Britain's Century: A Social and Political History, 1815–1905*
    (1998).
Russell, A. K., *Liberal Landslide: The General Election of 1906* (Newton
    Abbot, 1973).
Russell, Alice, *Political Stability in later Victorian England: A Sociological
    Analysis and Interpretation* (Lewes, 1992).
St John, M., *The Demands of the People: Dundee Radicalism, 1850–70*

(Abertay Historical Society, Dundee, 1997).

Saunders, L. J., *Scottish Democracy, 1815–40: The Social and Intellectual Background* (Edinburgh, 1950).

Schoyen, A. R., *The Chartist Challenge: A Portrait of George Julian Harney* (1958).

Schwarzkopf, Jutta, *Women and the Chartist Movement* (1992).

Scotland, N., 'The National Agricultural Labourers' Union and the demand for a stake in the soil, 1872–96', in E. F. Biagini, ed., *Citizenship and Community: Liberals, Radicals and Collective Identities in the British Isles, 1865–1931* (Cambridge, 1996), pp. 151–67.

Searle, G. R., *Corruption in British Politics, 1895–1930* (Oxford, 1987).

——, *The Liberal Party: Triumph and Disintegration, 1886–1929* (Basingstoke, 1992).

Seymour, C., *Electoral Reform in England and Wales: The Development and Operation of the Parliamentary Franchise, 1832–85* (Newton Abbot, 1970; first published 1915).

Shannon, R., *The Crisis of Imperialism, 1865–1915* (1974).

——, *Gladstone, 1809–65* (1982).

——, *The Age of Disraeli, 1868–81: The Rise of Tory Democracy* (1992).

——, *The Age of Salisbury, 1881–1902: Unionism and Empire* (1996).

——, *Gladstone: Heroic Minister, 1865–98* (1999).

Shaw, J., 'Land, people and the nation: historicist voices in the Highland land campaign, c. 1850–83', in E. F. Biagini, ed., *Citizenship and Community: Liberals, Radicals and Collective Identities in the British Isles, 1865–1931* (Cambridge, 1996), pp. 305–24.

Smith, E. A., 'The Yorkshire elections of 1806 and 1807: a study in electoral management', *Northern History*, II (1967), 69–90.

——, *Lord Grey* (Oxford, 1990).

——, *The House of Lords in British Politics and Society, 1815–1911* (1992).

——, ed., *Reform or Revolution? – A Diary of Reform: England, 1830–2* (Stroud, 1992).

Smith, F. B., *The Making of the Second Reform Bill* (Cambridge, 1966).

Smith, J., *The Taming of Democracy: The Conservative Party, 1880–1924* (Cardiff, 1997).

Smith, J. Milton, 'Earl Grey's cabinet and the objects of Parliamentary Reform', *Historical Journal*, XV (1972), 55–74.

Smith, P., *Disraeli: A Brief Life* (Cambridge, 1996).

——, ed., *Lord Salisbury on Politics: A Selection from his Articles in the Quarterly Review, 1860–83* (Cambridge, 1972).

Southgate, D., *The Passing of the Whigs, 1832–86* (1962).

——, ed., *The Conservative Leadership, 1832–1932* (1974).

——, 'The Salisbury era, 1881–1902', in D. Southgate, ed., *The Conservative Leadership, 1832–1932* (1974).

——, 'Politics and representation in Dundee, 1832–1963', in J. M.

Jackson, ed., *The City of Dundee* (*Third Statistical Account of Scotland*, vol. XXV, Arbroath, 1979).

Steele, E. D., *Palmerston and Liberalism, 1855–65* (Cambridge, 1991).

——, *Lord Salisbury: A Political Biography* (1999).

Stephen, J. F., *Liberty, Equality, Fraternity* (ed. Stuart D. Warner, Indianapolis, 1993; first published 1873).

Stewart, R., *The Foundation of the Conservative Party, 1830–67* (1978).

——, *Party and Politics, 1830–52* (Basingstoke, 1989).

Sunter, R. M., *Patronage and Politics in Scotland, 1707–1832* (Edinburgh, 1986).

Swanson, R. N., ed., *Gender and Christian Religion* (*Studies in Church History*, XXXIV, Oxford, 1998).

Sykes, A., 'The radical right and the crisis of Conservatism before the First World War', *Historical Journal*, XXVI (1983), 661–76.

——, *The Rise and Fall of British Liberalism, 1776–1988* (1997).

Tanner, D., 'The parliamentary electoral system, the "fourth" Reform Act and the rise of Labour in England and Wales', *Bulletin of the Institute of Historical Research*, LVI (1983), 705–19.

——, *Political Change and the Labour Party, 1900–18* (Cambridge, 1990).

Taylor, A. J. P., *English History, 1914–45* (Oxford, 1965).

Taylor, M., *The Decline of British Radicalism, 1847–60* (Oxford, 1995).

——, 'Rethinking the Chartists: searching for synthesis in the historiography of Chartism', *Historical Journal*, XXXIX (1996), 479–95.

Taylor, P., *Popular Politics in Early Industrial Britain: Bolton, 1825–50* (Keele, 1995).

Thane, Pat, 'Women, liberalism and citizenship, 1918–30', in E. F. Biagini, ed., *Citizenship and Community: Liberals, Radicals and Collective Identities in the British Isles, 1865–1931* (Cambridge, 1996), pp. 66–92.

Tholfsen, T. R., 'The transition to democracy in mid–Victorian Britain', *International Review of Social History*, VI (1961), 226–48.

——, *Working-Class Radicalism in mid-Victorian England* (1976).

Thomas, J. A., 'The system of registration and the development of party organization, 1832–70', *History*, XXXV (1950), 81–98.

Thomas, W., *The Philosophic Radicals: Nine Studies in Theory and Practice, 1817–41* (Oxford, 1979).

Thomis, M., and P. Holt, *Threats of Revolution in Britain, 1789–1848* (1977).

Thompson, Dorothy, *The Chartists: Popular Politics in the Industrial Revolution* (Aldershot, 1986).

Thompson, E. P., *The Making of the English Working Class* (Harmondsworth, 1968; first published 1963).

Thorley, J., *Athenian Democracy* (1996).

Tilly, C., *Popular Contention in Great Britain, 1758–1834* (Cambridge, Mass., 1995).

Tocqueville, A. de, *Democracy in America* (ed. P. Renshaw, Ware, 1998;

first published 1835, 1840).

Todd, N., *The Militant Democracy: Joseph Cowen and Victorian Radicalism* (Whitley Bay, 1991).

Turberville, A. S., *The House of Lords in the Age of Reform, 1784–1837* (ed. R. J. White, 1958).

Turner, F. M., *The Greek Heritage in Victorian Britain* (New Haven, Conn., 1981).

Turner, J., *British Politics and the Great War: Coalition and Conflict, 1915–18* (New Haven, Conn., 1992).

Turner, M., *The Age of Unease: Government and Reform in Britain, 1782–1832* (Gloucester, 1999).

Ullswater, Viscount (J. W. Lowther), *A Speaker's Commentaries* (2 vols, 1925).

Verney, D. V., *Parliamentary Reform in Sweden, 1866–1921* (Oxford, 1957).

Vernon, J., *Politics and the People: A Study of English Political Culture, 1815–67* (Cambridge, 1993).

——, ed., *Re–Reading the Constitution: New Narratives in the Political History of England's Long Nineteenth Century* (Cambridge, 1996).

Vincent, J., *The Formation of the Liberal Party, 1857–68* (1966).

——, ed., *Pollbooks: How Victorians Voted* (Cambridge, 1967).

Wager, D. A., 'Welsh politics and parliamentary reform, 1780–1832', *Welsh History Review*, VII (1974–5), 427–49.

Wallace, R., *Organise! Organise! Organise!: A Study of Reform Agitations in Wales, 1840–86* (Cardiff, 1991).

Waller, P. J., *Democracy and Sectarianism: A Political and Social History of Liverpool, 1868–1939* (Liverpool, 1981).

Walton, J. K., *Chartism* (1999).

Ward, J. T., *Chartism* (1973).

——, ed., *Popular Movements, c. 1830–50* (1970).

Weisser, H., *British Working Class Movements and Europe, 1815–48* (Manchester, 1975).

Wellhofer, E. Spencer, *Democracy, Capitalism and Empire in later Victorian Britain, 1885–1910* (Basingstoke, 1996).

Weston, Corinne C., *English Constitutional Theory and the House of Lords, 1556–1832* (1965).

——, 'The Liberal leadership and the Lords' veto, 1907–10', *Historical Journal*, XI (1968), 508–37.

——, 'Salisbury and the Lords, 1868–95', *Historical Journal*, XXV (1982), 103–29.

——, *The House of Lords and Ideological Politics: Lord Salisbury's Referendal Theory and the Conservative Party, 1846–1922* (American Philosophical Society, Philadelphia, 1995).

Wiener, J. H., *Radicalism and Freethought in Nineteenth-Century Britain: The Life of Richard Carlile* (Westport, Conn., 1983).

Williams, C., *Democratic Rhondda: Politics and Society, 1885–1951* (Cardiff, 1996).

Williams, D., 'The Pembrokeshire elections of 1831', *Welsh History*

Review, I (1960–3), 37–64.

Wilson, A., *The Chartist Movement in Scotland* (Manchester, 1970).

Winter, J., *Robert Lowe* (Toronto, 1976).

Witmer, Helen E., *The Property Qualifications of Members of Parliament* (New York, 1943).

Wollstonecraft, Mary, *A Vindication of the Rights of Women* (Harmondsworth, 1982; first published 1792).

Wright, D. G., *Democracy and Reform, 1815–85* (1970).

Young, J. D., *The Rousing of the Scottish Working Class* (1976).

Young, K., *Local Politics and the Rise of Party: The London Municipal Society and the Conservative Intervention in Local Elections, 1894–1963* (Leicester, 1975).

——, and Patricia L. Garside, *Metropolitan London: Politics and Urban Change, 1837–1981* (1982).

Index